5/17:OX

DATE DUE

JUL 2 8 2007

THE
COLD
WAR

GREAT SPEECHES IN HISTORY

Louise I. Gerdes,
Book Editor

Daniel Leone, *President*

Bonnie Szumski, *Publisher*

Scott Barbour, *Managing Editor*

**GREENHAVEN
PRESS®**

THOMSON

GALE

San Diego • Detroit • New York • San Francisco • Cleveland
New Haven, Conn. • Waterville, Maine • London • Munich

LIBRARY OF CONGRESS CATALOGING-IN-PUBLICATION DATA

The Cold War / Louise I. Gerdes, book editor.
    p. cm. — (Greenhaven Press's great speeches in history)
    Includes bibliographical references and index.
    ISBN 0-7377-0869-7 (lib. : alk. paper) — ISBN 0-7377-0868-9 (pbk. : alk. paper)
    1. Cold War—History—Sources. 2. Speeches, addresses, etc. 3. United States—Foreign relations—Soviet Union—Sources. 4. Europe—Foreign relations—1945–—Sources. 5. Soviet Union—Foreign relations—United States—Sources. 6. World politics—1945–1989—History—Sources. I. Gerdes, Louise I. II. Great speeches in history series.
    D843 .C57724 2003
    909.82'5—dc21
                                                            2002034718

Printed in the United States of America

Contents

der to help relieve international tensions, the UN should consider Soviet proposals that support a policy of peaceful coexistence.

morally indefensible. To restore the nation's confidence, America's leaders must end the war.

Chapter 3: The Threat of Nuclear War

address the problems posed by nuclear weapons can prevent such a tragedy from occurring. The American people should share their concerns, help increase awareness of the problem, and aim for a commonsense solution.

Chapter 4: The Struggle for Peace

enslaved, neither Berlin nor the rest of the world will be free.

Foreword

I have a dream that one day this nation will rise up and live out the true meaning of its creed: "We hold these truths to be self-evident: that all men are created equal."

I have a dream that one day on the red hills of Georgia the sons of former slaves and the sons of former slave owners will be able to sit down together at the table of brotherhood.

I have a dream that one day even the state of Mississippi, a state sweltering with the heat of injustice, sweltering with the heat of oppression, will be transformed into an oasis of freedom and justice.

I have a dream that my four little children will one day live in a nation where they will not be judged by the color of their skin but by the content of their character.

Perhaps no speech in American history resonates as deeply as Martin Luther King Jr.'s "I Have a Dream," delivered in 1963 before a rapt audience of 250,000 on the steps of the Lincoln Memorial in Washington, D.C. Decades later, the speech still enthralls those who read or hear it, and stands as a philosophical guidepost for contemporary discourse on racism.

What distinguishes "I Have a Dream" from the hundreds of other speeches given during the civil rights era are King's eloquence, lyricism, and use of vivid metaphors to convey abstract ideas. Moreover, "I Have a Dream" serves not only as a record of history—a testimony to the racism that permeated American society during the 1960s—but it is also a historical event in its own right. King's speech, aired live on national television, marked the first time that the grave injustice of racism was fully articulated to a mass audience in a way that was both logical and evocative. Julian Bond, a fellow participant in the civil rights movement and student of King's, states that

> King's dramatic 1963 "I Have a Dream" speech before the Lincoln Memorial cemented his place as first among equals in civil rights leadership; from this first televised mass meeting, an American audience saw and heard the unedited oratory of America's finest preacher, and for the first time, a mass white audience heard the undeniable justice of black demands.

Moreover, by helping people to understand the justice of the civil rights movement's demands, King's speech helped to transform the nation. In 1964, a year after the speech was delivered, President Lyndon B. Johnson signed the Civil Rights Act, which outlawed segregation in public facilities and discrimination in employment. In 1965, Congress passed the Voting Rights Act, which forbids restrictions, such as literacy tests, that were commonly used in the South to prevent blacks from voting. King's impact on the country's laws illustrates the power of speech to bring about real change.

Greenhaven Press's Great Speeches in History series offers students an opportunity to read and study some of the greatest speeches ever delivered before an audience. Each volume traces a specific historical era, event, or theme through speeches—both famous and lesser known. An introductory essay sets the stage by presenting background and context. Then a collection of speeches follows, grouped in chapters based on chronology or theme. Each selection is preceded by a brief introduction that offers historical context, biographical information about the speaker, and analysis of the speech. A comprehensive index and an annotated table of contents help readers quickly locate material of interest, and a bibliography serves as a launching point for further research. Finally, an appendix of author biographies provides detailed background on each speaker's life and work. Taken together, the volumes in the Greenhaven Great Speeches in History series offer students vibrant illustrations of history and demonstrate the potency of the spoken word. By reading speeches in their historical context, students will be transported back in time and gain a deeper understanding of the issues that confronted people of the past.

Introduction

Over a period of at least forty-three years, the Communist nations of the East and the democratic nations of the West alternated back and forth between conflict and cooperation in a pattern of diplomatic relations that resembled a game of ping pong. Although no war was ever officially declared, East and West waged an ideological battle that sometimes led to physical conflict. The two bloodiest physical conflicts of this contest were the Korean and Vietnam Wars. The nations of East and West also supported covert military operations, including coups, revolutions, assassinations, and insurrections. Airplanes were shot down, ships and hostages were taken, and nuclear arms were developed and grew in number until the possibility of global destruction became a reality. These hostile nations imposed economic sanctions, boycotts, and quarantines; they erected blockades, built walls, and manipulated the price and production of oil. In assaults against each other both real and manufactured, the nations of East and West were clearly at war—a cold war.

Conflicting Ideology, Common Goals

However, despite vast ideological differences, the nations of East and West came to see the advantage, even the necessity, of cooperation. For example, in pursuit of technological superiority, the United States and the Soviet Union eventually developed substantial nuclear capabilities. As nuclear capabilities increased, these nations were forced to seek a mutual reduction in nuclear arms to avoid global nuclear war. Soviet and American scientists with a mutual interest in space exploration started to see the advantages in cooperating with one another on collaborative projects. Similarly, as Soviet expansion began to threaten Communist China's autonomy, China saw the wisdom of pursuing the United States as an ally in order to contain Soviet power. Despite serious differences of opinion, throughout the Cold War individuals as diverse as political leaders, aeronautical engineers, and ping-pong players would seek common ground.

A History of Conflict

The ideological conflict between East and West had deep roots. Well before the Cold War, the relationship between the United States and the Soviet Union was hostile. In the early 1920s, shortly after the Communist revolution in Russia, the United States provided famine relief to the Soviets, and American businessmen established commercial ties in the Soviet Union. By the time the United States established diplomatic relations in 1933, however, the totalitarian nature of Joseph Stalin's Soviet regime presented an obstacle to friendly relations with the West.

Despite deep-seated mistrust and hostility between the Soviet Union and the Western democracies, Nazi Germany's invasion of Russia in June 1941 during World War II created an instant alliance between the Soviets and the United States. Three months after the invasion, the United States extended economic assistance to the Soviets in November through its Lend-Lease Act of March 1941. The program did not prevent friction, however. The Soviets, who were fighting against Germany on the eastern front, were annoyed at what seemed to be the long delay by the Allies in opening a second offensive front against Germany from the west. After the successful Allied landings in Normandy, France, in 1944, which turned the tide in favor of the Allies, tension between the Soviet Union and the United States continued to increase over differences in postwar aims.

The Soviet Union's aggressive, antidemocratic intentions toward the nations of Eastern Europe created tensions even before World War II ended. Lend-Lease made it possible for the Soviet Union not only to push the Germans out of Soviet territory but Eastern Europe as well. At settlement conferences among the Allies in Tehran (1943), Yalta (February 1945), and Potsdam (July/August 1945), the Soviets made it clear that they intended to take over Eastern Europe. In 1946, this led Winston Churchill, former prime minister of Great Britain, to warn that an "iron curtain" was descending through the middle of Europe. Stalin deepened the East-West estrangement when he asserted, also in 1946, that World War II was an unavoidable and inevitable consequence of "capitalist imperialism" and implied that such a war might reoccur. The wartime alliance ended, and the Cold War began.

A World Divided

After World War II, leaders of both East and West had divided the world into opposing camps, and both sides accused the other of having designs on the world. Stalin described a world split into imperialist and capitalist regimes on the one hand and Communist governments on the other. The Soviet Union and the Communist People's Republic of China saw the United States as an imperialist nation, using the resources of emerging nations to increase its own profits. The Soviet Union and China envisioned themselves as crusaders for the working class and the peasants, saving the world from oppression by wealthy capitalists.

U.S. president Harry Truman also spoke of two diametrically opposed systems: one free and the other bent on subjugating struggling nations. The United States and other democratic nations accused the Soviet Union and China of imposing their philosophy on emerging nations to increase their power and sphere of influence. Western nations envisioned themselves as the champions of freedom and choice, saving the world for democracy.

Because of the intense mistrust that divided these nations, the road toward cooperation was a rocky one. The distinct differences in the political and economic systems of these countries often prevented them from reaching a mutual understanding on key policy issues. The 1954 "Kitchen Debate" between Vice President Richard Nixon and Soviet leader Nikita Khrushchev reflects the impasse created by these conflicting ideologies. Nixon was a staunch anti-Communist and Khrushchev believed that communism would eventually bury capitalism. However, the debate also reveals, if briefly, the desire for an exchange of ideas that would ultimately come to fruition.

During a visit to Moscow, Nixon went to the American National Exhibition and was surprised by Khrushchev who dropped by as Nixon stood before an exhibit of an American kitchen. During the exchange, each claimed his own style of government was best, and each saw the other as closed to new ideas:

> *Khrushchev:* In Russia, all you have to do to get a house is to be born in the Soviet Union. You are entitled to housing. In America, if you don't have a dollar you have a right to choose between sleeping in a house or on the pavement. Yet you say we are the slave to Communism. . . .

> *Nixon:* Diversity, the right to choose, the fact that we have 1,000 builders building 1,000 different houses is the most important thing. We don't have one decision made at the top by one government official. This is the difference.

> *Khrushchev:* On politics, we will never agree with you. For instance, Mikoyan likes very peppery soup. I do not. But this does not mean that we do not get along.

> *Nixon:* You can learn from us, and we can learn from you. There must be a free exchange. Let the people choose the kind of house, the kind of soup, the kind of ideas that they want. . . . You must not be afraid of ideas.

> *Khrushchev:* We're saying it is you who must not be afraid of ideas. We're not afraid of anything.

> *Nixon:* Well, then, let's have more exchange of them. We all agree on that, right?

> *Khrushchev:* Good. [Khrushchev turns to translator and asks:] Now, what did I agree on?[1]

Khrushchev's defensiveness at the end of this communication is also representative of East-West exchanges. Negotiations were often hampered by mistrust and suspicions. However, after this exchange, Nixon assured Khrushchev that he would be heard and understood in America, and eventually they shook hands. Even if Nixon and Khrushchev's exchange was merely rhetorical, it expresses the hope that despite different tastes, these two nations could at least get along.

A Pattern for Change

Although political leaders used a variety of methods to move from confrontation toward cooperation during the Cold War, their efforts did follow a general pattern. A leader from either the East or West would initiate an exchange that took many forms, from diplomatic visits to sporting events. Both would promise to negotiate, and some progress would be made. Often, however, negotiation was followed by a betrayal that would result in a setback. Every two steps toward cooperation appeared to be followed by a step back toward conflict.

One of the first examples of this pattern of hope, negotiation, and betrayal was the efforts made by U.S. president Dwight D. Eisenhower and Soviet premier Khrushchev to establish peace between their nations. In 1956, both Eisenhower and Khrushchev began to express the desire for cooperation. After Stalin's death, when Khrushchev became the leader of the Soviet Union, he stated that imperialism and capitalism could coexist without war. That same year Eisenhower decided to run for re-election and told a small group of friends, "I want to advance our chances for world peace, if only by a little, maybe only a few feet."[2]

Eisenhower and his secretary of state, John Foster Dulles, came up with the idea of an exchange of visits between Eisenhower and Khrushchev. On July 11, 1959, Eisenhower drafted a formal proposal that Khrushchev visit the United States and Eisenhower travel to the Soviet Union. The proposal was accepted, and in September Khrushchev became the first leader of the Soviet Union to visit the United States. Many Americans recall images of a brash and boastful Khrushchev traversing the United States, crowing of Russian military might and achievement in space while at the same time offering promises of peace and friendship.

The First Step in a Long Journey

Eisenhower, however, got a different view of Khrushchev during their talks at Camp David at the end of this visit. Not unlike many political leaders, Khrushchev was anxious to win the approval of his own people and also to be accepted into the society of legitimate statesmen. Khrushchev was therefore willing to divert armament spending to consumer production and move toward peace. On September 27, 1959, writing for the *Washington Post*, Chalmers M. Roberts revealed the cautious optimism of those who reported the Camp David meeting between Eisenhower and Khrushchev: "The chief accomplishment of the Eisenhower-Khrushchev talks is to open a lengthy period of East-West negotiations which should mitigate the cold war and lessen the risks of a shooting war. The key which opened the door to this prospect was Soviet Premier Nikita S. Khrushchev's agreement with president Eisenhower on a statement that all international disputes should be settled through negotiations and not by force."[3] The article went on to describe a hopeful future of summits, nuclear test ban talks, and Soviet-American trade.

However, Roberts also reminded readers that Khrushchev believed that he had found Utopia in communism and that the Soviet Union would soon overtake the United States, which had reached the peak of its achievements. Prophetically, the article cautioned, "The Camp David talks, to take the broadest possible view, have at least opened prospects of continuing peace through continuing negotiation. Given a determination on both sides to keep at it, negotiation can go on for a long time."[4] Negotiations between the United States and the Soviet Union did indeed go on for a long time—for another thirty years, at least.

At the conclusion of Khrushchev's visit, Eisenhower seemed optimistic about the Paris summit scheduled for May 1960. The summit, a conference between Western nations and leaders of the Soviet Union, was to focus on disarmament. Unfortunately, on May 1, an American U-2 spy plane, piloted by Gary Powers, was shot down over the Soviet Union. Khrushchev demanded an apology, but for six days Eisenhower continued to deny that it was a spy plane. When

Eisenhower refused to apologize for the incident, Khrushchev withdrew his invitation to Eisenhower to visit the Soviet Union. One of the first of many instances of betrayal and mistrust, the U-2 incident, some authorities claim, ruined the potential for peace at the East-West summit in Paris. Eisenhower never did travel to the Soviet Union.

An Uphill Battle

Over the next thirty years, the United States and the Soviet Union would meet and sign confidence-building agreements, then punctuate the accords with hostile acts that threatened broader conflict. East-West relations went through phases of alternating relaxation and confrontation. For example, in the early 1970s, Soviet leader Leonid Brezhnev took a less overtly hostile stance toward the United States, which resulted in the signing of Strategic Arms Limitation Talks (SALT) agreements. Brezhnev proclaimed in 1973 that peaceful coexistence was the normal, permanent, and irreversible state of relations between imperialist and Communist countries. However, in the late 1970s, internal repression of Soviet citizens and the Soviet invasion of Afghanistan led to a renewal of hostility between the Soviet Union and the United States.

In the 1980s, the *glasnost* (openness) and *perestroika* (restructuring) instituted by Soviet leader Mikhail Gorbachev ultimately led to the dismantling of the Soviet Union and what many term the end of the Cold War. However, this final period of the Cold War was also threatened by disagreement. President Ronald Reagan supported the domestic Strategic Defense Initiative (SDI), dubbed Star Wars. SDI increased defense spending to investigate ways of protecting the United States from incoming nuclear missiles. Reagan speculated that the United States could protect itself from Soviet missiles with defenses in space. In October 1986, when Gorbachev and Reagan met in Reykjavik, Iceland, to discuss disarmament, Gorbachev argued that the negotiations hinged on the United States discontinuing its SDI program. Gorbachev and Reagan could not reach an agreement and not until December 8, 1987, would the treaty eliminating intermediate range nuclear weapons (INF) be signed. Despite these setbacks, however, the

Cold War between the Soviet Union and the United States ended in 1989 with the dismantling of the Soviet Union.

The Race to Space

The "space race" between the Soviet Union and the United States provides one last example of the back and forth nature of relations between the two countries during the Cold War. Although many scientists believed that the reach toward space would be facilitated by cooperation among the scientists of the world, Cold War attitudes made the road to cooperation in the exploration of space as rocky as the earthbound quest for peace. Because the Soviet Union and the United States felt the need to demonstrate their superiority, the exploration of space became a "space race." The fear of the opposition's military superiority, which had threatened negotiations toward peace over the years, spilled over into each nation's space program. Because some believed the "conquest" of space to be as much a military advance as a technological one, any attempts at cooperation appeared to mirror the intensity of Cold War relations, alternating back and forth between cooperation and competition. Moreover, cooperative efforts were influenced by the same mistrust and betrayal that characterized political negotiations. Unfortunately, because each nation developed its space program independently, when the day for cooperation finally came, the technological obstacles at times seemed insurmountable.

Political and scientific goals often conflicted between the United States and the Soviet Union. For example, in 1960 U.S. scientists hoped for international participation in the Tiros weather satellite program, the goal of which was to improve satellite applications for earth-bound decisions such as whether people should evacuate because of an approaching hurricane. "It's part of our national policy that space research is for peaceful purposes," urged Arnold Frutkin, head of the National Aeronautics and Space Administration's (NASA's) Office of International Programs. "We want to have an open program. And the best way to prove this to other countries is to have them participate in our experiments."[5] Despite these assurances, after the U-2 incident, the

Soviets saw the Tiros program as another attempt to spy on the Soviet Union.

Within the United States, an attitude of cooperation seemed unlikely as well. At the time, political interests seemed to outweigh scientific ones. While running for president, John F. Kennedy characterized space exploration as a competition:

> We are in a strategic space race with the Russians, and we have been losing. The first man-made satellite to orbit the earth was named Sputnik. The first living creature in space was Laika. The first rocket to the moon carried a Red flag. The first photograph of the far side of the moon was made with a Soviet camera. If a man orbits earth this year his name will be Ivan. These are unpleasant facts that the Republican candidate [Richard M. Nixon] would prefer us to forget. Control of space will be divided in the next decade. If the Soviets control space they can control earth, as in past centuries the nation that controlled the seas dominated the continents. This does not mean that the United States desires more rights in space than any other nation. But we cannot run second in this vital race. To insure peace and freedom, we must be first.[6]

Once Kennedy was elected, he and James E. Webb, NASA's administrator, seemed convinced that second place in space exploration implied that the United States was second in military strength as well, an attitude that fostered competition over cooperation.

The Soviets did little to dispel this belief. After the one-orbit flight of Yuri Aleksyevich Gagarin on April 12, 1961, the Soviet Union continually stressed that the flight was evidence of the virtues of communism and Soviet superiority. Despite Soviet claims that they could translate the technology into military weapons, they stated that they wanted peace and disarmament. However, the United States considered the flight a blow to its image at home and abroad and saw these remarks as a challenge.

New hope for cooperation came from the efforts of Sir Bernard Lovell, a professor at the University of Manchester, in Great Britain, and an active member of the international astronautics community. In 1963, Lovell visited the Soviet Academy of Sciences and reported in a letter to Hugh L. Dryden, NASA's deputy administrator, that Soviet scientists were interested in cooperating with the West, including a joint moon flight. Mstislav Vsevolodovich Keldysh, director of the Soviet Academy of Science and the man who had launched the first Sputnik spacecraft into space, had encountered technological problems and as a result had postponed a manned Soviet moon flight. Lovell suggested Keldysh might revive the program if a cooperative effort could resolve the Soviet program's problems.

As a result of this information, President Kennedy surprised the UN General Assembly when he raised the possibility of a joint expedition to the moon. On this occasion, it was the scientists who opposed cooperation, but not for political reasons. NASA scientists believed that American space engineers had enough difficulties making hundreds of electrical, mechanical, and pyrotechnic connections between American launch vehicles and spacecraft without combining the hardware of two nations whose technology had developed independently. Comparing cooperation in space to joint exploration in Antarctica, Deputy Associate Administrator for Manned Space Flight George E. Mueller said that although scientists from both nations worked in the same region, "they got there in different ships."[7] Optimism regarding joint ventures turned into disillusionment.

The Apollo-Soyuz Test Project

The technological fears of NASA scientists abated during the presidential administration of Richard Nixon. In April 1972, after meeting with Soviet scientists and engineers, George Low, NASA's deputy administrator at the time, suggested that a 1975 joint docking mission with the Soviet Union was a realistic possibility. As a result of NASA's confidence, President Nixon and Premier Kosygin signed the Agreement Concerning Cooperation in the Exploration and Use of Outer Space for Peaceful Purposes on May 24, 1972.

To guarantee success, the accord that established the Apollo-Soyuz Test Project (ASTP) required that the engineers of the United States and the Soviet Union work without discord to meet a specific timetable. NASA was confident that scientists, engineers, astronauts, and cosmonauts could meet this timetable. However, members of the House Subcommittee on Science and Astronautics, who needed to justify the cost to the American people, questioned the Soviet ability to perform the joint mission. When the committee learned that the Soviets had been slow in providing some documents, Chet Lee, mission director on the NASA teams that launched six Apollo moon missions, explained that it was not that Soviet scientists had refused to provide information. Delivery was just slow because unlike NASA scientists, Soviet scientists lacked the freedom to make on-the-spot decisions. Lee was convinced of the genuine desire on the Soviets' part to make the mission a success.

Despite the subcommittee's lack of confidence, NASA was genuinely optimistic about prospects for a successful flight. By the end of 1973, the Soviet and American teams had made considerable technical progress despite the tight schedules and heavy workloads, and the two crews began to work out the details of joint training. ASTP appeared to be politically possible as well since no major international crises occurred while the ASTP project proceeded.

At last, the project was ready. The Soviets launched the cosmonauts aboard the *Soyuz 19* first, with the Americans following in the *Apollo 18* later the same day. Early in the morning of July 15, 1975, from Houston, Texas, Ross Lavroff interpreted the broadcast of the Soviet launch from Kalingrad:

> This is the Soviet Mission Control Center. Moscow time is 15 hours, 15 minutes. Everything is ready at the Cosmodrome for the Launch of the Soviet spacecraft Soyuz. Five minutes remaining for launch. Onboard systems are now under onboard control. The right control board . . . opposite the commander's couch is now turned on. The cosmonauts have strapped themselves in and reported that they are ready. They have lowered their face plates. The key for launch has been inserted. . . . The crew is ready for launch.[8]

The *Soyuz 19* launched five minutes later carrying cosmonauts Alexei Leonov and Valeriy Kubasov, and the flight was proceeding normally while the American astronauts slept.

Later that morning in the United States, at T minus 7 minutes, 52 seconds, Apollo crewmembers Vance Brand, Tom Stafford, and Deke Slayton finished their checkout of some 556 switches, 40 event indicators, and 71 lights on the console. Tom Stafford told Houston to tell Soyuz to get ready for them, "We'll be up there shortly."[9] Once in orbit, the Apollo spacecraft separated from the Saturn IB booster that held the docking module, which served as an airlock and corridor between the two unique spacecraft. The Apollo then doubled back to dock with the docking module. After doing so, Apollo fired up for the rendezvous with Soyuz.

A Handshake in Space

At 11:10 A.M. on July 17, 1975, the chase of Soyuz by Apollo had ended in a flawless docking. "Well done, Tom," congratulated Leonov, "It was a good show. We're looking forward now to shaking hands with you on board Soyuz."[10] At 2:17 P.M., Stafford opened the door that led into the Soyuz orbital module. With applause from the control centers in the background, Stafford looked into the Soviet craft and, seeing all their umbilicals and communications cables floating about, said, "Looks like they['ve] got a few snakes in there, too. . . . Alexei, our viewers are here. Come over here, please."[11] According to NASA commentators, the astronaut and the cosmonaut appeared to accept their amazing technical accomplishment with the same nonchalance that had characterized their practice sessions in the ground simulators. There were no grand speeches, just a friendly greeting from men who seemed to have done this every day of their lives. Stafford and Slayton said good-bye to Leonov and Kubasov at 5:47 P.M. and floated back through the tunnel into the docking module.

During the space flight and docking, the television media presented the mission in a favorable way, but some newspaper journalists were critical of what they termed a "costly space circus." Robert B. Holtz, editor-in-chief of *Aviation Week and Space Technology* editorialized:

> The real tragedy for this country was the decision to put its scarce space dollars into the political fanfare of Apollo-

Soyuz. . . . Now that it is over, it is apparent that the decision to fly Apollo-Soyuz, instead of another Skylab [a U.S. space station in orbit from 1973 to 1979] or whatever else could yield a good return on the Apollo investment already made, was as foolish and feckless as those other facets of the Nixon-Kissinger detente—the SALT talks, the trade deals and that great treaty that brought peace to Vietnam. Again, NASA's programs seemed to reflect the current environment of foreign affairs.[12]

To the scientists who worked on the project, however, the joint effort was something more. According to NASA flight director Glynn Lunney the real breakthrough made in ASTP was the bringing together of the Soviet and American teams to "implement, design, test and finally fly a project of this complexity."[13] Moreover, NASA had discovered many things about the Soviet space program and just how differently they had approached various aspects of manned space flight. NASA engineers could only hope that their efforts would lead to further cooperation rather than return them to an era of rivalry and competition. In many ways their hopes were realized when Gorbachev and Reagan continued this spirit of cooperation to help bring an end to the Cold War.

The Emergence of New Rivals

In the early years of the Cold War, the primary tension existed between the United States and the Soviet Union. However, during the 1950s, China emerged as a power in its own right. During the Communist revolution in China, Mao Tsetung organized the peasantry of China in a guerilla war against the Nationalist armies of Chiang Kai-shek. Mao's army used its rural foundation to overwhelm the Nationalists, and he proclaimed the People's Republic of China on October 1, 1949, establishing himself as chairman.

The relationship between Communist China and the United States was overtly hostile from the outset. None of the early talk of cooperation or hope of peace expressed between the Soviet Union and the United States seemed possible between China and the United Sates. In fact, the two primary physical conflicts of the Cold War—the Korean and

Vietnam Wars—pitted China and the United States against one another. China's overt involvement in Korea and Vietnam made clear China's interest in eliminating the "imperialist" influence of the United States in Southeast Asia.

The Korean War

When Communist North Korea invaded democratic South Korea in 1949, the United Nations (UN) authorized the sending of troops to defend South Korea. President Harry S. Truman named General Douglas MacArthur commander of the UN forces. In the zeal to eradicate Communist influence in Southeast Asia, MacArthur drove North Korean forces beyond the 38th parallel that had divided Korea to the Yalu River that divided North Korea from China despite warnings that it would provoke Chinese intervention. When China did, in fact, intervene, MacArthur asked permission to bomb Chinese bases in Manchuria. Fearing war with China and the Soviet Union, Truman opposed MacArthur's strategy.

The Chinese retaliation drove the UN forces back to the 38th parallel, and the war became a bloody stalemate. After two years both sides agreed to an armistice, and a truce was signed on July 27, 1953. Although the physical conflict was over, the ideological hostility remained. The United States saw its interests in the Pacific threatened by China, and China perceived U.S. interference in Southeast Asia as imperialist aggression. The two nations remained bitter rivals.

A War Divides America

U.S. involvement in Vietnam began when France, unable to withstand the growing influence of communism, concluded it could no longer maintain its Indochinese colonies. France signed an agreement with Communist forces that temporarily divided Vietnam at the 17th parallel until Communist North Vietnam and democratic South Vietnam elected their own leaders, becoming independent nations. Responding to the threat of Communist expansion, the United States formed the Southeast Asia Treaty Organization (SEATO), hoping to protect South Vietnam from a Communist takeover by North

Vietnam, which was being aided by its ally, China. China hoped to expand its sphere of influence by helping the North Vietnamese. In 1961, a team sent by President John F. Kennedy to examine the situation in Vietnam asked for increased military, technical, and economic aid to the troubled nation. Kennedy increased the level of U.S. military involvement but would not send troops.

After Kennedy's assassination in 1963, Lyndon Johnson assumed the presidency and increased the level of American involvement in Vietnam. On August 4, 1964, North Vietnam launched an attack on an American ship in the Gulf of Tonkin. Congress granted Johnson broad war powers, and the president responded with air attacks against North Vietnam. The war escalated under Johnson, who introduced combat troops to Vietnam in March 1965. As American servicemen began to die in Vietnam, sentiment in the United States began to change.

In 1967, American opposition to the Vietnam War began to increase. In October, fifty thousand protesters picketed the Pentagon in Washington, and in April, seven hundred thousand marched down Fifth Avenue in New York. Despite this opposition, Johnson ordered more U.S. troops into Vietnam. By 1967, nearly sixteen thousand U.S. servicemen had been killed in the war. As casualties mounted, an ideological rift began to divide the nation. Many in the United States believed that America should not use its military strength to act as the planet's police force, believing military intervention was immoral. Others continued to support the war, and Richard Nixon, who succeeded Johnson as president, expanded the Vietnam War into neighboring Laos and Cambodia in an effort to eliminate Communist supply routes. When in May 1970 students protesting the invasions were killed at Kent State in Ohio and Jackson State in Mississippi, horrified Americans who had once supported the war in Vietnam began to question U.S. involvement. Fortunately, as the nation tried to heal its internal wounds, an ideological rift between the world's most powerful Communist powers would force the United States and China to look at each other in a new light. This shift in relations would enable both parties to agree on an end to the Vietnam War.

A Rift in the East

Most of the Western world viewed China and the Soviet Union as two versions of the same evil, but in reality, Sino-Soviet relations, not unlike those between the Soviet Union and the United States, had been historically uneasy. The two nations shared the longest land border in the world, the source of border disputes since the seventeenth century. Moreover, during the Communist revolution, the Soviet Union had initially supported Chiang Kai-shek rather than Mao Tse-tung. However, in 1950, Mao signed a Treaty of Friendship, Alliance, and Mutual Assistance with the Soviet Union, which offered the newly Communist China some security against the United States while it increased in strength. However, while the Soviet Union was considering peaceful coexistence with the United States, China favored continued aggression toward "imperialist" nations. These differences escalated as both the Soviet Union and China vied for control of satellite states.

During the late 1960s, the Soviet invasion of Czechoslovakia and the buildup of forces in the Soviet Far East raised China's suspicion of Soviet intentions toward China. Border clashes along the Ussuri River that separates Manchuria from the Soviet Union reached a peak in 1969, and for several months, China and the Soviet Union teetered on the brink of a nuclear conflict. Fortunately, negotiations between Soviet premier Kosygin and Chinese premier Zhou En-lai defused the crisis. However, Zhou and Mao began to rethink China's geopolitical strategy. The desire to drive imperialist nations from Asia had brought China into conflict with the United States in two of the bloodiest clashes of the Cold War, the Korean and Vietnam Wars. However, when the Soviets began to make efforts to cooperate with the United States, China's vigorous opposition to Western imperialism drove a wedge between the Soviet Union and China. Ironically, this Sino-Soviet rift eventually drove China and the United States toward cooperation in mutual defense against a common enemy—the Soviet Union. When President Richard Nixon showed signs of reducing if not eliminating the American presence in Vietnam, China began to see normalization of relations with the United States as a way of safeguarding its security.

A Secret Visit

However, the rocky road from confrontation to cooperation with China was long and difficult to navigate. Some negotiations with China, for example, were conducted without the knowledge of the American people. On July 9, 1971, U.S. secretary of state Henry Kissinger boarded a plane from Pakistan to Beijing where he spent two days in discussions with Premier Zhou. Once Kissinger's true destination was revealed, the American people were told that the purpose of Kissinger's visit was to prepare for Nixon's visit in the spring of 1972. Americans later learned, however, that much of the dialogue between Kissinger and Zhou focused on Vietnam and the Nixon administration's "decent interval" solution to American withdrawal from South Vietnam. U.S. troop withdrawals from Vietnam would be accompanied by a North Vietnamese cease-fire and some attempt at negotiation with South Vietnam. If these negotiations broke down, North Vietnam would not move to overthrow South Vietnam for a "decent interval." Records between Kissinger and Zhou reveal that Kissinger told Zhou, "What we require is a transition period between the military withdrawal and the political evolution. . . . If after complete American withdrawal, the Indochinese people change their government, the US will not interfere."[14] At the same time, the Nixon administration encouraged the Saigon regime in South Vietnam to sign the Paris Peace Accord, ending open hostilities between the United States and North Vietnam. South Vietnamese forces tried to keep Communist forces at bay without U.S. assistance, but Saigon fell on April 30, 1975.

Whether or not the sacrifice of South Vietnam to communism in exchange for a unified force against the Soviet Union was a necessary or appropriate strategy remains the subject of debate. Nevertheless, internal division in the United States and China's fear of being subsumed by the Soviet Union drove unlikely allies to seek common ground.

Ping-Pong Diplomacy

Although high diplomacy was deemed necessary to resolve the Vietnam War, a simple sports contest proved to be an equally effective anodyne to the tensions between China and the United States. Before Secretary of State Henry Kissinger's secret meetings with Zhou and Mao in July 1971 and Nixon's well-publicized visit in February 1972, fifteen American table tennis players and three journalists made a historic visit to Beijing. This time, however, it was "hostile" China, not "peace-seeking" United States, that initiated diplomatic negotiations.

In April 1971, while in Nagoya, Japan, for the World Table Tennis Championship, the American table tennis team received a surprise invitation from the Chinese team to visit China in what *Time* magazine called "the ping heard round the world."[15] While watching the tournament in Nagoya, Zhou noticed that there was no intense rivalry between the teams and that the game was friendly and sportsmanlike. After the tournament, Chairman Mao invited the team to play in China. This method of dealing with an isolated, possibly hostile country, made without any direct contact with political leaders, came to be called "ping-pong diplomacy."

The U.S. table tennis team arrived on April 14. The team, led by IBM programmer Jack Howard, was made up of Americans from many walks of life, including, among others, a personnel supervisor, a chemist, a university professor, a student, an immigrant, a United Nations employee, and a housewife. The players engaged in a competition at Tsinghua University, watched by eighteen thousand Chinese citizens. The Chinese players dressed in red jumpsuits while each American dressed in his or her own unique way. The Chinese won the men's games 5-3 and the women's 5-4. American team members noted later, however, that the Chinese seemed to be trying very hard not to embarrass the American players by defeating them too handily.

During their visit, U.S. team members reported that they were treated like royalty. They traveled to many places, including Shanghai, the Great Wall, and a summer palace outside Beijing. The Chinese government allowed American journalists to film the visit and waived its rule that Chinese officials develop and inspect the film. The players reported that the people were kind, but reticent and seemed to be curious about the United States. A year later, the Chinese world champion table tennis team arrived in the United States for a series of matches and a tour of ten U.S. cities. Commenting on the success of the visits Zhou remarked, "Never before in history has a sport been used so effectively as a tool of international diplomacy."[16] Although some remained skeptical that China and the United States could find common ground, the U.S. media presented these visits as a positive first step toward normalization of relations with China.

Many of the political and cultural leaders whose decisions shaped Cold War policies in the nations of East and West share their social, economic, and political philosophies in *Great Speeches in History: The Cold War*. The perspectives in the following collection reflect the back and forth nature of Cold War diplomacy and the cycle of conflict and cooperation that marked this stressful period in international affairs.

Notes

1. Vice President Richard Nixon and Soviet premier Nikita Khrushchev, "The Kitchen Debate," CNN.com, July 24, 1954. www.cnn.com.

2. "Man of the Year: Dwight D. Eisenhower," *Time*, January 4, 1960. www.time.com.

3. Chalmers M. Roberts, "Accord on Talks May Ease Tensions," *Washington Post*, September 27, 1959. www.washingtonpost.com.

4. Ibid.

5. Quoted in Edward Clinton Ezell and Linda Neuman Ezell, *The Partnership: A History of the Apollo-Soyuz Test Project*, Washington, DC: NASA, 1978, p. 27.

6. Ibid., pp. 27–28.

7. Ibid., p. 52.

8. Ibid., p. 317.

9. Ibid., p. 319.

10. Ibid., p. 328.

11. Ibid., p. 329.

12. Ibid., p. 353.

13. Ibid., p. 354.

14. Quoted in Jussi M. Hanhimaki, "Some More 'Smoking Guns'? The Vietnam War and Kissinger's Summitry with Moscow and Beijing, 1971–73," www.ohio.edu/hafr/NEWS/2001/DEC/SMOKING.htm.

15. Quoted in David DeVoss, "Ping-Pong Diplomacy," *Smithsonian Magazine*, April 2002. www.smithsonianmag.si.edu.

16. Ibid.

CHAPTER
ONE

The Fear of
Communist
Aggression

An Iron Curtain Divides Europe

Winston Churchill

Winston Churchill, born on November 30, 1874, was a
prominent British statesman, renowned orator, and Nobel
Prize–winning author who served as Great Britain's prime
minister from 1940 to 1945, and 1951 to 1955.
Churchill led Britain from near defeat to victory over
Nazi Germany during World War II and is considered
one of the greatest political figures of the twentieth century. Churchill's foreign policy consisted of three goals:
preserving the British Empire, smashing the Axis powers
(Nazi Germany, Fascist Italy, and Imperial Japan), and
preventing the Soviet Union from dominating Eastern Europe. Churchill accomplished his first two goals but was
compelled by Soviet leader Joseph Stalin and President
Franklin D. Roosevelt to concede a Soviet-dominated
Eastern Europe.

Even though Churchill had been voted out of office
in 1945, President Harry S. Truman invited him to the
United States to speak of his fears of communism. On
March 5, 1946, before a crowd at Westminster College in
Fulton, Missouri, Churchill delivered one of the most famous speeches of the twentieth century. Not only is the
speech remembered for its impact on foreign policy, it is
considered by many authorities to be technically brilliant
as well. Although veiled in vague language, Churchill essentially accuses the Soviets of expansionist policies that
could lead to world domination and calls for an alliance
between the British Commonwealth and the United States
in order to stop Soviet expansion.

Winston Churchill, "The Sinews of Peace," Westminster College, Fulton, Missouri, March 5, 1946.

Although fears of Communist expansion developed during World War II, some authorities credit the speech as the beginning of the Cold War. The passage on "the iron curtain" attracted immediate international attention and, despite opposition, galvanized the West into forging the North Atlantic Treaty Organization (NATO). Although Stalin respected Churchill, he was furious about the speech and attacked Churchill's views. Some suggest the speech itself may have forced Stalin into conflict with the United States or at least threatened the Soviet Union and gave Stalin an excuse to increase his control of Eastern Europe.

T he United States stands at this time at the pinnacle of world power. It is a solemn moment for the American Democracy. For with primacy in power is also joined an awe-inspiring accountability to the future. If you look around you, you must feel not only the sense of duty done but also you must feel anxiety lest you fall below the level of achievement. Opportunity is here now, clear and shining for both our countries. To reject it or ignore it or fritter it away will bring upon us all the long reproaches of the after-time. It is necessary that constancy of mind, persistency of purpose, and the grand simplicity of decision shall guide and rule the conduct of the English-speaking peoples in peace as they did in war. We must, and I believe we shall, prove ourselves equal to this severe requirement.

When American military men approach some serious situation they are wont to write at the head of their directive the words "over-all strategic concept." There is wisdom in this, as it leads to clarity of thought. What then is the over-all strategic concept which we should inscribe today? It is nothing less than the safety and welfare, the freedom and progress, of all the homes and families of all the men and women in all the lands. And here I speak particularly of the myriad cottage or apartment homes where the wage-earner strives amid the accidents and difficulties of life to guard his wife and children from privation and bring the family up in the fear of the Lord, or upon ethical conceptions which often play their potent part.

Shielding the People from War

To give security to these countless homes, they must be shielded from the two giant marauders, war and tyranny. We all know the frightful disturbances in which the ordinary family is plunged when the curse of war swoops down upon the bread-winner and those for whom he works and contrives. The awful ruin of Europe, with all its vanished glories, and of large parts of Asia glares us in the eyes. When the designs of wicked men or the aggressive urge of mighty States dissolve over large areas the frame of civilized society, humble folk are confronted with difficulties with which they cannot cope. For them all is distorted, all is broken, even ground to pulp.

When I stand here this quiet afternoon I shudder to visualize what is actually happening to millions now and what is going to happen in this period when famine stalks the earth. None can compute what has been called "the unestimated sum of human pain." Our supreme task and duty is to guard the homes of the common people from the horrors and miseries of another war. We are all agreed on that.

Our American military colleagues, after having proclaimed their "over-all strategic concept" and computed available resources, always proceed to the next step—namely, the method. Here again there is widespread agreement. A world organization has already been erected for the prime purpose of preventing war, UNO [United Nations Organization], the successor of the League of Nations, with the decisive addition of the United States and all that means, is already at work. We must make sure that its work is fruitful, that it is a reality and not a sham, that it is a force for action, and not merely a frothing of words, that it is a true temple of peace in which the shields of many nations can some day be hung up, and not merely a cockpit in a Tower of Babel. Before we cast away the solid assurances of national armaments for self-preservation we must be certain that our temple is built, not upon shifting sands or quagmires, but upon the rock. Anyone can see with his eyes open that our path will be difficult and also long, but if we persevere together as we did in the two world wars—though not, alas, in the interval between them—I cannot doubt that we shall achieve our common purpose in the end. . . .

The Danger of Tyranny

Now I come to the second danger of these two marauders which threatens the cottage, the home, and the ordinary people—namely, tyranny. We cannot be blind to the fact that the liberties enjoyed by individual citizens throughout the British Empire are not valid in a considerable number of countries, some of which are very powerful. In these States control is enforced upon the common people by various kinds of all-embracing police governments. The power of the State is exercised without restraint, either by dictators or by compact oligarchies operating through a privileged party and a political police. It is not our duty at this time when difficulties are so numerous to interfere forcibly in the internal affairs of countries which we have not conquered in war. But we must never cease to proclaim in fearless tones the great principles of freedom and the rights of man which are the joint inheritance of the English-speaking world and which through Magna Carta, the Bill of Rights, the Habeas Corpus, trial by jury, and the English common law find their most famous expression in the American Declaration of Independence.

All this means that the people of any country have the right, and should have the power by constitutional action, by free unfettered elections, with secret ballot, to choose or change the character or form of government under which they dwell; that freedom of speech and thought should reign; that courts of justice, independent of the executive, unbiased by any party, should administer laws which have received the broad assent of large majorities or are consecrated by time and custom. Here are the title deeds of freedom which should lie in every cottage home. Here is the message of the British and American peoples to mankind. Let us preach what we practice—let us practice what we preach.

I have now stated the two great dangers which menace the homes of the people: War and Tyranny. I have not yet spoken of poverty and privation which are in many cases the prevailing anxiety. But if the dangers of war and tyranny are removed, there is no doubt that science and co-operation can bring in the next few years to the world, certainly in the next few decades newly taught in the sharpening school of war, an expansion of material well-being beyond anything that has yet occurred in human experience. Now, at this sad and breathless moment, we are plunged in the hunger and distress which are the aftermath of our stupendous struggle; but this will pass and may pass quickly, and there is no reason except human folly or sub-human crime which should deny to all the nations the inauguration and enjoyment of an age of plenty. I have often used words which I learned fifty years ago from a great Irish-American orator, a friend of mine, Mr. Bourke Cockran. "There is enough for all. The earth is a generous mother; she will provide in plentiful abundance food for all her children if they will but cultivate her soil in justice and in peace." So far I feel that we are in full agreement. . . .

A shadow has fallen upon the scenes so lately lighted by the Allied victory. Nobody knows what Soviet Russia and its Communist international organization intends to do in the immediate future, or what are the limits, if any, to their expansive and proselytizing tendencies. I have a strong admiration and regard for the valiant Russian people and for my wartime comrade, Marshal [Joseph] Stalin. There is deep sympathy and goodwill in Britain—and I doubt not here also—towards the peoples of all the Russias and a resolve to persevere through many differences and rebuffs in establishing lasting friendships. We understand the Russian need to be secure on her western frontiers by the removal of all possibility of German aggression. We welcome Russia to her rightful place among the leading nations of the world. We welcome her flag upon the seas. Above all, we welcome constant, frequent, and growing contacts between the Russian people and our own people on both sides of the Atlantic. It is my duty, however, for I am sure you would wish me to state the facts as I see them to you, to place before you certain facts about the present position in Europe.

From Stettin in the Baltic to Trieste in the Adriatic, an iron curtain has descended across the Continent. Behind that line lie all the capitals of the ancient states of Central and Eastern Europe. Warsaw, Berlin, Prague, Vienna, Budapest, Belgrade, Bucharest, and Sofia, all these famous cities and the populations around them, lie in what I must call the Soviet sphere, and all are subject in one form or another, not only to Soviet influence but to a very high and, in many cases, increasing measure of control from Moscow. Athens alone—Greece with its immortal glories—is free to decide its future at an election under British, American, and French observation. The Russian-dominated Polish Government has been encouraged to make enormous and wrongful inroads upon Germany, and mass expulsions of millions of Germans on a scale grievous and undreamed-of are now taking place. The Communist parties, which were very small in all these Eastern States of Europe, have been raised to pre-eminence and power far beyond their numbers and are seeking everywhere to obtain totalitarian control. Police governments are prevailing in nearly every case, and so far, except in Czechoslovakia, there is no true democracy. Turkey and Persia are both profoundly alarmed and disturbed at the claims which are being made upon them and at the pressure being exerted by the Moscow Government. An attempt is being made by the Russians in Berlin to build up a quasi-Communist party in their zone of Occupied Germany by showing special favors to groups of left-wing German leaders. At the end of the fighting, last June [1945], the American and British Armies withdrew westwards, in accordance with an earlier agreement, to a depth at some points of 150 miles upon a front of nearly four hundred miles, in order to allow our Russian allies to occupy this vast expanse of territory which the Western Democracies had conquered.

If now the Soviet Government tries, by separate action, to build up a pro-Communist Germany in their areas, this will cause new serious difficulties in the British and American zones, and will give the defeated Germans the power of putting themselves up to auction between the Soviets and the Western Democracies. Whatever conclusions may be drawn from these facts—and facts they are—this is certainly not the Liberated Europe we fought to build up. Nor is it one which contains the essentials of permanent peace.

The safety of the world requires a new unity in Europe,

from which no nation should be permanently outcast. It is from the quarrels of the strong parent races in Europe that the world wars we have witnessed, or which occurred in former times, have sprung. Twice in our own lifetime we have seen the United States, against their wishes and their traditions, against arguments, the force of which it is impossible not to comprehend, drawn by irresistible forces, into these wars in time to secure the victory of the good cause, but only after frightful slaughter and devastation had occurred. Twice the United States has had to send several millions of its young men across the Atlantic to find the war; but now war can find any nation, wherever it may dwell between dusk and dawn. Surely we should work with conscious purpose for a grand pacification of Europe, within the structure of the United Nations and in accordance with its Charter. That I feel is an open cause of policy of very great importance.

A Challenge to the Cause of Freedom

In front of the iron curtain which lies across Europe are other causes for anxiety. In Italy the Communist Party is seriously hampered by having to support the Communist-trained Marshal [Josip Broz] Tito's claims to former Italian territory at the head of the Adriatic. Nevertheless the future of Italy hangs in the balance. Again one cannot imagine a regenerated Europe without a strong France. All my public life I have worked for a strong France and I never lost faith in her destiny, even in the darkest hours. I will not lose faith now. However, in a great number of countries, far from the Russian frontiers and throughout the world, Communist fifth columns are established and work in complete unity and absolute obedience to the directions they receive from the Communist center. Except in the British Commonwealth and in the United States where Communism is in its infancy, the Communist parties or fifth columns constitute a growing challenge and peril to Christian civilization. These are somber facts for anyone to have to recite on the morrow of a victory gained by so much splendid comradeship in arms and in the cause of freedom and democracy; but we should be most unwise not to face them squarely while time remains.

The outlook is also anxious in the Far East and especially in Manchuria. The Agreement which was made at Yalta,[1] to which I was a party, was extremely favorable to Soviet Russia, but it was made at a time when no one could say that the German war might not extend all through the summer and autumn of 1945 and when the Japanese war was expected to last for a further 18 months from the end of the German war. In this country you are all so well-informed about the Far East, and such devoted friends of China, that I do not need to expatiate on the situation there.

I have felt bound to portray the shadow which, alike in the west and in the east, falls upon the world. I was a high minister at the time of the Versailles Treaty and a close friend of Mr. [David] Lloyd-George, [British prime minister, 1916–1922], who was the head of the British delegation at Versailles. I did not myself agree with many things that were done, but I have a very strong impression in my mind of that situation, and I find it painful to contrast it with that which prevails now. In those days there were high hopes and unbounded confidence that the wars were over, and that the League of Nations would become all-powerful. I do not see or feel that same confidence or even the same hopes in the haggard world at the present time.

A United Defense

On the other hand I repulse the idea that a new war is inevitable; still more that it is imminent. It is because I am sure that our fortunes are still in our own hands and that we hold the power to save the future that I feel the duty to speak out now that I have the occasion and the opportunity to do so. I do not believe that Soviet Russia desires war. What they desire is the fruits of war and the indefinite expansion of their power and doctrines. But what we have to consider here to-day while time remains, is the permanent prevention of war and the es-

1. From February 4 to February 11, 1945, Joseph Stalin, Winston Churchill, and Franklin D. Roosevelt met at Yalta in the Crimea to discuss the organization of postwar Europe. The Soviet Union agreed to enter the war against Japan in exchange for the occupation of Eastern Europe. The Agreement established the United Nations and divided Germany among Britain, France, the Soviet Union, and the United States.

tablishment of conditions of freedom and democracy as rapidly as possible in all countries. Our difficulties and dangers will not be removed by closing our eyes to them. They will not be removed by mere waiting to see what happens; nor will they be removed by a policy of appeasement. What is needed is a settlement, and the longer this is delayed, the more difficult it will be and the greater our dangers will become.

From what I have seen of our Russian friends and Allies during the war, I am convinced that there is nothing they admire so much as strength, and there is nothing for which they have less respect than for weakness, especially military weakness. For that reason the old doctrine of a balance of power is unsound. We cannot afford, if we can help it, to work on narrow margins, offering temptations to a trial of strength. If the Western Democracies stand together in strict adherence to the principles of the United Nations Charter, their influence for furthering those principles will be immense and no one is likely to molest them. If however they become divided or falter in their duty and if these all-important years are allowed to slip away then indeed catastrophe may overwhelm us all.

Last time I saw it all coming and cried aloud to my own fellow-countrymen and to the world, but no one paid any attention. Up till the year 1933 or even 1935, Germany might have been saved from the awful fate which has overtaken her and we might all have been spared the miseries Adolf Hitler let loose upon mankind. There never was a war in all history easier to prevent by timely action than the one which has just desolated such great areas of the globe. It could have been prevented in my belief without the firing of a single shot, and Germany might be powerful, prosperous, and honored today; but no one would listen and one by one we were all sucked into the awful whirlpool. We surely must not let that happen again. This can only be achieved by reaching now, in 1946, a good understanding on all points with Russia under the general authority of the United Nations Organization and by the maintenance of that good understanding through many peaceful years, by the world instrument, supported by the whole strength of the English-speaking world and all its connections. There is the solution which I respectfully offer to you in this Address to which I have given the title "The Sinews of Peace."

Let no man underrate the abiding power of the British Empire and Commonwealth. Because you see the 46 millions in our island harassed about their food supply, of which they only grow one half, even in war-time, or because we have difficulty in restarting our industries and export trade after six years of passionate war effort, do not suppose that we shall not come through these dark years of privation as we have come through the glorious years of agony, or that half a century from now, you will not see 70 or 80 millions of Britons spread about the world and united in defense of our traditions, our way of life, and of the world causes which you and we espouse. If the population of the English-speaking Commonwealths be added to that of the United States with all that such co-operation implies in the air, on the sea, all over the globe, and in science and in industry, and in moral force, there will be no quivering, precarious balance of power to offer its temptation to ambition or adventure. On the contrary, there will be an overwhelming assurance of security. If we adhere faithfully to the Charter of the United Nations and walk forward in sedate and sober strength seeking no one's land or treasure, seeking to lay no arbitrary control upon the thoughts of men; if all British moral and material forces and convictions are joined with your own in fraternal association, the high-roads of the future will be clear, not only for us but for all, not only for our time, but for a century to come.

Protecting Greece and Turkey from Communist Aggression

Harry S. Truman

Shortly after becoming the nation's vice president and less than one month prior to the end of World War II in Europe, Harry S. Truman became the United States's thirty-third president when President Franklin D. Roosevelt died on April 12, 1945. Having received little to no briefing, Truman was forced to deal with wartime problems. Soon after victory in Europe, the war against Japan was also drawing to a close, but Japan would not agree to end the war. Truman therefore ordered atomic bombs dropped on Hiroshima and Nagasaki, and shortly thereafter, Japan surrendered.

Although World War II brought the Soviet Union and the Western democracies into an alliance to defeat Nazi Germany and Japan, the Soviet Union's aggressive, antidemocratic policy toward Eastern Europe had been creating tensions all during the war. On February 27, 1947, Truman gathered together several congressional leaders to discuss the Soviet threat. Secretary of State George C. Marshall and his undersecretary Dean Acheson described for the gathering the threat of Communist expansion in Europe and Asia, suggesting that the United States provide aid to Greece and Turkey so that these countries would not fall to communism. Acheson explained that if Greece and Turkey should fall, communism would likely

---

Harry S. Truman, speech before a joint session of Congress, Washington, DC, March 12, 1947.

spread south to Iran and as far east as India. Profoundly affected by the remarks of these men, the congressional leaders urged Truman to speak to Congress.

Truman was not normally an impressive speaker, but his speech before Congress on March 12, 1947, was delivered with authority. Although the speech only lasted eighteen minutes, it was met by a standing ovation. Truman described the desperate situation in Greece and Turkey and defined for Congress and the American people the nature of the Cold War and what came to be known as the Truman Doctrine of containment. Truman's speech, which asked Congress to provide financial aid to Greece and Turkey, was met with enthusiastic support, and Congress overwhelmingly approved the plan.

T he gravity of the situation which confronts the world today necessitates my appearance before a joint session of the Congress.

The foreign policy and the national security of this country are involved.

One aspect of the present situation, which I present to you at this time for your consideration and decision, concerns Greece and Turkey.

An Appeal from Greece

The United States has received from the Greek Government an urgent appeal for financial and economic assistance. Preliminary reports from the American Economic Mission now in Greece and reports from the American Ambassador in Greece corroborate the statement of the Greek Government that assistance is imperative if Greece is to survive as a free nation.

I do not believe that the American people and the Congress wish to turn a deaf ear to the appeal of the Greek Government.

Greece is not a rich country. Lack of sufficient natural resources has always forced the Greek people to work hard to make both ends meet. Since 1940, this industrious, peace loving country has suffered invasion, four years of cruel enemy occupation, and bitter internal strife.

When forces of liberation entered Greece they found that the retreating Germans had destroyed virtually all the railways, roads, port facilities, communications, and merchant marine. More than a thousand villages had been burned. Eighty-five percent of the children were tubercular. Livestock, poultry, and draft animals had almost disappeared. Inflation had wiped out practically all savings.

As a result of these tragic conditions, a militant minority, exploiting human want and misery, was able to create political chaos which, until now, has made economic recovery impossible.

Greece is today without funds to finance the importation of those goods which are essential to bare subsistence. Under these circumstances the people of Greece cannot make progress in solving their problems of reconstruction. Greece is in desperate need of financial and economic assistance to enable it to resume purchases of food, clothing, fuel, and seeds. These are indispensable for the subsistence of its people and are obtainable only from abroad. Greece must have help to import the goods necessary to restore internal order and security so essential for economic and political recovery.

The Greek Government has also asked for the assistance of experienced American administrators, economists, and technicians to insure that the financial and other aid given to Greece shall be used effectively in creating a stable and self-sustaining economy and in improving its public administration.

The very existence of the Greek state is today threatened by the terrorist activities of several thousand armed men, led by Communists, who defy the government's authority at a number of points, particularly along the northern boundaries. A Commission appointed by the United Nations Security Council is at present investigating disturbed conditions in northern Greece and alleged border violations along the frontier between Greece on the one hand and Albania, Bulgaria, and Yugoslavia on the other.

Meanwhile, the Greek Government is unable to cope with the situation. The Greek army is small and poorly equipped. It needs supplies and equipment if it is to restore authority to the government throughout Greek territory.

Greece must have assistance if it is to become a self-supporting and self-respecting democracy.

The United States must supply this assistance. We have already extended to Greece certain types of relief and economic aid but these are inadequate.

There is no other country to which democratic Greece can turn.

No other nation is willing and able to provide the necessary support for a democratic Greek government.

The British Government, which has been helping Greece, can give no further financial or economic aid after March 31, 1947. Great Britain finds itself under the necessity of reducing or liquidating its commitments in several parts of the world, including Greece.

We have considered how the United Nations might assist in this crisis. But the situation is an urgent one requiring immediate action, and the United Nations and its related organizations are not in a position to extend help of the kind that is required.

It is important to note that the Greek Government has asked for our aid in utilizing effectively the financial and other assistance we may give to Greece, and in improving its public administration. It is of the utmost importance that we supervise the use of any funds made available to Greece, in such a manner that each dollar spent will count toward making Greece self-supporting, and will help to build an economy in which a healthy democracy can flourish.

No government is perfect. One of the chief virtues of a democracy, however, is that its defects are always visible and under democratic processes can be pointed out and corrected. The government of Greece is not perfect. Nevertheless it represents 85 percent of the members of the Greek Parliament who were chosen in an election in 1946. Foreign observers, including 692 Americans, considered this election to be a fair expression of the views of the Greek people.

The Greek Government has been operating in an atmosphere of chaos and extremism. It has made mistakes. The extension of aid by this country does not mean that the United States condones everything that the Greek Government has done or will do. We have condemned in the past, and we condemn now, extremist measures of the right or the left. We have in the past advised tolerance, and we advise tolerance now.

Maintaining Turkey's National Integrity

Greece's neighbor, Turkey, also deserves our attention.

The future of Turkey as an independent and economically sound state is clearly no less important to the freedom-loving peoples of the world than the future of Greece. The circumstances in which Turkey finds itself today are considerably different from those of Greece. Turkey has been spared the disasters that have beset Greece. And during the war, the United States and Great Britain furnished Turkey with material aid.

Nevertheless, Turkey now needs our support.

Since the war Turkey has sought additional financial assistance from Great Britain and the United States for the purpose of effecting that modernization necessary for the maintenance of its national integrity.

That integrity is essential to the preservation of order in the Middle East.

The British Government has informed us that, owing to its own difficulties, it can no longer extend financial or economic aid to Turkey.

As in the case of Greece, if Turkey is to have the assistance it needs, the United States must supply it. We are the only country able to provide that help.

I am fully aware of the broad implications involved if the United States extends assistance to Greece and Turkey, and I shall discuss these implications with you at this time.

The Objectives of Foreign Aid

One of the primary objectives of the foreign policy of the United States is the creation of conditions in which we and other nations will be able to work out a way of life free from coercion. This was a fundamental issue in the war with Germany and Japan. Our victory was won over countries which sought to impose their will, and their way of life, upon other nations.

To ensure the peaceful development of nations, free from coercion, the United States has taken a leading part in establishing the United Nations. The United Nations is designed to make possible lasting freedom and independence for all its members. We shall not realize our objectives, however, unless we are willing to help free peoples to maintain their free institutions and their national integrity against aggressive movements that seek to impose upon them totalitarian regimes. This is no more than a frank recognition that totalitarian regimes imposed upon free peoples, by direct or indirect aggression, undermine the foundations of international peace and hence the security of the United States.

Harry S. Truman

The peoples of a number of countries of the world have recently had totalitarian regimes forced upon them against their will. The Government of the United States has made frequent protests against coercion and intimidation, in violation of the Yalta agreement, [which required those who signed the agreement to help occupied nations establish their own governments through free elections], in Poland, Rumania, and Bulgaria. I must also state that in a number of other countries there have been similar developments.

At the present moment in world history nearly every nation must choose between alternative ways of life. The choice is too often not a free one.

One way of life is based upon the will of the majority, and is distinguished by free institutions, representative government, free elections, guarantees of individual liberty, freedom of speech and religion, and freedom from political oppression.

The second way of life is based upon the will of a minority forcibly imposed upon the majority. It relies upon terror and oppression, a controlled press and radio, fixed elections, and the suppression of personal freedoms.

I believe that it must be the policy of the United States to support free peoples who are resisting attempted subjugation by armed minorities or by outside pressures.

I believe that we must assist free peoples to work out their own destinies in their own way.

I believe that our help should be primarily through economic and financial aid which is essential to economic stability and orderly political processes.

The world is not static, and the *status quo* is not sacred. But we cannot allow changes in the *status quo* in violation of the Charter of the United Nations by such methods as coercion, or by such subterfuges as political infiltration. In helping free and independent nations to maintain their freedom, the United States will be giving effect to the principles of the Charter of the United Nations.

Protecting Free Nations

It is necessary only to glance at a map to realize that the survival and integrity of the Greek nation are of grave importance in a much wider situation. If Greece should fall under the control of an armed minority, the effect upon its neighbor, Turkey, would be immediate and serious. Confusion and disorder might well spread throughout the entire Middle East.

Moreover, the disappearance of Greece as an independent state would have a profound effect upon those countries in Europe whose peoples are struggling against great difficulties to maintain their freedoms and their independence while they repair the damages of war.

It would be an unspeakable tragedy if these countries, which have struggled so long against overwhelming odds, should lose that victory for which they sacrificed so much. Collapse of free institutions and loss of independence would be disastrous not only for them but for the world. Discouragement and possibly failure would quickly be the lot of neighboring peoples striving to maintain their freedom and independence.

Should we fail to aid Greece and Turkey in this fateful hour, the effect will be far reaching to the West as well as to the East.

We must take immediate and resolute action.

I therefore ask the Congress to provide authority for assistance to Greece and Turkey in the amount of $400,000,000 for the period ending June 30, 1948. In requesting these funds, I have taken into consideration the maximum amount of relief assistance which would be furnished to Greece out of the $350,000,000 which I recently requested that the Congress authorize for the prevention of starvation and suffering in countries devastated by the war.

In addition to funds, I ask the Congress to authorize the detail of American civilian and military personnel to Greece and Turkey, at the request of those countries, to assist in the tasks of reconstruction, and for the purpose of supervising the use of such financial and material assistance as may be furnished. I recommend that authority also be provided for the instruction and training of selected Greek and Turkish personnel.

Finally, I ask that the Congress provide authority which will permit the speediest and most effective use, in terms of needed commodities, supplies, and equipment, of such funds as may be authorized.

Investing in Peace

If further funds, or further authority, should be needed for the purposes indicated in this message, I shall not hesitate to bring the situation before the Congress. On this subject the Executive and Legislative branches of the Government must work together.

This is a serious course upon which we embark.

I would not recommend it except that the alternative is much more serious.

The United States contributed $341,000,000,000 toward winning World War II. This is an investment in world freedom and world peace.

The assistance that I am recommending for Greece and Turkey amounts to little more than $1/10$ of 1 percent of this investment. It is only common sense that we should safeguard this investment and make sure that it was not in vain.

The seeds of totalitarian regimes are nurtured by misery

and want. They spread and grow in the evil soil of poverty and strife. They reach their full growth when the hope of a people for a better life has died.

We must keep that hope alive.

The free peoples of the world look to us for support in maintaining their freedoms.

If we falter in our leadership, we may endanger the peace of the world—and we shall surely endanger the welfare of this Nation.

Great responsibilities have been placed upon us by the swift movement of events.

I am confident that the Congress will face these responsibilities squarely.

The State Department Is Infested with Communists

Joseph R. McCarthy

Joseph R. McCarthy was born on November 14, 1908, in
Grand Chute, Wisconsin. He became a U.S. senator in
1946 when he defeated twenty-two-year incumbent
Robert La Follette Jr. McCarthy's early years as a junior
senator were characterized by his disregard of the Senate's rules, customs, and procedures. He often used
threats and personal attacks to serve his purposes. His
career in the Senate was rather unremarkable, however,
until he spoke at an Abraham Lincoln birthday celebration at the Women's Republican Club in Wheeling, West
Virginia, on February 9, 1950.

One of the most significant in America's Cold War
history, McCarthy's speech came at a time when Americans were faced with the threat of Communist expansion:
China had been "lost" to communism, South Korea faced
the threat of invasion by Communist North Korea, and
the nations of Eastern Europe were succumbing to Soviet
Communist influence. In the following excerpt from a similar address delivered the following day in Salt Lake City,
Utah, McCarthy exploits the public's fear of communism
by providing alarming statistics on the spread of Communist influence in the world. However, what made his
speech notorious was his claim that Communists had infil-
trated the U.S. State Department. In the Wheeling speech,

Joseph R. McCarthy, speech in Salt Lake City, Utah, February 10, 1950.

McCarthy claimed he had a list of 205 State Department employees who were Communists. In his Salt Lake City speech, however, McCarthy changed the number to fifty-seven for unknown reasons. He specifically names several employees working within the State Department, describing their crimes and their relationships with others in government in detail. Some of those he accused lost their jobs although McCarthy never proved their guilt.

After Republicans took control of the White House and Congress in 1953, McCarthy was named chairman of the Committee on Government Operations and its Subcommittee on Investigations. In widely publicized hearings on Communist subversion in America, McCarthy used his position to make reckless accusations with the help of unidentified informers; careers were ruined on the flimsiest evidence. His bullying of witnesses turned public opinion against McCarthy, and his methods also came under attack by his Republican colleagues. On December 2, 1954, the Senate voted to censure him, describing his acts as "contrary to senatorial traditions." The term *McCarthyism* came to mean similar political assaults involving sensational tactics and unsubstantiated accusations.

Tonight as we celebrate the 141st birthday of one of the great men in American history, I would like to be able to talk about what a glorious day today is in the history of the world. As we celebrate the birth of this man, who with his whole heart and soul hated war, I would like to be able to speak of peace in our time, of war being outlawed, and of worldwide disarmament. These would be truly appropriate things to be able to mention as we celebrate the birthday of Abraham Lincoln.

Five years after a world war has been won, men's hearts should anticipate a long peace, and men's minds should be free from the heavy weight that comes with war. But this is not such a period—for this is not a period of peace. This is a time of the Cold War. This is a time when all the world is split into two vast, increasingly hostile armed camps—a time of a great armaments race. Today we can almost physically hear the mutterings and rumblings of an invigorated god of war. You can see it, feel it, and hear it all the way from the hills of Indochina, from the shores of Formosa right over into the very heart of Europe itself. . . .

A Showdown Between Democracy and Communism

Today we are engaged in a final, all-out battle between communistic atheism and Christianity. The modern champions of communism have selected this as the time. And, ladies and gentlemen, the chips are down—they are truly down.

Lest there be any doubt that the time has been chosen, let us go directly to the leader of communism today—Joseph Stalin. Here is what he said—not back in 1928, not before the war, not during the war—but two years after the last war was ended: "To think that the communist revolution can be carried out peacefully, within the framework of a Christian democracy, means one has either gone out of one's mind and lost all normal understanding, or has grossly and openly repudiated the communist revolution."

And this is what was said by Lenin in 1919, which was also quoted with approval by Stalin in 1947: "We are living," said Lenin, "not merely in a state but in a system of states, and the existence of the Soviet Republic side by side with Christian states for a long time is unthinkable. One or the other must triumph in the end. And before that end supervenes, a series of frightful collisions between the Soviet Republic and the bourgeois states will be inevitable."

Ladies and gentlemen, can there be anyone here tonight who is so blind as to say that the war is not on? Can there be anyone who fails to realize that the communist world has said, "The time is now"—that this is the time for the showdown between the democratic Christian world and the communist atheistic world? Unless we face this fact, we shall pay the price that must be paid by those who wait too long.

Six years ago [in October 1944], at the time of the first conference to map out peace—Dumbarton Oaks [a mansion in Washington, D.C., where the first blueprint of the UN was prepared]—there was within the Soviet orbit 180 million people. Lined up on the anti-totalitarian side there were in the world at that time roughly 1.625 billion people. Today, only six years later, there are 800 million people under the absolute domination of Soviet Russia—an increase of over 400 percent. On our side, the figure has shrunk to around 500 million. In other words, in less than six years the odds have changed from 9 to 1 in our favor to 8 to 5 against us. This indicates the swiftness of the tempo of communist victories and American defeats in the Cold War. As one of our outstanding historical figures once said, "When a great democracy is destroyed, it will not be because of enemies from without but rather because of enemies from within." The truth of this statement is becoming terrifyingly clear as we see this country each day losing on every front.

At war's end we were physically the strongest nation on Earth and, at least potentially, the most powerful intellectually and morally. Ours could have been the honor of being a beacon in the desert of destruction, a shining, living proof that civilization was not yet ready to destroy itself. Unfortunately, we have failed miserably and tragically to arise to the opportunity.

Who Are the Traitors?

The reason why we find ourselves in a position of impotency is not because our only powerful, potential enemy has sent men to invade our shores, but rather because of the traitorous actions of those who have been treated so well by this nation. It has not been the less fortunate or members of minority groups who have been selling this nation out, but rather those who have had all the benefits that the wealthiest nation on earth has had to offer—the finest homes, the finest college education, and the finest jobs in government we can give.

This is glaringly true in the State Department. There the bright young men who are born with silver spoons in their mouths are the ones who have been worst.

Now I know it is very easy for anyone to condemn a particular bureau or department in general terms. Therefore, I would like to cite one rather unusual case—the case of a man who has done much to shape our foreign policy.

When Chiang Kai-shek [who led the Nationalists against the rising communist forces, but was driven from mainland China to Taiwan in 1949] was fighting our war, the State Department had in China a young man named John S. Service. His task, obviously, was not to work for the communization of China. Strangely, however, he sent official reports back to the State Department urging that we torpedo our ally Chiang Kai-shek and stating, in effect, that communism was the best hope of China.

Later, this man—John Service—was picked up by the Federal Bureau of Investigation for turning over to the communists secret State Department information. Strangely, however, he was never prosecuted. However, Joseph Grew, the undersecretary of state, who insisted on his prosecution, was forced to resign. Two days after, Grew's successor, Dean Acheson, took over as undersecretary of state, this man— John Service—who had been picked up by the FBI and who had previously urged that communism was the best hope of China, was not only reinstated in the State Department but promoted; and finally, under Acheson, placed in charge of all placements and promotions. Today, ladies and gentlemen, this man Service is on his way to represent the State Department and Acheson in Calcutta—by far and away the most important listening post in the Far East.

Now, let's see what happens when individuals with communist connections are forced out of the State Department. Gustave Duran, who was labeled as, I quote, "a notorious international communist," was made assistant secretary of state in charge of Latin American affairs. He was taken into the State Department from his job as a lieutenant colonel in the Communist International Brigade. Finally, after intense congressional pressure and criticism, he resigned in 1946 from the State Department—and, ladies and gentlemen, where do you think he is now? He took over a high-salaried job as chief of Cultural Activities Section in the office of the assistant secretary-general of the United Nations. . . .

This, ladies and gentlemen, gives you somewhat of a picture of the type of individuals who have been helping to shape our foreign policy. In my opinion the State Department, which is one of the most important government departments, is thoroughly infested with communists.

I have in my hand 57 cases of individuals who would appear to be either card-carrying members or certainly loyal to the Communist Party, but who nevertheless are still helping to shape our foreign policy.

One thing to remember in discussing the communists in our government is that we are not dealing with spies who get 30 pieces of silver to steal the blueprints of new weapons. We are dealing with a far more sinister type of activity because it permits the enemy to guide and shape our policy.

The Influence of Alger Hiss

This brings us down to the case of one Alger Hiss, who is important not as an individual anymore but rather because he is so representative of a group in the State Department. It is unnecessary to go over the sordid events showing how he sold out the nation which had given him so much. Those are rather fresh in all of our minds. However, it should be remembered that the facts in regard to his connection with this international communist spy ring were made known to the then-Undersecretary of State [Adolf] Berle three days after [Adolf] Hitler and [Joseph] Stalin signed the Russo-German Alliance Pact. At that time one Whittaker Chambers—who was also part of the spy ring—apparently decided that with Russia on Hitler's side, he could no longer betray our nation to Russia. He gave Undersecretary of State Berle—and this is all a matter of record—practically all, if not more, of the facts upon which Hiss' conviction was based.

Undersecretary Berle promptly contacted Dean Acheson and received word in return that Acheson, and I quote, "could vouch for Hiss absolutely"—at which time the matter was dropped. And this, you understand, was at a time when Russia was an ally of Germany. This condition existed while Russia and Germany were invading and dismembering Poland, and while the communist groups here were screaming "warmonger" at the United States for their support of the Allied nations.

Again in 1943, the FBI had occasion to investigate the facts surrounding Hiss' contacts with the Russian spy ring. But even after that FBI report was submitted, nothing was done.

Then, late in 1948—on August 5—when the Un-American Activities Committee called Alger Hiss to give an accounting, President [Harry S.] Truman at once issued a presidential directive ordering all government agencies to refuse to turn over any information whatsoever in regard to the communist activities of any government employee to a congressional committee.

Incidentally, even after Hiss was convicted, it is interesting to note that the president still labeled the exposé of Hiss as a "red herring."

If time permitted, it might be well to go into detail about the fact that Hiss was Roosevelt's chief adviser at Yalta [a conference during which the Soviet Union was allowed to occupy Eastern Europe] when Roosevelt was admittedly in ill health and tired physically and mentally . . . and when, according to the secretary of state, Hiss and [Andrei] Gromyko [Soviet Ambassador to the UN] drafted the report on the conference.

According to the then-Secretary of State [Edward] Stettinius, here are some of the things that Hiss helped to decide at Yalta: (1) the establishment of a European High Commission; (2) the treatment of Germany—this you will recall was the conference at which it was decided that we would occupy Berlin with Russia occupying an area completely encircling the city, which as you know, resulted in the Berlin airlift which cost 31 American lives; (3) the Polish question; (4) the relationship between UNRRA [United Nations Relief and Rehabilitation Administration] and the Soviet; (5) the rights of Americans on control commissions of Rumania, Bulgaria, and Hungary; (6) Iran; (7) China—here's where we gave away Manchuria; (8) Turkish Straits question; (9) international trusteeships; (10) Korea.

Of the results of this conference, Arthur Bliss Lane of the State Department had this to say: "As I glanced over the document, I could not believe my eyes. To me, almost every line spoke of a surrender to Stalin."

As you hear this story of high treason, I know that you are saying to yourself, "Well, why doesn't the Congress do something about it?" Actually, ladies and gentlemen, one of the important reasons for the graft, the corruption, the dishonesty, the disloyalty, the treason in high government positions—one of the most important reasons why this continues—is a lack of moral uprising on the part of the 140 million American people. In the light of history, however, this is not hard to explain.

It is the result of an emotional hangover and a temporary moral lapse which follows every war. It is the apathy to evil which people who have been subjected to the tremendous evils of war feel. As the people of the world see mass murder, the destruction of defenseless and innocent people, and all of the crime and lack of morals which go with war, they become numb and apathetic. It has always been thus after war. However, the morals of our people have not been destroyed. They still exist. This cloak of numbness and apathy has only needed a spark to rekindle them. Happily, this spark has finally been supplied.

As you know, very recently the secretary of state [Dean Acheson] proclaimed his loyalty to a man [Alger Hiss] guilty of what has always been considered as the most abominable of all crimes—of being a traitor to the people who gave him a position of great trust. The secretary of state, in attempting to justify his continued devotion to the man who sold out the Christian world to the atheistic world, referred to Christ's Sermon on the Mount as a justification and reason therefore, and the reaction of the American people to this would have made the heart of Abraham Lincoln happy. When this pompous diplomat in striped pants, with a phony British accent, proclaimed to the American people that Christ on the Mount endorsed communism, high treason, and betrayal of a sacred trust, the blasphemy was so great that it awakened the dormant indignation of the American people.

He has lighted the spark which is resulting in a moral uprising and will end only when the whole sorry mess of twisted, warped thinkers are swept from the national scene so that we may have a new birth of national honesty and decency in government.

Trial by Accusation Is Dangerous to the Nation

Margaret Chase Smith

Margaret Chase Smith was born in Skowhegan, Maine,
on December 14, 1897. Smith was elected to the U.S.
House of Representatives in 1940, succeeding her husband after his death. She became a U.S. senator in 1948
and was the first woman nominated for the U.S. presidency, placing second to Barry Goldwater, who was defeated by Lyndon Johnson in November 1964. During
her career Smith earned a reputation for expertise in international relations. She was a member of both the
Armed Services and Appropriations Committees and, as a
supporter of the space program, served as a charter member of the Senate Aeronautical and Space Committee.

Smith gained national attention when she gave the
following speech before the Senate denouncing the ex-
cesses of her fellow Republican senator, Joseph McCarthy
of Wisconsin, in his crusade to purge the government of
Communists. Smith said, "If I am to be remembered in
history, it will not be because of legislative accomplishments, but for an act I took as a legislator in the U.S.
Senate when on June 1, 1950, I spoke . . . in condemnation of McCarthyism, when the junior Senator from Wisconsin had the Senate paralyzed with fear that he would
purge any Senator who disagreed with him." Smith sub-
sequently became the victim of McCarthy's vengeance:
He dropped her from a key investigation subcommittee
and supported an attempt to defeat her reelection.

Margaret Chase Smith, speech before the U.S. Senate, Washington, DC, June 1,
1950.

Notwithstanding McCarthy's actions, Maine voters returned Smith to office.

Smith was the only woman in the Senate when she
signed a declaration made by seven Republican senators
that denounced McCarthy's tactics. Her address to Congress, "The Declaration of Conscience," questions the
Senate's right to make accusations without recourse to
the law and challenges the Senate's abuse of freedom of
speech. Smith claims that the right to criticize, protest,
and hold unpopular beliefs is one of the fundamental
principles of democracy. Smith's address speaks to the
Senate from several perspectives: As a Republican, she
questions the success of a party that exploits fear to succeed; as a woman, she fears the effect of unfounded accusation on the families of those who have been accused; as
a senator, she is ashamed that the Senate would place political gain before integrity; and, as an American, she
fears the danger posed to the country by such abuses.
Both liberals and moderates hailed the declaration, but
not until December 2, 1954, did the Senate officially censure McCarthy.

Mr. President, I would like to speak briefly and simply about a serious national condition. It is a national feeling of fear and frustration that could result in national suicide and the end of everything that we
Americans hold dear. It is a condition that comes from the
lack of effective leadership either in the legislative branch or
the executive branch of our government. That leadership is
so lacking that serious and responsible proposals are being
made that national advisory commissions be appointed to
provide such critically needed leadership.

I speak as briefly as possible because too much harm has
already been done with irresponsible words of bitterness and
selfish political opportunism. I speak as simply as possible
because the issue is too great to be obscured by eloquence. I
speak simply and briefly in the hope that my words will be
taken to heart.

Mr. President, I speak as a Republican. I speak as a woman. I speak as a United States senator. I speak as an American.

A Forum for Character Assassination

The United States Senate has long enjoyed worldwide respect as the greatest deliberative body in the world. But recently that deliberative character has too often been debased to the level of a forum of hate and character assassination sheltered by the shield of congressional immunity.

It is ironical that we senators can in debate in the Senate, directly or indirectly, by any form of words, impute to any American who is not a senator any conduct or motive unworthy or unbecoming an American—and without that non-senator American having any legal redress against us—yet if we say the same thing in the Senate about our colleagues we can be stopped on the grounds of being out of order.

It is strange that we can verbally attack anyone else without restraint and with full protection, and yet we hold ourselves above the same type of criticism here on the Senate floor. Surely the United States Senate is big enough to take self-criticism and self-appraisal. Surely we should be able to take the same kind of character attacks that we dish out to outsiders.

I think that it is high time for the United States Senate and its members to do some real soul searching and to weigh our consciences as to the manner in which we are performing our duty to the people of America and the manner in which we are using or abusing our individual powers and privileges.

I think it is high time that we remembered that we have sworn to uphold and defend the Constitution. I think it is high time that we remembered that the Constitution, as amended, speaks not only of the freedom of speech but also of trial by jury instead of trial by accusation.

Whether it be a criminal prosecution in court or a character prosecution in the Senate, there is little practical distinction when the life of a person has been ruined.

Those of us who shout the loudest about Americanism in making character assassinations are all too frequently those who, by our own words and acts, ignore some of the basic principles of Americanism: the right to criticize; the right to hold unpopular beliefs; the right to protest; the right of independent thought.

The exercise of these rights should not cost one single American citizen his reputation or his right to a livelihood nor should he be in danger of losing his reputation or livelihood merely because he happens to know someone who holds unpopular beliefs. Who of us does not? Otherwise none of us could call our souls our own. Otherwise thought control would have set in.

The American people are sick and tired of being afraid to speak their minds lest they be politically smeared as communists or fascists by their opponents. Freedom of speech is not what it used to be in America. It has been so abused by some that it is not exercised by others.

The American people are sick and tired of seeing innocent people smeared and guilty people whitewashed. But there have been enough proved cases . . . to cause nationwide distrust and strong suspicion that there may be something to the unproved, sensational accusations. . . .

A Nation Divided by Suspicion

Today our country is being psychologically divided by the confusion and the suspicions that are bred in the United States Senate to spread like cancerous tentacles of "know nothing, suspect everything" attitudes. . . .

The record of the present Democratic administration has provided us with sufficient campaign issues without the necessity of resorting to political smears. America is rapidly losing its position as leader of the world simply because the Democratic administration has pitifully failed to provide effective leadership. . . .

The Democratic administration has greatly lost the confidence of the American people by its complacency to the threat of communism here at home and the leak of vital secrets to Russia through key officials of the Democratic administration. There are enough proved cases to make this point without diluting our criticism with unproved charges. . . .

Surely it is clear that this nation will continue to suffer so long as it is governed by the present ineffective Democratic administration. Yet to displace it with a Republican regime embracing a philosophy that lacks political integrity or intellectual honesty would prove equally disastrous to the nation. The nation sorely needs a Republican victory. But I do not want to see the Republican party ride to political victory on the Four Horsemen of Calumny—fear, ignorance, bigotry, and smear.

Chapter
TWO

Coercion,
Conflict,
and Crisis

Appeasing China Means Surrendering to Communism

Douglas MacArthur

Often remembered for his corn-cob pipe and Ray-Ban sunglasses, General Douglas MacArthur was an American war hero who led U.S. armed forces to defeat Japan during World War II. When North Korean premier Kim Il Sung sent troops to South Korea in 1949 to force the reunification of North and South Korea as one Communist-ruled country, President Harry S. Truman named MacArthur commander of the United Nations forces. MacArthur drove North Korean forces beyond the 38th parallel that divided North and South Korea to the Yalu River that separated North Korea from China. This drive to the Chinese border provoked Chinese intervention, and MacArthur asked permission to bomb Chinese bases in Manchuria. Fearing war with China and the Soviet Union, Truman opposed MacArthur's strategy. MacArthur made his disagreement with Truman public, and Truman removed him from command in April 1951.

Public reaction to MacArthur's dismissal was strong, and on his return from Korea, MacArthur was given a hero's welcome. However, Democrats believed that MacArthur's public disapproval of the commander in chief undermined the president's authority. When MacArthur asked to address the nation in a televised speech before Congress, Democratic leaders agreed; they hoped that MacArthur, known for his theatrics, would criticize the president and provoke a backlash of presidential support.

Douglas MacArthur, speech before the U.S. Congress, Washington, DC, April 19, 1951.

However, on April 19, 1951, MacArthur spoke calmly,
barely using his notes, and when delivering his final lines,
spectators were hanging onto his every word. When
MacArthur whispered his final "goodbye," the gallery
was silent, and some had tears in their eyes.

Considered by many to be one of the great moments
in the early days of television, MacArthur's address de-
fends his strategy pertaining to the defense of Korea. In
the years that followed MacArthur's address, the Korean
conflict continued with no side gaining advantage. A
truce was finally signed on July 27, 1953.

I stand on this rostrum with a sense of deep humility and
great pride—humility in the wake of those great archi-
tects of our history who have stood here before me, pride
in the reflection that this home of legislative debate represents human liberty in the purest form yet devised.

Here are centered the hopes and aspirations and faith of
the entire human race.

I do not stand here as advocate for any partisan cause,
for the issues are fundamental and reach quite beyond the
realm of partisan considerations. They must be resolved on
the highest plane of national interest, if our course is to prove
sound and our future protected.

I trust, therefore, that you will do me the justice of receiving that which I have to say as solely expressing the considered viewpoint of a fellow American.

I address you with neither rancor nor bitterness in the
fading twilight of life, with but one purpose in mind: to serve
my country.

A Global Threat

The issues are global, and so interlocked that to consider the
problems of one sector oblivious to those of another is to
court disaster for the whole. While Asia is commonly referred to as the gateway to Europe, it is no less true that Europe is the gateway to Asia, and the broad influence of the

one cannot fail to have its impact upon the other.

There are those who claim our strength is inadequate to protect on both fronts, that we cannot divide our effort. I can think of no greater expression of defeatism.

If a potential enemy can divide his strength on two fronts, it is for us to counter his efforts. The Communist threat is a global one. Its successful advance in one sector threatens the destruction of every other sector. You cannot appease or otherwise surrender to Communism in Asia without simultaneously undermining our efforts to halt its advance in Europe.

Beyond pointing out these general truisms, I shall confine my discussion to the general areas of Asia.

While I was not consulted prior to the President's decision to intervene in support of the Republic of Korea, that decision, from a military standpoint, proved a sound one. As I say, it proved a sound one, as we hurled back the invader and decimated his forces. Our victory was complete, and our objectives within reach, when Red China intervened with numerically superior ground forces.

Opposing Chinese Intervention

This created a new war and an entirely new situation, a situation not contemplated when our forces were committed against the North Korean invaders; a situation which called for new decisions in the diplomatic sphere to permit the realistic adjustment of military strategy. Such decisions have not been forthcoming. While no man in his right mind would advocate sending our ground forces into continental China, and such was never given a thought, the new situation did urgently demand a drastic revision of strategic planning, if our political aim was to defeat this new enemy as we had defeated the old.

Apart from the military need, as I saw it, to neutralize the sanctuary protection given the enemy north of the Yalu, I felt that military necessity in the conduct of the war made necessary:

1. The intensification of our economic blockade against China.
2. The imposition of a naval blockade against the China coast.

3. Removal of restrictions on air reconnaissance of China's coastal area and of Manchuria.
4. Removal of restrictions on the forces of the Republic of China on Formosa, with logistical support to contribute to their effective operations against the Chinese mainland.

For entertaining these views, all professionally designed to support our forces committed to Korea and to bring hostilities to an end with the least possible delay and at a saving of countless American and Allied lives, I have been severely criticized in lay circles, principally abroad, despite my understanding that, from a military standpoint, the above views have been fully shared in the past by practically every military leader concerned with the Korean campaign, including our own Joint Chiefs of Staff.

I called for reinforcements, but was informed that reinforcements were not available. I made clear that if not permitted to destroy the enemy built-up bases north of the Yalu, if not permitted to utilize the friendly Chinese force of some six hundred thousand men on Formosa, if not permitted to blockade the China coast to prevent the Chinese Reds from getting succor from without, and if there were to be no hope of major reinforcements, the position of the command from the military standpoint forbade victory.

We could hold in Korea by constant maneuver and at an approximate area where our supply-line advantages were in balance with the supply-line disadvantages of the enemy, but we could hope at best for only an indecisive campaign with its terrible and constant attrition upon our forces if the enemy utilized his full military potential.

I have constantly called for the new political decisions essential to a solution. Efforts have been made to distort my position. It has been said, in effect, that I was a warmonger. Nothing could be further from the truth.

I know war as few other men now living know it, and nothing to me is more revolting! I have long advocated its complete abolition, as its very destructiveness on both friend and foe has rendered it useless as a means of settling international disputes.

Indeed, on the second day of September, 1945, just following the surrender of the Japanese nation on the battleship *Missouri*, I formally cautioned as follows:

> Men since the beginning of time have sought peace. Various methods through the ages have been attempted to devise an international process to prevent or settle disputes between nations. From the very start, workable methods were found in so far as individual citizens were concerned, but the mechanics of an instrumentality of larger international scope have never been successful.
>
> Military alliances, balances of power, leagues of nations, all in turn failed, leaving the only path to be by way of the crucible of war. The utter destructiveness of war now blocks out this alternative. We have had our last chance. If we will not devise some greater and more equitable system, our Armageddon will be at our door. The problem basically is theological and involves a spiritual recrudescence, an improvement of human character that will synchronize with our almost matchless advances in science, art, literature, and all material and cultural developments of the past two thousand years. It must be of the spirit if we are to save the flesh.

But once war is forced upon us, there is no other alternative than to apply every available means to bring it to a swift end. War's very object is victory, not prolonged indecision. In war, there is no substitute for victory.

There are some who, for varying reasons, would appease Red China. They are blind to history's clear lesson, for history teaches with unmistakable emphasis that appeasement but begets new and bloodier war. It points to no single instance where this end has justified that means, where appeasement has led to more than a sham peace. Like blackmail, it lays the basis for new and successively greater demands until, as in blackmail, violence becomes the only other alternative.

Why, my soldiers asked of me, surrender military advantages to an enemy in the field? I could not answer.

Some may say to avoid spread of the conflict into an all-out war with China. Others, to avoid Soviet intervention.

Neither explanation seems valid, for China is already engaging with the maximum power it can commit, and the Soviet [Union] will not necessarily mesh its actions with our moves. Like a cobra, any new enemy will more likely strike whenever it feels that the relativity in military or other potential is in its favor on a world-wide basis.

The tragedy of Korea is further heightened by the fact that its military action is confined to its territorial limits. It condemns that nation, which it is our purpose to save, to suffer the devastating impact of full naval and air bombardment, while the enemy's sanctuaries are fully protected from such attack and devastation.

Of the nations of the world Korea alone, up to now, is the sole one which has risked its all against communism. The magnificence of the courage and fortitude of the Korean people defies description. They have chosen to risk death rather than slavery. Their last words to me were: "Don't scuttle the Pacific."

I have just left your fighting sons in Korea. They have met all tests there, and I can report to you without reservation that they are splendid in every way. It was my constant effort to preserve them and end this savage conflict honorably and with the least loss of time and a minimum sacrifice of life. Its growing bloodshed has caused me the deepest anguish and anxiety. Those gallant men will remain often in my thoughts and in my prayers always.

I am closing my fifty-two years of military service. When I joined the army, even before the turn of the century, it was the fulfillment of all of my boyish hopes and dreams.

The world has turned over many times since I took the oath on the plain at West Point, and the hopes and dreams have long since vanished, but I still remember the refrain of one of the most popular barracks ballads of that day which proclaimed most proudly that "old soldiers never die; they just fade away." And like the old soldier of that ballad, I now close my military career and just fade away, an old soldier who tried to do his duty as God gave him the light to see that duty.

Good-bye.

A Victory over U.S. Aggression in Korea

Mao Tse-tung

Mao Tse-tung was born in the Hunan province of China on December 26, 1893. The son of a prosperous peasant, Mao received enough schooling to spark in him an interest in education, but while he was attending a training college for teachers, the Chinese empire collapsed. Mao became active in radical student groups and in 1921 became a founding member of the Chinese Communist Party. Mao also founded the Red Army of workers and peasants that opposed the Nationalist armies of Chiang Kai-shek between 1927 and 1945. Chiang Kai-shek drove Mao's armies to the northwest, but later, when the Chinese civil war resumed, Mao's Red Army overwhelmed the Nationalists. Mao proclaimed the People's Republic of China on October 1, 1949, establishing himself as Chairman of the party.

Both China and the Soviet Union supported North Korean premier Kim Il Sung, who in 1949 sent troops to South Korea to force the reunification of Korea as one Communist-ruled country. However, Chinese forces did not officially intervene until United Nation's forces, led by General Douglas MacArthur, drove North Korean forces to the Chinese border. These retaliatory Chinese forces then drove the UN forces back to the 38th parallel that divided North and South Korea after World War II. In 1951, the war had become a bloody stalemate. It was another two years before either side agreed to an armistice, and not until July 27, 1953, was a truce signed. This agreement again divided Korea at the 38th

Mao Tse-tung, "Our Great Victory in the War to Resist U.S. Aggression and Aid Korea and Our Future Tasks," September 12, 1953.

parallel; the division and tension remain today.

In the following speech, delivered at the twenty-fourth session of the Central People's Government Council on September 12, 1953, Mao explains the reasons for the success of Chinese and Korean armies against "the forces of U.S. aggression." He describes the strengths of the Communist troops and points out the internal weaknesses of the enemy. Mao emphasizes the importance of victory: Not only have the people been protected from the threat of imperialism, but the aggressors themselves are now aware of the strength of the Chinese people. If U.S. imperialists begin a new war, says Mao, the people of China must again make short-term economic sacrifices to protect their long-term interests.

A fter three years we have won a great victory in the war to resist U.S. aggression and aid Korea. It has now come to a halt.

To what was this victory due? Just now fellow members [of the Central People's Government Council] put it down to correct leadership. Leadership is one factor; nothing can succeed without correct leadership. But we won mainly because ours was a people's war, the whole nation gave it support and the people of China and Korea fought shoulder to shoulder.

The Sources of Success

We fought U.S. imperialism, an enemy wielding weapons many times superior to ours, and yet we were able to win and compelled it to agree to a truce. Why was the truce possible?

First, militarily the U.S. aggressors were in an unfavourable position and were on the receiving end. If they had not accepted the truce, their whole battle line would have been broken through and Seoul would have fallen into the hands of the Korean people. This situation became evident in the summer of last year [1952].

Each belligerent calls his own battle line a bastion of iron. Ours is truly a bastion of iron. Our soldiers and cadres are resourceful and brave and dare to look death in the face. In contrast the U.S. aggressor troops are afraid of death, and their officers are rather rigid, not very flexible. Their battle line is not solid and is anything but a bastion of iron.

The problems facing our side were first whether we could fight, then whether we could hold our lines, later whether we could ensure the flow of supplies, and finally whether we could foil the germ warfare. These four problems came one after the other and were all solved. Our troops grew from strength to strength in fighting. This summer [1953] we were already able to break through an enemy position with its front of twenty-one kilometres within an hour, fire several hundred thousand shells in a concentrated attack and penetrate the enemy area up to eighteen kilometres. If we had kept this up and mounted two, three or four more attacks, his whole battle line would have been cut to pieces.

Second, politically the enemy had many insoluble internal contradictions, and the people the world over demanded peace.

Third, economically the enemy spent vast sums in the war of aggression against Korea, and his budgetary revenues and expenditures were not balanced.

All these causes combined to force the enemy to come to terms. The first was the primary cause, and in its absence a truce with the enemy would have been difficult. The U.S. imperialists are very arrogant; if at all possible, they always refuse to talk reason, and will do so after a fashion only when driven into a tight corner.

In the Korean war the enemy suffered 1,090,000 in killed and wounded. Naturally we paid a price too. Nevertheless, our casualties were far fewer than anticipated and they became still fewer after tunnels were built. We grew stronger and stronger through fighting. The Americans failed to undermine our positions; on the contrary, their units were always wiped out by us.

The Contributions of the Masses

Just now you all mentioned the factor of leadership. In my view, leadership is one factor, but the most important factor is the contribution of ideas by the masses. Our cadres and soldiers thought up all sorts of ways to fight the enemy. Let me give one example. In the first month of the war our losses in trucks were tremendous. What was to be done? While the leadership devised counter-measures, we relied mainly on the masses to come up with ideas. Over ten thousand people were posted on both sides of the highway to fire signal shots to warn of approaching enemy planes. On hearing these signals, our drivers would dodge or find places in which to hide their trucks. In the meantime the roads were widened and many new ones built so that trucks could run in both directions unimpeded. Thus the losses in trucks dropped from 40 per cent at the beginning to less than 1 per cent. Later on, underground storehouses and even underground auditoriums were built. While enemy bombs fell from overhead, we went on with our meetings underground. When they picture the Korean battlefield, people living in Peking feel it must have been very dangerous. True, there was danger, but it was not so terrible as long as everyone contributed ideas.

Our experience is that reliance on the people together with a fairly correct leadership enables us to defeat a better-equipped enemy with our inferior equipment.

The Significance of Victory

The victory in the war to resist U.S. aggression and aid Korea is a great one and has major significance. First, together with the Korean people we have fought our way back to the 38th Parallel [which in 1945 divided Soviet occupied North Korea from U.S. occupied South Korea] and held on there. This is very important. If we had not fought back to the 38th Parallel and our front lines had remained along the Yalu and Tumen Rivers [bordering China], it would have been impossible for the people in Shenyang, Anshan and Fushun [cities in China] to carry on production free from worry.

Second, we have gained military experience. The ground, air and naval forces, the infantry, artillery, engineer, tank, railway, air defence and signal corps and also the medical and logistic units, etc., of the Chinese People's Volunteers have all gained practical experience in fighting the U.S. aggressor troops. This time we have taken the measure of the

U.S. armed forces. If you have never taken them on, you are liable to be scared of them. We have fought them for thirty-three months and got to know them for what they are worth. U.S. imperialism is not terrifying, nothing to make a fuss about. Such is our experience, indeed an invaluable piece of experience.

Third, the people of the whole country have heightened their political awareness.

From the above three points a fourth can be deduced: a new imperialist war of aggression against China and a third world war have been put off.

A Willingness to Fight Back

The imperialist aggressors ought to bear this in mind: the Chinese people are now organized, they are not to be trifled with. Once they are provoked to anger, things can get very tough.

The enemy may resume the war, and even if he doesn't, he is sure to make trouble in all sorts of ways, such as by sending in secret agents to carry out wrecking activities. He has set up a vast network of secret services in places like Taiwan, Hongkong and Japan. But we have gained experience in the movement to resist U.S. aggression and aid Korea, and so long as we mobilize the masses and rely on the people, we know how to cope with the enemy.

For us the present situation is different from that in the winter of 1950. Were the U.S. aggressors then on the other side of the 38th Parallel? No, they were not. They were on the other side of the Yalu and Tumen Rivers. Did we then have any experience in fighting the U.S. aggressors? No, we did not. Did we then know much about the U.S. troops? No, we did not. Now, all this has changed. Supposing U.S. imperialism does not put off its new war of aggression and says: "I'll fight!", then we can cope with it by relying on the first three points. But supposing it says: "I'll not fight!", then the fourth point will hold good. Here is proof of the superiority of our people's democratic dictatorship.

Are we going to invade others? No, we will invade no one anywhere. But if others invade us, we will fight back and fight to a finish.

The Chinese people adhere to this stand: we are for peace, but are not afraid of war; we are ready for both. We have the support of the people. In the war to resist U.S. aggression and aid Korea, people fell over each other to join up. The conditions for enrolment were stiff, only one in a hundred was chosen. People said the conditions were stricter than those for choosing a husband for one's daughter. If U.S. imperialism wants to resume the fighting, we will take it on again.

The Economic Policies of War

War costs money. Yet the war to resist U.S. aggression and aid Korea did not cost us too much. It went on for several years, but the expenses incurred were less than a single year's industrial and commercial taxes. Of course, it would have been better if we had not had to fight the war and spend this money. For construction in the country today calls for expenditure and the peasants still have difficulties. Last year [1952] and the year before last [1951], the agricultural tax was a shade on the heavy side, and so this set some friends talking. They demanded a "policy of benevolence", as if they represented the interests of the peasants. Did we favour this view? No, we didn't. At that time we had to do our utmost to win victory in the war to resist U.S. aggression and aid Korea. For the peasants, for the people of the whole country, which was in their interest? To endure austerity for the time being and strive for victory? Or not to resist U.S. aggression and aid Korea and so save a few coppers? Undoubtedly winning the war was in their interest. It was because the war required money that we collected a bit more in agricultural tax last year and the year before. This year it is different. We have not increased the agricultural tax and have put a ceiling on its volume.

Speaking of the "policy of benevolence", we are of course for it. But what was the policy of maximum benevolence? To resist U.S. aggression and aid Korea. To carry out this policy of maximum benevolence sacrifices had to be made, money spent and more collected in agricultural tax. Just because more was collected, some people raised an outcry. They even claimed to represent the interests of the peasants. I just don't approve of such talk.

To resist U.S. aggression and aid Korea was to implement the policy of benevolence, and to carry on industrial construction today is likewise to implement this policy.

Considering Long-Term Interests

Policies of benevolence are of two kinds. One is concerned with the people's immediate interests. The other is concerned with their long-term interests, such as resisting U.S. aggression and aiding Korea and building heavy industry. The first is a policy of lesser benevolence and the second a policy of greater benevolence. Both must be taken into consideration and it is wrong not to do so. Where then is the emphasis to be placed? On the policy of greater benevolence. At present the emphasis in our policy of benevolence should be on the construction of heavy industry. Construction takes money. Therefore, much as the livelihood of the people needs to be improved, this cannot be done to any great extent for the time being. In other words, while we have to improve the people's livelihood, we must not try to do too much, and while we have to make some allowance for it, we must not make too much. To make allowance for the policy of lesser benevolence at the expense of the policy of greater benevolence is to go off the right track.

Now some friends put lop-sided stress on the policy of lesser benevolence; in effect, they wanted us to give up the war to resist U.S. aggression and aid Korea, and now they want us to give up the building of heavy industry. We must criticize this erroneous view. It is also to be found in the Communist Party; we came across it in Yenan. In 1941 we collected 200,000 piculs [150 kg.] of grain in the Shensi-Kansu-Ningsia Border Region, and some people began to yell that the Communist Party was not being considerate of the peasants. A few leading cadres in the Party also brought up this issue of the policy of benevolence. I criticized this view even then. What was the policy of maximum benevolence at that time? To overthrow Japanese imperialism. If we had slashed the amount of grain to be collected from the peasants, we would have had to cut down the size of the Eighth Route and New Fourth Armies. That would have been to the advantage of Japanese imperialism. So those who held this view were actually speaking on behalf of Japanese imperialism and doing it a service.

Now the war to resist U.S. aggression and aid Korea has come to a halt. If the United States wants to resume the war, we will fight on. In that case, we will have to collect grain from the peasants, do work on them and persuade them to make their contribution. To act thus would be truly to serve the interests of the peasants. To raise outcries would actually be to serve the interests of U.S. imperialism.

There are major as well as minor principles. The people's standard of living in the whole country should be raised yearly, but not too much. If it had been raised too much, we could not have fought the war to resist U.S. aggression and aid Korea, or at least not in such grim earnest. We have fought this war resolutely and earnestly and with all our might. Whatever was available at home the Korean front could have for the asking. That has been the case for the last few years.

American Colonialism Threatens World Peace

Nikita Khrushchev

The son of a miner, Nikita Khrushchev was born in Kalinovka, Russia, in 1894. Khrushchev began working at an early age and was fired at eighteen after helping a group of workers organize a strike protesting working conditions. He joined the Communist Party and the Red Army in 1918. He advanced rapidly in the party and, after the death of Joseph Stalin in 1953, Khrushchev became the head of the Communist Party of the Soviet Union.

Although Khrushchev continued to maintain the Soviet Union's strong control over Eastern Europe, he advocated peaceful coexistence with the West. In 1959, Khrushchev toured the United States and met with President Dwight D. Eisenhower at Camp David. However, the relationship between Khrushchev and the United States remained tense. In the following speech, delivered before the UN General Assembly on September 23, 1960, Khrushchev discusses one incident that exacerbated the tension between the two nations.

On May 1, 1960, a U.S. reconnaissance plane was shot down by Soviet military authorities inside the Soviet Union. Khrushchev points to the U-2 incident as evidence that U.S. militarists are provoking peace-loving nations. He claims that U.S. colonialism threatens the economic and political independence of many nations throughout

Nikita Khrushchev, address before the United Nations General Assembly, New York, September 23, 1960.

the world. Khrushchev appeals to the United Nations to uphold the sovereign right of states and to stop impeding the participation of the People's Republic of China and other newly emerging nations in the UN simply because their political and social philosophy differs from Western countries. Khrushchev also presents the Soviet Union's strategy for disarmament, which calls for complete prohibition of nuclear weapons.

O ur century is the century of the struggle for freedom, the century in which nations are liberating themselves from foreign domination. The peoples desire a worthwhile life and are fighting to secure it.

Victory has already been won in many countries and lands. But we cannot rest on our laurels, for we know that tens of millions of human beings are still languishing in colonial slavery and are suffering grave hardships. . . .

Every intelligent individual gives some thought to what scientific progress, what this great twentieth century, is bringing mankind. Some rightly say that the world has been given new horizons, unlimited opportunities for the creation of abundant material wealth and for the ample satisfaction of human needs. With no less justification, others point to the great danger of scientific and technical achievements being used, not for these beneficial purposes, but primarily for the production of appalling means of destruction. These means of destruction are not being used at the present time. But, in the last analysis, they are produced to be used.

A Conflict Between International Policies

This argument between optimists and pessimists reflects the facts of our times. The most important of these facts is the conflict between two trends or lines of policy in international relations. I am not, of course, referring here to differences in social systems, since this is a domestic issue, which can and must be settled only by nations and States themselves. . . .

These two lines of policy in international relations have

long been in opposition. Although parallel lines never meet in elementary geometry they may come into collision in international affairs. That would be a fearful moment indeed. Only ten or fifteen years ago, few could predict the outcome of the struggle between these two lines of international policy. In the year 1960, however, only the blind can fail to see how the majority of peoples are becoming more and more positively and plainly convinced of the need to maintain peace.

The peoples of all countries—workers, peasants, intellectuals and the bourgeoisie, excluding a small handful of militarists and monopolists—want not war but peace, and peace alone. And if, therefore, the peoples actively fight to tie the hands of the militarist and monopolist circles, peace can be ensured. . . .

No one can dispute the fact that the Soviet Union has been unsparing in its efforts to ensure the continuation of this welcome trend in the development of international relations. But the sinister forces which profit from the maintenance of international tension are clinging tenaciously to their positions. Though only a handful of individuals is involved, they are quite powerful and exert a strong influence on the policy of their respective States. A major effort is therefore required to break their resistance. As soon as the policy of easing international tension begins to yield tangible results, they immediately resort to extreme measures in order to ensure that the people should feel no relief; they strain every nerve to plunge the world back again and again into an atmosphere of gloom and to exacerbate international tension.

The Threat of U.S. Militarists and Monopolists

We saw a dangerous manifestation of the work of these forces last spring [May 1960] when the aircraft of one of the largest States Members of the United Nations, the United States of America, treacherously invaded the air space of the Soviet Union and that of other States.[1] What is more, the

1. Khrushchev refers to the U-2 incident, in which the Soviet military shot down an unarmed reconnaisance plane, the U-2, piloted by Francis Gary Powers. Authorities argue that Khrushchev used the incident to sabotage a summit meeting of leaders from the United States, the Soviet Union, France, and the United Kingdom.

United States has elevated such violations of international law into a principle of deliberate State policy.

The aggressive intrusion into our country by a United States aircraft and the whole course of the United States Government's subsequent behaviour showed the peoples that they were dealing with a calculated policy on the part of the United States Government, which was trying to substitute brigandage for international law and treachery for honest negotiations between sovereign and equal States. . . .

The flights by the United States spy aircraft are also instructive in another respect. They have shown up the danger to peace presented by the network of United States bases in which dozens of States in Europe, Asia, Africa and Latin America are enmeshed.

Like a deep-seated form of acute infection in a living organism, these bases disrupt the normal political and economic life of the States upon which they have been foisted. They hinder the establishment of normal relations between those States and their neighbours. How, indeed, can there be any question of normal relations if the people of these neighbouring countries cannot sleep peacefully, if they have to live with the threat of being subjected to an annihilating blow whenever the United States militarists take it into their heads to embark on fresh acts of provocation? . . .

United States relations with Cuba are illuminating. As you know, before the victory of the popular revolution, all branches of the Cuban economy were wholly dominated by United States monopolies which earned vast profits from exploiting the working people of Cuba and the wealth of their fertile soil.

Some people in the United States occasionally like to boast that the standard of living in their country is higher than that in other countries. There is no gainsaying the fact that the standard of living in the United States is now higher than in Cuba, but why is that so? Is it because the Cuban people are less industrious or because the Cuban soil is less fertile? No, this of course is not the reason. The Cuban people are well known for their industry and for their attachment to their country and to their soil. The explanation is entirely different. For many years the fruits of the Cuban people's toil were enjoyed not by the Cuban people but by United States monopolies. Is it therefore surprising that in 1958, for example, the per capita income in Cuba was 6.5 times lower than in the United States? This telling fact speaks for itself. . . .

We are all witnesses to the fact that many peoples are being continually subjected to hostile acts and crude pressure by a certain group of States which seek to set at naught the legitimate interests and rights of other countries. This is why the international situation is fraught with acute conflicts, the danger of which is intensified by the mounting arms race.

Violating the Sovereign Rights of States

It is quite evident that international relations cannot continue on such a basis, as that would mean a headlong descent to the abyss. It is the sacred duty of the United Nations to uphold the sovereign rights of States and to press for the reestablishment of international relations on a sound legal basis and for the ending of the arms race.

Unfortunately, the policy of violating the inalienable rights of peoples is still in evidence in the United Nations itself.

Take, for instance, the question of the representation in the United Nations of the Chinese people. To impede the reinstatement of the People's Republic of China in its legitimate rights in the United Nations, simply because the socialist regime of that State is not to the taste of the leading circles of certain Western countries, and in particular of the United States, is to disregard the facts; it betokens the absence of any desire for a relaxation of international tension; it means that the interests of strengthening world peace and of developing international cooperation are being sacrificed to the narrow political calculations of a small group of States. This situation is inimical to peace and is degrading to the United Nations. . . .

Is the solution of major international problems really conceivable today without the participation of the People's Republic of China? Is it possible to solve these problems without the participation of India, Indonesia, Burma, Ceylon, the United Arab Republic, Iraq, Ghana, Guinea and the other States? If anyone has this idea, let him try to disregard the opinion and the votes of the representatives of the Asian, African and Latin American States here in the United Nations. It is true that the appearance of the new Asian and African States in the United Nations is giving rise to apprehension in certain Western countries. More than that, people are beginning to discuss ways of limiting the further influx of newly-emerging States into the United Nations.

Abolishing Colonialism

As regards the Soviet Union, I can say frankly that we are glad to see a great number of new States making their appearance in the United Nations. We have always opposed and we shall continue to oppose any curtailment of the rights of peoples who have won their national independence. We share with these States the desire to preserve and strengthen peace, to create on our planet conditions for the peaceful co-existence and co-operation of countries regardless of their political and social structure, in accordance with the peaceful principles proclaimed at the Conference of African and Asian States at Bandung [Indonesia.] The facts show that the liberation of nations and peoples under colonial domination leads to an improvement in international relations, an increase in international co-operation and the reinforcement of world peace. . . .

It would be difficult to exaggerate the vast significance which the abolition of the colonial system would have for the entire world. Everyone knows that the economics of the colonies and the Trust Territories are at present subordinated to the mercenary interests of foreign monopolies, and the industrialization of these countries is being deliberately impeded. Imagine that the situation has changed and that these countries and territories, having become independent, are in a position to make ample use of their rich natural resources and to proceed with their industrialization, and that a better life has begun for their peoples. This would lead to a tremendous growth in the capacity of the world market, which would no doubt have a beneficial effect, not only on the economic development of the countries of the East but also on the economies of the industrially developed countries of the West. . . .

Impeding the Progress of Disarmament

A year has elapsed since the General Assembly adopted the resolution on general and complete disarmament. Having regard to the present pace of life, that is a comparatively long period of time and we need have no doubt that those engaged in the production of weapons and in the perfection and invention of new lethal means have not let it go to waste.

But in the sphere of disarmament not the slightest progress has been made in the past year. What are the reasons for this state of affairs to which we are forced to refer with great regret and serious concern? Who is preventing the implementation of the General Assembly resolution on general and complete disarmament, perhaps the most important and outstanding decision in the history of the United Nations? Who is making it impossible to break the deadlock on the problem of disarmament?

The facts show that the absence of any progress towards the solution of the disarmament problem is the consequence of the position taken by the United States and by certain other States linked with it through NATO.

Throughout the work of the Ten-Nation Committee on Disarmament, the Western Powers refused to start working out a treaty on general and complete disarmament and in every way avoided discussion of the substance of the Soviet programme of general and complete disarmament, which the General Assembly had referred to the Committee for detailed consideration. For their part, they made proposals which provided for neither general nor complete disarmament, nor any disarmament at all, but only for measures of control over armaments; i.e., control without disarmament. However, one cannot but see that the establishment of control without disarmament would be tantamount to setting up an international espionage system which, far from contributing to the consolidation of peace, could, on the contrary, make it easier for a potential aggressor to realize his plans which pose a threat to the peoples. . . .

The Soviet Government, together with the Governments of a number of other States, was compelled to suspend its participation in the work of the Ten-Nation Committee, which the Western Powers had turned into a screen for concealing the arms race. It was not easy for the Soviet Government to take this decision, because it was precisely our country that had first raised the issue of general and complete disarmament, and had been doing its utmost to achieve in the Committee a constructive solution to the problem, in strict conformity with the General Assembly resolution. In the circumstances, however, staying on in the Committee would only have meant helping the opponents of disarmament. It was impossible to tolerate attempts to make the great cause of disarmament an object of speculation for purposes inimical to the interests of universal peace.

The Soviet Proposal

That is why the Soviet Government has placed the question of disarmament before the United Nations General Assembly, a considerable majority of whose members have no interest whatever in the arms race and sincerely wish to see it brought to an end. . . .

The new Soviet proposal on the question of general and complete disarmament, which is based on the provisions of the proposal dated 2 June 1960, submitted by the Soviet Government to all the Governments of the world for consideration, has been drafted with due regard for all the useful ideas expressed in the past year in the course of the discussions on this question in political and public circles in various countries. This proposal goes a long way towards meeting the position of the Western Powers and this we hope will make for early agreement on disarmament.

We now provide, in particular, that all means of delivering nuclear weapons to their targets should be eliminated in the very first stage of general and complete disarmament; we have worked out detailed measures for effective international control at all stages; and we have taken into account the wish of certain Western Powers that, from the outset, there should be provision for reduction in the strength of armed forces and in conventional armaments. We have also introduced quite a number of other amendments to and modifications of our programme. In our view all these amendments render the programme of general and complete disarmament more concrete and even more realistic and practicable. . . .

The Soviet Government is deeply convinced that only a radical solution of the problem of disarmament, providing for the complete prohibition of nuclear weapons together with the cessation of their manufacture and testing and the destruction of all accumulated stockpiles of these weapons, can accomplish the task of delivering mankind from the threat of nuclear war which hangs over it. This is precisely the aim which the Soviet Union is pursuing in consistently and resolutely advocating general and complete disarmament.

All this, in our view, leads to one important conclusion. In order finally to break the deadlock on the disarmament problem, the General Assembly should call to order those who are hindering its solution and are trying to replace business-like negotiations on disarmament by empty beating about the bush. . . .

A Policy of Peaceful Coexistence

The peoples of the Soviet Union and the Soviet Government are striving unremittingly to have the principles of peaceful coexistence firmly established in relations between States and to ensure that these principles become the fundamental law of life for the whole of modern society. There is no communist-devised "trick" behind these principles but simple truths dictated by life itself, such as that relations between all States should develop peacefully, without the use of force, without war and without interference in each other's internal affairs.

I am revealing no secret when I say that we have no liking for capitalism. But we do not want to impose our system on other peoples by force. Let those, then, who determine the policy of States with a different social system from ours, renounce their fruitless and dangerous attempts to dictate their will. It is time they also recognized that the choice of a particular way of life is the domestic concern of every people. Let us build up our relations having regard to actual realities. That is true peaceful coexistence. . . .

The policy of peaceful coexistence assumes a readiness to

solve all outstanding issues without resort to force, by means of negotiations and reasonable compromises. We all know that during the cold war years such questions for the most part did not find a solution, and that led to the creation of dangerous foci of tension in Europe, Asia and other parts of the world.

The Korean Question

The Soviet Union considers that, in order to strengthen peace in the Far East and throughout the world, it is most essential to settle the Korean question.

Only madmen could think of settling the Korean question by armed force. The only correct proposal, namely to leave the solution of the question of the peaceful reunification of Korea to the Koreans themselves with no interference from outside, is finding ever wider acceptance. An essential condition for this is the immediate and complete withdrawal of all United States troops from South Korea, for their presence poisons the atmosphere not only in Korea but throughout the Far East and has made possible such shameful facts as the rigging of elections in South Korea. The proposal of the Government of the Democratic People's Republic of Korea to establish a confederation of North and South Korea is just as reasonable as the proposal of the Government of the German Democratic Republic to set up a confederation of the two German States. It is the only way to lay a sound foundation for the reunification of these States. . . .

We are now firmly convinced that the time has come to take steps to create conditions for an improved functioning both of the United Nations as a whole and of the Organization's executive, working organ. I repeat, the matter relates primarily to the Secretary-General and his staff. We must particularly bear in mind the necessity for certain changes and improvements, with a view to the immediate future. . . .

We consider it reasonable and just for the executive organ of the United Nations to consist not of a single person—the Secretary-General—but of three persons invested with the highest trust of the United Nations, persons representing the States belonging to the three basic groups I have mentioned. The point at issue is not the title of the organ but that this executive organ should represent the States belonging to the military block of the Western Powers, the socialist States and the neutralist States. This composition of the United Nations executive organ would create conditions for a more correct implementation of the decisions taken. . . .

The Soviet Government hopes that the proposals it has raised for questions to be considered at the present session of the General Assembly will meet with support and understanding, since they are prompted by a sincere desire to secure a better life and tranquillity on our planet. . . .

The Soviet Government is ready to do its utmost in order that colonial servitude may be destroyed here and now, that here and now the problems of disarmament may find their concrete and effective solution.

The Soviet Government is ready to do its utmost in order that the testing of nuclear weapons may be prohibited here and now, that this means of mass destruction may be prohibited and destroyed.

It could be said that these are complicated problems and that they cannot be solved at one stroke. But these are problems posed by life itself and they must be solved before it is too late. Their solution cannot be evaded.

In concluding my statement I wish to emphasize once again that the Soviet Government, guided by the interests of the Soviet people, by the interests of the citizens of a free socialist State, once again proposes to all: let us talk, let us argue, but let us settle the questions of general and complete disarmament and let us bury colonialism that is accursed of all mankind.

Communist Nations Threaten Freedom Worldwide

Dean Rusk

Dean Rusk was born in Cherokee County, Georgia, on
February 9, 1909. He received a Rhodes Scholarship that
allowed him to study at Oxford, where he focused on international affairs. After World War II, Rusk served in
several positions within the Department of State and was
appointed secretary of state by John F. Kennedy after the
1960 election and remained in this position until 1969.

On July 10, 1961, early in his career as secretary of
state, Rusk gave the following speech before the National
Press Club in Washington, D.C. In this speech Rusk de-
fines what he believes is the central issue of the Cold
War: the desire on the part of China and the Soviet
Union to impose communism onto free nations. The
United Nations, says Rusk, was created as a community
of independent nations who choose to cooperate on matters of common interest but are free to develop their own
institutions. Rather than abide by the spirit of the UN,
claims Rusk, the Soviet Union has distorted the language
of post–World War II war policies to support its desire
for expansion. In order to combat Communist expansion,
argues Rusk, developed nations who choose freedom
must work together, forming their own revolution of political freedom and economic progress to support struggling nations that want to remain free.

Dean Rusk, address before the National Press Club, Washington, DC, July 10,
1961.

L et us start from where we ourselves are and what we in this country should like to achieve in our relations with the rest of the world. Since World War II we have had more than one so-called great debate about foreign policy. Actually, the greatest debate of all occurred during that war, and the most eloquent voice was the war itself. Before the fighting was over we had concluded as a nation that we must throw ourselves into the building of a decent world order in which such conflagrations could not occur.

Building a New World Order

The nature of that world order was set forth succinctly in the charter of the United Nations, a charter backed by an overwhelming majority of the Senate and supported by an overwhelming majority of the Nation. It called for a community of independent nations, each free to work out its own institutions as it saw fit but cooperating effectively and loyally with other nations on matters of common interest and concern. The inevitable disputes were to be settled by peaceful means; and let us not forget that the charter supposed that the tried processes of negotiation, mediation and adjudication were to be preferred over violent or fruitless debate. But parties in serious dispute were to seek the help of the broader international community in order that disinterested judgments could be brought to bear upon sensitive or inflamed issues.

As such a world order grew in strength and effectiveness, the limitation and reduction of arms would become possible, cooperation on economic and social problems would improve the lot of man, human rights would be strengthened, and the role of law would steadily take over from the law of the jungle. On matters of political arrangements, the underlying thesis was that the people themselves should play the decisive role as the principle of self-determination was brought to bear. It was then, and remains, our hope that man can take up once again the ancient aspirations of the race and move to free himself from the burdens of war, tyranny and misery.

With deference to our shortcomings, I think it can be properly said that the United States threw itself with honesty and diligence into this great effort. It rapidly demobilized—

more rapidly than events proved wise. It offered its atomic weapons to international control. It committed vast resources to the reconstruction of war-torn nations. It cooperated both in the large and in detail with the great cooperative ventures of the community of nations. Most important of all, it turned aside from the ambitions and appetites which have historically been associated with great power and conformed its national aims to those I have just described.

Undermining the International Community

What has gone wrong? Why, after fifteen years, is there so much tension and danger in a world which had hoped for so much just yesterday? To be fair, let us not suppose that all of our problems are traceable to a single source. Under the best of conditions, the surging tides of nationalism and the insistent demands for economic and social improvement would have required great skill and understanding to handle the inevitable changes which were bound to come in our postwar world. But these were manageable, and there is no reason to suppose that they could not be accommodated in the processes of peaceful change.

The underlying crisis of our generation arises from the fact that the Soviet Union did not join the United Nations in fact, as well as in form, and lend itself to the commitments they and the rest of us made in the midst of a great war. The possession of power was transformed once more to ambition for more power. The capacity to defy law became a contempt for law. Doctrines were revised and adapted to promote an imperialism as old as the tragic history of man. An entire people was sealed off from the rest of the world, and secrecy became a prime strategic weapon. The institutions of the international community were either ignored or undermined from within. The Soviet Union has just cast its ninety-fifth veto in the Security Council of the United Nations.

In the process the very language of international intercourse became distorted and contrived. "Peace" has become a word to describe whatever condition would promote their world revolution. "Aggression" is whatever stands in its way. "People's

Democracy" is a term applied to regimes no one of which has been chosen by free election. Self-determination is loudly espoused but only in areas not under Communist control.

The normally attractive word "negotiation" is used as a weapon, for the only subjects to be negotiated are further concessions to Communist appetite. Agreements are offered but against the background of a long and sobering list of broken promises; an agreement is apparently a rest camp, where one pauses and refits for a further advance. New assurances are offered in the very act of withdrawing those earlier given. Law, as one of their spokesmen put it, "is like the tongue of a wagon—it goes in the direction in which it is pointed." And the gains of lawlessness are cited as the "new conditions" which justify new invasions of the rights of others.

A Policy of Expansion and Coercion

Neutrality is temporary, a pasture growing green for future grazing. On January 6, Mr. [Nikita] Khrushchev said, "The revolutionary emergence of more and more peoples into the world arena creates exceptionally favorable conditions for an unprecedented broadening of the sphere of influence of Marxism-Leninism. The time is not far away when Marxism-Leninism will possess the minds of the majority of the world's population." Apparently, according to one of his homely maxims, "Every vegetable has its season."

The underlying crisis is not an ideological conflict between nineteenth-century capitalism and nineteenth-century Marxism. It does not result from a bilateral conflict between the Soviet Union and the United States.

The central issue of the crisis is the announced determination to impose a world of coercion upon those not already subjected to it. If this seems exaggerated simplicity, let us not be misled by our own reluctance to believe what they say, for on this point they have proved that they mean it. At stake is the survival and growth of the world of free choice and of the free cooperation pledged in the charter. There is no "troika" on this issue—it is posed between the Sino-Soviet empire and all the rest, whether allied or neutral; and it is now posed in every continent.

The underlying crisis has shown itself in many forms—from the cynical disregard of the pledges on liberated areas, made at Yalta, to the latest threats to West Berlin. The calendar of conflict between these two dates is filled with unceasing attempts to expand an empire—some successful but many repelled by those determined to be free.

Strengthening Western Solidarity

President [John F.] Kennedy has taken up his great task with a deep awareness of the nature of the crisis and of the actions required by the continuing struggle for freedom.

It is essential to get on with the building of the world community designed by the charter. This we would do in any event; but it is here that the breadth and depth of the crisis are fully revealed, and it is here that those who would not be coerced can act together for a world of peace. We speak of uncommitted nations, and we usually mean those who are committed to neither of the principal blocs on the present scene. But all nations have commitments arising out of their own interests and out of their own hopes for the future. In the United Nations commitments to the charter can weave the fabric of common interest which, by reaching beyond the cold war, may determine its outcome.

No less essential is the strengthening of the solidarity of NATO and of the Western community—possessed of enormous capacity to shape the course of events. The political, economic and military strengthening of the Western community is an urgent matter to which the administration is giving full attention. The President has also seen that the Western World must recapture the leadership of its own revolution of political freedom. It is a revolution which the West itself has taken into every continent and which continues to stir men to action. This struggle for freedom in the West itself was not painless; nor will it be in other places in our own time. But we dare not yield its leadership to those who would seize it, subvert it, and use it to destroy us.

The President is also asking us, and other economically advanced free nations, to reassert our leadership of the revolution of economic and social progress. The world of coercion is offering tempting bait for those who are determined to shake off their misery and want. We believe that freedom and progress are historic partners and that the alleged choice between rapid progress and free institutions is false. But this we must prove. This is the meaning of the President's Alliance for Progress, which is stirring the hopes and the hard thinking of the nations of our own hemisphere. This is the meaning of the rapidly growing effort of the Western community to throw substantial resources behind the economic and social development of less favored nations. This is why the President is asking for thoughtful planning, effective leadership, and determined self-help from those who need external assistance for national growth. And this is why the President is asking the Congress for aid legislation and appropriations which will put us in a position to help generate the momentum of development—aid which must be provided, in association with others, in the amounts and for the periods of time required to achieve enduring and satisfying results.

During these first months the President has established direct contact with the leadership of many nations in order to give us as quickly as possible an accurate understanding of their interests and views. In his own discussions with them, through the Vice President [Lyndon B. Johnson], Ambassador [Adlai] Stevenson and others, he has been able to lay the basis for the greater unity of our several alliances and the greater effort which will be required to deal with the continuing crisis.

The President has recognized the changes which are occurring in the strategic problems which we and our allies must face and is moving, in consultation with other governments, to bring the free world's capabilities up to the needs of the variety of dangers which have to be confronted.

Working Toward Freedom

Despite the continuing crisis, we have felt it necessary to work diligently and realistically at the possibilities of disarmament. Even though the political atmosphere is not encouraging, an imaginative effort must be made to relieve the tensions arising from the arms race itself. We cannot understand how the Soviet Union, which has expended so much eloquence on disarmament, could have rejected the reasonable and workable treaty for the ban of nuclear testing which was tabled at Geneva this spring. "General and complete disarmament" are apparently among those words given a special meaning in the glossary of their world revolution. For reasonable people would suppose that the way to get there is to start and that the steps along the way must be such as to leave no one, in Aristide Briand's words, as "dupes or victims." Nevertheless our work goes forward, and we earnestly hope that the Congress will support the recent proposals of the President to make it effective.

Let me conclude by saying that the agenda of our foreign relations is filled with problems requiring and getting urgent attention. If there are those looking for still waters, we are not yet there. We can move on with confidence if we are prepared to do what has to be done. The free world has enormous strength, including the inner strength of purposes which are deeply rooted in the nature of man.

The world of coercion has its problems too. Dissensions within its ranks, national resistance to this modern imperialism, and a growing demand for freedom are among them. It has learned that economic aid does not buy puppets, that intimidation awakens its own resistance, that the United Nations is tougher than it thought, and that those who set out to "possess the minds" of man have set themselves against the course of history.

Our democracy must have its turbulent debate. Free nations will, of course, differ among themselves as they move to build a common interest out of disparate circumstances and varied responsibility. But the underlying crisis is becoming more widely understood, and out of it will come the responses which men must make when their freedom is at stake.

Saying "No" to Yankee Imperialism

Ernesto "Che" Guevara

Ernesto "Che" Guevara was a revolutionary and Cuban political leader born in Rosario, Argentina, on June 14, 1928. Guevara studied at the University of Buenos Aires where he took part in riots opposing Argentine dictator Juan Perón. In his travels to Guatemala, while witnessing the CIA influence in the overthrow of Jacobo Arbenz, he developed his philosophy that only armed insurrection would lead to successful revolutions against imperialism. From Guatemala, Guevara went to Mexico where he met Fidel Castro. He followed Castro to Cuba first as a doctor and later as a successful guerrilla officer. When Castro's revolutionaries succeeded in overthrowing Cuban dictator Fulgencio Batista in 1959, Guevara became Castro's second in command and was appointed governor of the national bank. In 1961, Guevara was made minister of industry and became increasingly hostile toward the United States while strengthening his relationship with the Soviet Union.

Guevara's disdain for the United States is evident in the following address delivered at the Presidential Palace in Havana, Cuba, on July 10, 1960. When explaining Cuba's success in repelling an attack by U.S. imperialists shortly after the Cuban revolution, Guevara compares the United States to a predator who has lost its prey. The United States has failed in its duty to protect Cuba, says Guevara, instead imposing its will on the Cuban people. He cites further evidence of U.S. treachery by listing Latin American dictators the U.S. has supported. Guevara ex-

Ernesto "Che" Guevara, speech before the Presidential Palace, Havana, Cuba, July 10, 1960.

plains that the Cuban people must be prepared to use atomic weapons against the United States.

Guevara's threats against the United States continued long after his speech. During the Cuban Missile Crisis, in which the United States set up a naval blockade to prevent Soviet shipments of offensive missiles to Cuba, Guevara advocated nuclear confrontation. While traveling around the world with his wife, however, he became disillusioned with the weakness of Soviet communism. Guevara's outspoken frustration with Soviet communism forced Castro to remove Guevara from office. During a final attempt at revolution against Bolivian dictator General René Barrientos, Guevara was captured and executed on October 9, 1967.

O nce again we are gathered together in this tribunal, which of all the revolutionary tribunals of Cuba is the one which best represents the dignity of her people, the dignity and the fighting spirit of Cuba.

At the dawn of this Revolution, when the people, having just won the battle for their liberty, were exercising revolutionary justice, their enemies, encouraged by the foreign press, attempted to diminish that justice and shorten its reach. Then, for the first time, the people gathered here said *no* to foreign intervention, and revolutionary justice took its inexorable course. At the same time it followed the course of the deepening revolution, until Cuba was converted into the vanguard of America.

It was at that moment that imperialism loosed its pack of hounds, themselves sons of this people. From Florida they pounced on a defenseless Havana, and in one single day of darkness, killed and wounded her helpless children. And once more the people came together in this tribunal to pit their militant faith against foreign intervention of any kind. The Revolution continued to grow more profound. Although they tried to halt it with increasingly severe economic measures, it continued forward despite everything. Then, once and for all, they removed their mask, revealing hidden beneath it the garrote, used so often in America. Nor did they disguise it with pretty words. They no longer even talk about freedom; now they talk about their lost prey. And they threaten more and more violently, with the impotent rage of the wild beast, who, although she has watched the gradual escape of the prey from her claws on every continent of this planet, yet she wishes to maintain in the backyards of all her colonial possessions, each and every sinecure upon which the American way of life was erected. North American diplomacy, crippled physically and mentally, is staggering.

A New World Position for Cuba

Today Cuba is no longer becoming, as she was until recently, the vanguard of America. Today we hold a position of still greater danger and greater glory. Today we are practically, because of the compelling circumstances, the arbiters of world peace. The immense responsibility of the position which Cuba occupies is of tremendous importance, for the world is going too fast for the limited capacity of North American diplomacy.

We planned to gather here to proclaim once again that we could not be bowed, that to attack Cuba would mean sending a torrent of blond invaders to certain death in every house and every field on this privileged island. We have discovered, however, that the warning of the Prime Minister of the Union of Soviet Socialist Republics has changed the character of our threat. The invasion of Cuba now would signify more than the destruction of all her buildings by enemy bombs, more even than the massacre of our children, our women, and all our people by the enormous superiority of the enemy and its air power. It would also mean something else, something that must make the Northern hierarchs stop to think; it would mean that atomic rockets could erase, once and forever, the country that today incarnates colonial avariciousness.

Let them take heed, those sons of the Pentagon and of North American monopolies who until now have paraded their arrogance up and down the lands of America; let them think it over carefully. Cuba is no longer a solitary island in the middle of the ocean, defended only by the vulnerable

breasts of her sons and the generous breasts of all the helpless of the world. Cuba is now, in addition, a proud Caribbean island defended by the missiles of the greatest military
power in history.

The United States Fails Its Duty

But they have responded to the Soviet warning with renewed
boasting. The former President of the United States [Franklin
D. Roosevelt] was questioned at the retreat where he has
spent the last trying years of what could have been a glorious
life, what could have been the incarnation of democracy
fighting against European fascism. He answered that, despite
Soviet warnings, the United States will fulfill its duty with respect to Cuba. And we all know the nature of that duty. It is
the same duty that took to account a sovereign nation, as is
Mexico, for its expression of indignation at the violent and
bestial economic aggression unleashed against Cuba. This
duty of the United States is the same duty that compelled it
to assassinate the patriot [Augusto C.] Sandino and put into
power in Nicaragua the justly hated [Anastasio] Somoza.
The duty of the United States was to give arms and planes,
first to [Fulgencio] Batista and then to those who continue
his work. But the greatest and most brilliant of American duties has been to place and maintain in power for thirty years
our "good friend" [Rafael] Trujillo.

Thus do the rulers of the most powerful nation of this
hemisphere understand their duties. These are our "good
neighbors," those who would defend us, who place a military
base on our soil and pay us two thousand pesos a year for it;
the sower of atomic bases on all the world's continents, the
barons of oil, tin, copper, and sugar—the heirs of monopoly.

The greatest aspiration of our people is to win all our victories with the strength of our own children. We cannot rest on
the laurels of others, for we do not know the lengths to which
our powerful neighbors will be carried by their madness.

And if, disdaining all our admonitions, they still want to
come to trample this Cuban territory, they are caught in an
extraordinary new world situation. The balance of power
has shifted definitively, and the forces of peace and peaceful

coexistence have triumphed. The strength of these forces is increasing daily, as every day their retaliatory power becomes more and more terrible.

Displaying Cuba's Strength

Yet we cannot be tranquil by any means; first, because this people won its own liberty, and each conquest of its freedom was accomplished with the sweat and work and blood of its sons. We see the risk of the whole world becoming a huge atomic bonfire, and we must be prepared for that day. If others, more powerful than we, take it upon themselves to destroy great concentrations of troops, we must be ready to destroy, in our turn, all types of physical aggression against our country. Our militias must be more vigilant than ever, our army more cautious, our entire people must be ready at all times to repel aggression, even if it does not occur. And if the shadowy danger of war passes away definitely and forever, we must remain united and vigilant in order to continue the economic battle for the right to call ourselves a free nation. We must keep working, we must keep striving to produce more and more, to be self-supporting, to achieve technical advances, to make culture more accessible to all, and to unite our people in a single column to march toward the future.

But if anyone has doubts; if anyone in this country believes all this is mere boasting in the face of the powerful ones who intend to attack us; and if even our friends think that our people are not able to withstand the approaching pressures; we must demonstrate rapidly that we are.

And today, as proof of this, as a message to all of them and also as a message to our highest leader, who is not with us today, as the total expression of the will of a people, let us raise our voices and make Fidel Castro's radio vibrate. From every Cuban mouth a single shout: "Cuba sí, Yankees no! Cuba sí, Yankees no!"

Facing the Cuban Missile Crisis

John F. Kennedy

John F. Kennedy was born on May 29, 1917, in Brookline, Massachusetts. After graduating from Harvard in 1940, Kennedy joined the navy, serving in the Pacific as the skipper of a patrol torpedo (PT) boat during World War II. After the war, Kennedy entered politics and was elected to Congress in 1946, becoming a senator in 1952. Kennedy became the nation's thirty-fifth president in 1960, winning by a narrow margin.

Although the Cold War spanned the terms of at least nine presidencies, Kennedy arguably faced some of its most memorable crises. One of the most severe threats to peace under Kennedy's administration was the Cuban Missile Crisis. On October 16, 1962, the president was shown aerial reconnaissance photographs of Soviet missile bases under construction in Cuba. Soviet diplomats denied that these installations were for offensive missiles, but Kennedy's advisors remained concerned. After seven days of debate and discussion among members of his administration, Kennedy announced the discovery and his decision to act in a televised address on October 22, 1962. During his speech, Kennedy explained the threat, announced his decision to impose a naval quarantine on Cuba to prevent further shipments of offensive military weapons, and stated that the United States would consider any missile launched from Cuba an attack by the Soviet Union.

In the days that followed Kennedy's address to the nation, the United States kept its armed forces at combat readiness. For an anxious week, the world waited as the

John F. Kennedy, televised address to the American people, Washington, DC, October 22, 1962.

threat of thermonuclear war loomed. During this time,
Soviet leader Nikita Khrushchev and Kennedy communi-
cated both formally and informally about the nature of
Soviet intentions. Finally, on October 28, Khrushchev announced that he would dismantle the installations and return them to the Soviet Union if the United States would
not invade Cuba. The two nations held further negotiations to implement the agreement and tensions began to
ease. Some claim that this was a major victory for the
West in the Cold War and credit Kennedy for its success.

This Government, as promised, has maintained the clos-
est surveillance of the Soviet Military buildup on the
island of Cuba. Within the past week, unmistakable
evidence has established the fact that a series of offensive missile sites is now in preparation on that imprisoned island. The
purpose of these bases can be none other than to provide a
nuclear strike capability against the Western Hemisphere.

Upon receiving the first preliminary hard information of
this nature last Tuesday morning [October 16, 1962] at 9 A.M.,
I directed that our surveillance be stepped up. And having now
confirmed and completed our evaluation of the evidence and
our decision on a course of action, this Government feels
obliged to report this new crisis to you in fullest detail.

Deliberate Defiance and Deception

The characteristics of these new missile sites indicate two distinct types of installations. Several of them include medium
range ballistic missiles capable of carrying a nuclear warhead
for a distance of more than 1,000 nautical miles. Each of
these missiles, in short, is capable of striking Washington,
D.C., the Panama Canal, Cape Canaveral, Mexico City, or
any other city in the southeastern part of the United States,
in Central America, or in the Caribbean area.

Additional sites not yet completed appear to be designed
for intermediate range ballistic missiles—capable of traveling
more than twice as far—and thus capable of striking most of

the major cities in the Western Hemisphere, ranging as far north as Hudson Bay, Canada, and as far south as Lima, Peru. In addition, jet bombers, capable of carrying nuclear weapons, are now being uncrated and assembled in Cuba, while the necessary air bases are being prepared.

This urgent transformation of Cuba into an important strategic base—by the presence of these large, long range, and clearly offensive weapons of sudden mass destruction—constitutes an explicit threat to the peace and security of all the Americas, in flagrant and deliberate defiance of the Rio Pact of 1947, the traditions of this Nation and hemisphere, the joint resolution of the 87th Congress, the Charter of the United Nations, and my own public warnings to the Soviets on September 4 and 13 [1962]. This action also contradicts the repeated assurances of Soviet spokesmen, both publicly and privately delivered, that the arms buildup in Cuba would retain its original defensive character, and that the Soviet Union had no need or desire to station strategic missiles on the territory of any other nation. . . .

The Threat of Nuclear War

Neither the United States of America nor the world community of nations can tolerate deliberate deception and offensive threats on the part of any nation, large or small. We no longer live in a world where only the actual firing of weapons represents a sufficient challenge to a nation's security to constitute maximum peril. Nuclear weapons are so destructive and ballistic missiles are so swift, that any substantially increased possibility of their use or any sudden change in their deployment may well be regarded as a definite threat to peace.

For many years both the Soviet Union and the United States, recognizing this fact, have deployed strategic nuclear weapons with great care, never upsetting the precarious status quo which insured that these weapons would not be used in the absence of some vital challenge. Our own strategic missiles have never been transferred to the territory of any other nation under a cloak of secrecy and deception; and our history—unlike that of the Soviets since the end of World War II—demonstrates that we have no desire to dominate or conquer any other nation or impose our system upon its people. Nevertheless, American citizens have become adjusted to living daily on the Bull's-eye of Soviet missiles located inside the U.S.S.R. or in submarines.

In that sense, missiles in Cuba add to an already clear and present danger—although it should be noted the nations of Latin America have never previously been subjected to a potential nuclear threat.

But this secret, swift, and extraordinary buildup of Communist missiles—in an area well known to have a special and historical relationship to the United States and the nations of the Western Hemisphere, in violation of Soviet assurances, and in defiance of American and hemispheric policy—this sudden, clandestine decision to station strategic weapons for the first time outside of Soviet soil—is a deliberately provocative and unjustified change in the status quo which cannot be accepted by this country, if our courage and our commitments are ever to be trusted again by either friend or foe. . . .

Taking Defensive Steps

Acting, therefore, in the defense of our own security and of the entire Western Hemisphere, and under the authority entrusted to me by the Constitution as endorsed by the resolution of the Congress, I have directed that the following initial steps be taken immediately:

First: To halt this offensive buildup, a strict quarantine on all offensive military equipment under shipment to Cuba is being initiated. All ships of any kind bound for Cuba from whatever nation or port will, if found to contain cargoes of offensive weapons, be turned back. This quarantine will be extended, if needed, to other types of cargo and carriers. We are not at this time, however, denying the necessities of life as the Soviets attempted to do in their Berlin blockade of 1948.

Second: I have directed the continued and increased close surveillance of Cuba and its military buildup. The foreign ministers of the OAS [Organization of American States], in their communique of October 6 [1962], rejected secrecy in such matters in this hemisphere. Should these offensive military preparations continue, thus increasing the threat to the hemisphere, further action will be justified. I have directed the Armed Forces to prepare for any eventualities; and I trust that in the interest of both the Cuban people and the Soviet technicians at the sites, the hazards to all concerned in continuing this threat will be recognized.

Third: It shall be the policy of this Nation to regard any nuclear missile launched from Cuba against any nation in the Western Hemisphere as an attack by the Soviet Union on the United States, requiring a full retaliatory response upon the Soviet Union.

Fourth: As a necessary military precaution, I have reinforced our base at Guantanamo, evacuated today the dependents of our personnel there, and ordered additional military units to be on a standby alert basis.

Fifth: We are calling tonight for an immediate meeting of the Organ of Consultation under the Organization of

In a televised address to the American public, Kennedy announced the discovery of Soviet missile bases in Cuba.

American States, to consider this threat to hemispheric security and to invoke articles 6 and 8 of the Rio Treaty in support of all necessary action. The United Nations Charter allows for regional security arrangements—and the nations of this hemisphere decided long ago against the military presence of outside powers. Our other allies around the world have also been alerted.

Sixth: Under the Charter of the United Nations, we are asking tonight that an emergency meeting of the Security Council be convoked without delay to take action against this latest Soviet threat to world peace. Our resolution will call for the prompt dismantling and withdrawal of all offensive weapons in Cuba, under the supervision of U.N. observers, before the quarantine can be lifted.

Seventh and finally: I call upon Chairman [Nikita] Khrushchev to halt and eliminate this clandestine, reckless and provocative threat to world peace and to stable relations between our two nations. I call upon him further to abandon this course of world domination, and to join in an historic effort to end the perilous arms race and to transform the history of man. He has an opportunity now to move the world back from the abyss of destruction—by returning to his government's own words that it had no need to station missiles outside its own territory, and withdrawing these weapons from Cuba—by refraining from any action which will widen or deepen the present crisis—and then by participating in a search for peaceful and permanent solutions.

This Nation is prepared to present its case against the Soviet threat to peace, and our own proposals for a peaceful world, at any time and in any forum—in the OAS, in the United Nations, or in any other meeting that could be useful—without limiting our freedom of action. We have in the past made strenuous efforts to limit the spread of nuclear weapons. We have proposed the elimination of all arms and military bases in a fair and effective disarmament treaty. We are prepared to discuss new proposals for the removal of tensions on both sides—including the possibility of a genuinely independent Cuba, free to determine its own destiny. We have no wish to war with the Soviet Union—for we are a peaceful people who desire to live in peace with all other peoples.

But it is difficult to settle or even discuss these problems in an atmosphere of intimidation. That is why this latest Soviet threat—or any other threat which is made either independently or in response to our actions this week—must and will be met with determination. Any hostile move anywhere in the world against the safety and freedom of peoples to whom we are committed—including in particular the brave people of West Berlin—will be met by whatever action is needed. . . .

A Difficult Path

My fellow citizens: let no one doubt that this is a difficult and dangerous effort on which we have set out. No one can see precisely what course it will take or what costs or casualties will be incurred. Many months of sacrifice and self-discipline lie ahead—months in which our patience and our will will be tested—months in which many threats and denunciations will keep us aware of our dangers. But the greatest danger of all would be to do nothing.

The path we have chosen for the present is full of hazards, as all paths are—but it is the one most consistent with our character and courage as a nation and our commitments around the world. The cost of freedom is always high—and Americans have always paid it. And one path we shall never choose, and that is the path of surrender or submission.

Our goal is not the victory of might, but the vindication of right—not peace at the expense of freedom, but both peace and freedom, here in this hemisphere, and, we hope, around the world. God willing, that goal will be achieved.

The Vietnam War Is Indefensible

Eugene McCarthy

Eugene McCarthy, born in Watkins, Minnesota, in 1916, began his political career as a Democratic member of the U.S. House of Representatives, becoming a senator in 1959. His opposition to President Lyndon B. Johnson's policies in Vietnam won McCarthy the support of many liberals, and in 1967 he announced his candidacy for the Democratic nomination. Backed by a large number of college students, McCarthy was very successful in early primaries. However, he lost the nomination to Hubert Humphrey at the Democratic National Convention in Chicago, during which antiwar protests led to a riot with police.

U.S. involvement in Vietnam began when France concluded it could no longer maintain Indochinese colonies and formed an agreement with Communist forces that temporarily divided Vietnam at the 17th parallel. Fearing Communist expansion, the United States formed the Southeast Asia Treaty Organization (SEATO), hoping to protect southern Vietnam from communism. The regime of South Vietnamese president Ngo Dinh Diem, however, met with opposition from within and without. In 1961, a team sent by President John F. Kennedy to examine the situation in Vietnam asked for increased military, technical, and economic aid to the troubled nation. Kennedy increased the level of U.S. military involvement but would not send troops. After Kennedy's assassination, Lyndon B. Johnson assumed the presidency. On August 4, 1964, North Vietnam launched an attack on an American ship in the Gulf of Tonkin. As a result, Congress granted John-

Eugene McCarthy, address before the Conference of Concerned Democrats, Chicago, Illinois, December 2, 1967.

son broad war powers, and Johnson responded with air attacks against North Vietnam. The war escalated under Johnson, who introduced combat troops to Vietnam in March 1965. As American servicemen began to die in Vietnam, sentiment in the United States began to change. In 1967, opposition to the Vietnam War began to increase. In October, 50,000 protesters picketed the Pentagon in Washington, and in April, 700,000 marched down Fifth Avenue in New York. Despite this opposition, Johnson ordered more U.S troops into Vietnam. By 1967, 15,997 U.S. servicemen had been killed in the war.

In the following address before the Conference of Concerned Democrats, in Chicago, Illinois, on December 2, 1967, McCarthy outlines his opposition to the war in Vietnam. According to McCarthy, the United States should not use its military strength to act as the planet's police force. He claims that it is wrong for the United States to impose its will by violent military intervention. Moreover, the nation's great generals warned against involvement in a land war in Asia, says McCarthy. He explains that those who support the war have been unable to prove that the good that may come from victory is worth the loss of life, and he calls for the government to end the war.

Richard Nixon, who succeeded Johnson as president, expanded the Vietnam War into neighboring Laos and Cambodia in an effort to eliminate Communist supply routes. Opposition to the war increased at home, and in 1970, students protesting the invasions were killed at Kent State University in Ohio and Jackson State University in Mississippi. In early 1973, the Nixon administration encouraged the Saigon regime to sign the Paris Peace Accord, ending open hostilities between the United States and North Vietnam. South Vietnamese forces tried to keep Communist forces at bay without U.S. assistance, but Saigon fell on April 30, 1975.

I n 1952, in this city of Chicago, the Democratic party nominated as its candidate for the presidency Adlai Stevenson.

His promise to his party and to the people of the country then was that he would talk sense to them. And he did in the clearest tones. He did not speak above the people, as his enemies charged, but he raised the hard and difficult questions and proposed the difficult answers. His voice became the voice of America. He lifted the spirit of this land. The country, in his language, was purified and given direction.

Before most other men, he recognized the problem of our cities and called for action.

Before other men, he measured the threat of nuclear war and called for a test-ban treaty.

Before other men, he anticipated the problem of conscience which he saw must come with maintaining a peacetime army and a limited draft and urged the political leaders of this country to put their wisdom to the task.

From Optimism to Distrust

In all of these things he was heard by many but not followed, until under the presidency of John F. Kennedy his ideas were revived in new language and in a new spirit. To the clear sound of the horn was added the beat of a steady and certain drum.

John Kennedy set free the spirit of America. The honest optimism was released. Quiet courage and civility became the mark of American government, and new programs of promise and of dedication were presented: the Peace Corps, the Alliance for Progress, the promise of equal rights for all Americans—and not just the promise, but the beginning of the achievement of that promise.

All the world looked to the United States with new hope, for here was youth and confidence and an openness to the future. Here was a country not being held by the dead hand of the past, nor frightened by the violent hand of the future which was grasping at the world.

This was the spirit of 1963.

What is the spirit of 1967? What is the mood of America and of the world toward America today?

It is a joyless spirit—a mood of frustration, of anxiety, of uncertainty.

In place of the enthusiasm of the Peace Corps among the

young people of America, we have protests and demonstrations.

In place of the enthusiasm of the Alliance for Progress, we have distrust and disappointment.

Instead of the language of promise and of hope, we have in politics today a new vocabulary in which the critical word is *war*: war on poverty, war on ignorance, war on crime, war on pollution. None of these problems can be solved by war but only by persistent, dedicated, and thoughtful attention.

But we do have one war which is properly called a war—the war in Vietnam, which is central to all of the problems of America.

Questioning the War

A war of questionable legality and questionable constitutionality.

A war which is diplomatically indefensible; the first war in this century in which the United States, which at its founding made an appeal to the decent opinion of mankind in the Declaration of Independence, finds itself without the support of the decent opinion of mankind.

A war which cannot be defended in the context of the judgment of history. It is being presented in the context of an historical judgment of an era which is past. Munich [which symbolizes Britain's appeasement of Hitler in the late 1930s] appears to be the starting point of history for the secretary of state [Dean Rusk] and for those who attempt to support his policies. What is necessary is a realization that the United States is a part of the movement of history itself; that it cannot stand apart, attempting to control the world by imposing covenants and treaties and by violent military intervention; that our role is not to police the planet but to use military strength with restraint and within limits, while at the same time we make available to the world the great power of our economy, of our knowledge, and of our good will.

A war which is not defensible even in military terms; which runs contrary to the advice of our greatest generals—[Dwight D.] Eisenhower, [Matthew] Ridgway, [Omar] Bradley, and [Douglas] MacArthur—all of whom admonished us against becoming involved in a land war in Asia. Events have proved them right, as estimate after estimate as to the time of success and the military commitment necessary to success has had to be revised—always upward: more troops, more extensive bombing, a widening and intensification of the war. Extension and intensification have been the rule, and projection after projection of success have been proved wrong.

The Administration's Objectives

With the escalation of our military commitment has come a parallel of overleaping of objectives: from protecting South Vietnam, to nation building in South Vietnam, to protecting all of Southeast Asia, and ultimately to suggesting that the safety and security of the United States itself is at stake.

Finally, it is a war which is morally wrong. The most recent statement of objectives cannot be accepted as an honest judgment as to why we are in Vietnam. It has become increasingly difficult to justify the methods we are using and the instruments of war which we are using as we have moved from limited targets and somewhat restricted weapons to greater variety and more destructive instruments of war, and also have extended the area of operations almost to the heart of North Vietnam.

Even assuming that both objectives and methods can be defended, the war cannot stand the test of proportion and of prudent judgment. It is no longer possible to prove that the good that may come with what is called victory, or projected as victory, is proportionate to the loss of life and property and to other disorders that follow from this war. . . .

The Price of Peace

Those of us who are gathered here tonight [at the Conference of Concerned Democrats] are not advocating peace at any price. We are willing to pay a high price for peace—for an honorable, rational, and political solution to this war, a solution which will enhance our world position, which will permit us to give the necessary attention to our other commitments abroad, both military and nonmilitary, and leave us with both human and physical resources and with moral energy to deal effectively with the pressing domestic problems of the United States itself.

I see little evidence that the administration has set any limits on the price which it will pay for a military victory which becomes less and less sure and more hollow and empty in promise.

The scriptural promise of the good life is one in which the old men see visions and the young men dream dreams. In the context of this war and all of its implications, the young men of America do not dream dreams, but many live in the nightmare of moral anxiety, of concern and great apprehension; and the old men, instead of visions which they can offer to the young, are projecting, in the language of the secretary of state, a specter of one billion Chinese threatening the peace and safety of the world—a frightening and intimidating future.

Sending a New Message

The message from the administration today is a message of apprehension, a message of fear—yes, even a message of fear of fear.

This is not the real spirit of America. I do not believe that it is. This is a time to test the mood and spirit:

To offer in place of doubt—trust.

In place of expediency—right judgment.

In place of ghettos, let us have neighborhoods and communities.

In place of incredibility—integrity.

In place of murmuring, let us have clear speech; let us again hear America singing.

In place of disunity, let us have dedication of purpose.

In place of near despair, let us have hope.

This is the promise of greatness which was stated for us by Adlai Stevenson and which was brought to form and positive action in the words and actions of John Kennedy.

Let us pick up again these lost strands and weave them again into the fabric of America.

Let us sort out the music from the sounds and again respond to the trumpet and the steady drum.

GREAT
SPEECHES
IN
HISTORY

The Threat of Nuclear War

The Menace of
Mass Destruction

Albert Einstein

Albert Einstein was born in Ulm, Germany, on March 14,
1879. By 1913, Einstein had won international fame as a
theoretical physicist and is often identified as the father
of the theory of relativity. He was also a major contributor to quantum theory and in 1921 won the Nobel Prize
in physics for his study of photoelectric effect. After his
property was confiscated by the Nazi government in
1934 because Einstein was Jewish, he took a position at
Princeton University in New Jersey, which he held until
his death in 1955.

Einstein was a pacifist, but as a witness to the rise of
the Nazis, he came to advocate military preparedness and
wrote a famous letter to President Franklin D. Roosevelt
urging him to initiate a nuclear research program. However, as the atomic era progressed, Einstein realized that
nuclear weapons were a profound risk to humanity. During the last decade of his life, he was an advocate of nuclear disarmament and international cooperation to prevent war.

In the following speech before the Foreign Press Association delivered on November 11, 1947, Einstein questions the effectiveness of using government negotiations
to resolve the problem posed by atomic weapons. Rather
than treat the problem as an epidemic of disease, in
which experts from all nations would be brought together to share their knowledge and come up with an objective solution, says Einstein, the problem remains in the
hands of those whose thinking is corrupted by national-

Albert Einstein, address before the Second Annual Dinner of the Foreign Press
Association to the General Assembly and Security Council of the United Nations,
New York, November 11, 1947. Copyright © 1947 by the Philosophical Library.
Reproduced by permission.

ism in a divided world. According to Einstein, there is little hope for a solution when those who are best suited to solve the problem remained separated by international politics.

One week before his death Einstein wrote a letter to renowned philosopher and fellow pacifist Bertrand Russell agreeing to put his name on a manifesto that urged all nations to give up nuclear weapons—one of the final acts of a man dedicated to international peace.

Everyone is aware of the difficult and menacing situation in which human society—shrunk into one community with a common fate—finds itself, but only a few act accordingly. Most people go on living their everyday life: half frightened, half indifferent, they behold the ghostly tragicomedy that is being performed on the international stage before the eyes and ears of the world. But on that stage, on which the actors under the floodlights play their ordained parts, our fate of tomorrow, life or death of the nations, is being decided.

It would be different if the problem were not one of things made by man himself, such as the atomic bomb and other means of mass destruction equally menacing all peoples. It would be different, for instance, if an epidemic of bubonic plague were threatening the entire world. In such a case conscientious and expert persons would be brought together and they would work out an intelligent plan to combat the plague. After having reached agreement upon the right ways and means, they would submit their plan to the governments. Those would hardly raise serious objections but rather agree speedily on the measures to be taken. They certainly would never think of trying to handle the matter in such a way that their own nation would be spared whereas the next one would be decimated.

But could not our situation be compared to one of a menacing epidemic? People are unable to view this situation in its true light, for their eyes are blinded by passion. General fear and anxiety create hatred and aggressiveness. The adaptation to warlike aims and activities has corrupted the mentality of man; as a result, intelligent, objective, and humane thinking has hardly any effect and is even suspected and persecuted as unpatriotic.

There are, no doubt, in the opposite camps enough people of sound judgment and sense of justice who would be capable and eager to work out together a solution for the factual difficulties. But the efforts of such people are hampered by the fact that it is made impossible for them to come together for informal discussions. I am thinking of persons who are accustomed to the objective approach to a problem and who will not be confused by exaggerated nationalism or other passions. This forced separation of the people of both camps I consider one of the major obstacles to the achievement of an acceptable solution of the burning problem of international security.

As long as contact between the two camps is limited to the official negotiations, I can see little prospect for an intelligent agreement being reached, especially since considerations of national prestige as well as the attempt to talk out of the window for the benefit of the masses are bound to make reasonable progress almost impossible. What one party suggests officially is for that reason alone suspected and even made unacceptable to the other. Also behind all official negotiations stands—though veiled—the threat of naked power. The official method can lead to success only after spade-work of an informal nature has prepared the ground; the conviction that a mutually satisfactory solution can be reached must be gained first; then the actual negotiations can get under way with a fair promise of success.

We scientists believe that what we and our fellow men do or fail to do within the next few years will determine the fate of our civilization. And we consider it our task untiringly to explain this truth, to help people realize all that is at stake, and to work, not for appeasement, but for understanding and ultimate agreement between peoples and nations of different views.

The Peaceful Use of Atomic Power

Dwight D. Eisenhower

Dwight D. Eisenhower was an American general and the thirty-fourth president of the United States. Eisenhower is credited with the success of the Allied invasion of Europe during World War II. After heading the European occupation forces for six months, Eisenhower succeeded George C. Marshall as army chief of staff and in 1949 accepted the presidency of Columbia University in New York. In 1950, President Harry S. Truman recalled Eisenhower to active duty to command the North Atlantic Treaty Organization forces in Europe, a post he held until May 1952, when he won the Republican presidential nomination. Eisenhower defeated Adlai Stevenson in the election.

Some authorities claim Eisenhower's stand on atomic power was inconsistent. Others claim it simply reflected the tension of the atomic age. Although nuclear weapons evoked the fear of mass destruction, he believed that nuclear power offered progress and hope. In the following speech, for example, Eisenhower explains the extent of the buildup of atomic weapons and their potential for destruction; however, Eisenhower proposes a program to extend aid to other countries to establish nuclear reactors for peaceful research. In addition, he asks those nations with nuclear weapons to relinquish a portion of their stockpiles to a newly created International Atomic Energy Agency in an effort to reduce atomic materials used for military purposes.

In 1946, the General Assembly of the United Nations

Dwight D. Eisenhower, address before the General Assembly of the United Nations, New York, December 8, 1953.

set up an atomic energy commission to examine proposals for the peaceful uses of atomic energy. It also tried to
pass a plan to create an international agency to control
atomic power and weapons, but the plan was vetoed by
the Soviet Union. In 1952, the UN formed a disarmament
commission and, in 1953, set up a subcommittee consisting of Canada, France, Great Britain, the United States,
and the Soviet Union. Western nations in the subcommittee believed on-site inspection should be instituted before
disarmament could proceed while the Soviet Union believed this action would result in inspection without disarmament and insisted on an immediate ban on nuclear
weapons. Disagreements on how to proceed with nuclear
weapons and nuclear energy continued throughout the
Cold War and after.

I know that the American people share my deep belief that
if a danger exists in the world, it is a danger shared by
all—and equally, that if hope exists in the mind of one
nation, that hope should be shared by all.

If there is to be advanced any proposal designed to ease
even by the smallest measure the tensions of today's world,
what more appropriate audience could there be than the
members of the General Assembly of the United Nations?

I feel impelled to speak today in a language that in a sense
is new—one which I, who have spent so much of my life in
the military profession, would have preferred never to use.

That new language is the language of atomic warfare.

The atomic age has moved forward at such a pace that
every citizen of the world should have some comprehension,
at least in comparative terms, of the extent of this development of the utmost significance to every one of us. Clearly, if
the peoples of the world are to conduct an intelligent search
for peace, they must be armed with the significant facts of today's existence.

My recital of atomic danger and power is necessarily
stated in United States terms, for these are the only incontro-
vertible facts that I know. I need hardly point out to this As-

sembly, however, that this subject is global, not merely national, in character.

On July 16, 1945, the United States set off the world's first atomic explosion. Since that date in 1945, the United States of America has conducted 42 test explosions.

Atomic bombs today are more than 25 times as powerful as the weapons with which the atomic age dawned, while hydrogen weapons are in the range of millions of tons of TNT equivalent.

Today, the United States' stockpile of atomic weapons, which, of course, increases daily, exceeds by many times the explosive equivalent of the total of all bombs and all shells that came from every plane and every gun in every theatre of war in all of the years of World War II.

A single air group, whether afloat or land-based, can now deliver to any reachable target a destructive cargo exceeding in power all the bombs that fell on Britain in all of World War II.

In size and variety, the development of atomic weapons has been no less remarkable. The development has been such that atomic weapons have virtually achieved conventional status within our armed services. In the United States, the Army, the Navy, the Air Force, and the Marine Corps are all capable of putting this weapon to military use.

But the dread secret, and the fearful engines of atomic might, are not ours alone.

In the first place, the secret is possessed by our friends and allies, Great Britain and Canada, whose scientific genius made a tremendous contribution to our original discoveries, and the designs of atomic bombs.

The secret is also known by the Soviet Union.

The Soviet Union has informed us that, over recent years, it has devoted extensive resources to atomic weapons. During this period, the Soviet Union has exploded a series of atomic devices, including at least one involving thermonuclear reactions.

If at one time the United States possessed what might have been called a monopoly of atomic power, that monopoly ceased to exist several years ago. Therefore, although our earlier start has permitted us to accumulate what is today a great quantitative advantage, the atomic realities of today comprehend two facts of even greater significance.

The Significance of Atomic Power

First, the knowledge now possessed by several nations will eventually be shared by others—possibly all others.

Second, even a vast superiority in numbers of weapons, and a consequent capability of devastating retaliation, is no preventive, of itself, against the fearful material damage and toll of human lives that would be inflicted by surprise aggression.

The free world, at least dimly aware of these facts, has naturally embarked on a large program of warning and defense systems. That program will be accelerated and expanded.

But let no one think that the expenditure of vast sums for weapons and systems of defense can guarantee absolute safety for the cities and citizens of any nation. The awful arithmetic of the atomic bomb does not permit of any such easy solution. Even against the most powerful defense, an aggressor in possession of the effective minimum number of atomic bombs for a surprise attack could probably place a sufficient number of his bombs on the chosen targets to cause hideous damage.

Should such an atomic attack be launched against the United States, our reactions would be swift and resolute. But for me to say that the defense capabilities of the United States are such that they could inflict terrible losses upon an aggressor—for me to say that the retaliation capabilities of the United States are so great that such an aggressor's land would be laid waste—all this, while fact, is not the true expression of the purpose and the hope of the United States.

To pause there would be to confirm the hopeless finality of a belief that two atomic colossi are doomed malevolently to eye each other indefinitely across a trembling world. To stop there would be to accept helplessly the probability of civilization destroyed—the annihilation of the irreplaceable heritage of mankind handed down to us generation from generation—and the condemnation of mankind to begin all over again the age-old struggle upward from savagery toward decency, and right, and justice.

Surely no sane member of the human race could discover victory in such desolation. Could anyone wish his name to be coupled by history with such human degradation and destruction?

Occasional pages of history do record the faces of the "Great Destroyers" but the whole book of history reveals mankind's never-ending quest for peace, and mankind's God-given capacity to build.

Taking Steps Toward Peace

It is with the book of history, and not with isolated pages, that the United States will ever wish to be identified. My country wants to be constructive, not destructive. It wants agreements, not wars, among nations. It wants itself to live in freedom, and in the confidence that the people of every other nation enjoy equally the right of choosing their own way of life.

So my country's purpose is to help us move out of the dark chamber of horrors into the light, to find a way by which the minds of men, the hopes of men, the souls of men everywhere, can move forward toward peace and happiness and well being.

In this quest, I know that we must not lack patience.

I know that in a world divided, such as ours today, salvation cannot be attained by one dramatic act.

I know that many steps will have to be taken over many months before the world can look at itself one day and truly realize that a new climate of mutually peaceful confidence is abroad in the world.

But I know, above all else, that we must start to take these steps—*now.*

The United States and its allies, Great Britain and France, have over the past months tried to take some of these steps. Let no one say that we shun the conference table.

On the record has long stood the request of the United States, Great Britain, and France to negotiate with the Soviet Union the problems of a divided Germany.

On that record has long stood the request of the same

three nations to negotiate an Austrian Peace Treaty.

On the same record still stands the request of the United Nations to negotiate the problems of Korea.

Most recently, we have received from the Soviet Union what is in effect an expression of willingness to hold a Four Power Meeting. Along with our allies, Great Britain and France, we were pleased to see that this note did not contain the unacceptable preconditions previously put forward.

As you already know from our joint Bermuda communiqué, the United States, Great Britain, and France have agreed promptly to meet with the Soviet Union.

The Government of the United States approaches this conference with hopeful sincerity. We will bend every effort of our minds to the single purpose of emerging from that conference with tangible results toward peace—the only true way of lessening international tension.

Seeking a Free Europe

We never have, we never will, propose or suggest that the Soviet Union surrender what is rightfully theirs.

We will never say that the peoples of Russia are an enemy with whom we have no desire ever to deal or mingle in friendly and fruitful relationship.

On the contrary, we hope that this coming Conference may initiate a relationship with the Soviet Union which will eventually bring about a free intermingling of the peoples of the East and of the West—the one sure, human way of developing the understanding required for confident and peaceful relations.

Instead of the discontent which is now settling upon Eastern Germany, occupied Austria, and the countries of Eastern Europe, we seek a harmonious family of free European nations, with none a threat to the other, and least of all a threat to the peoples of Russia.

Beyond the turmoil and strife and misery of Asia, we seek peaceful opportunity for these peoples to develop their natural resources and to elevate their lives.

These are not idle words or shallow visions. Behind them lies a story of nations lately come to independence, not as a result of war, but through free grant or peaceful negotiation. There is a record, already written, of assistance gladly given by nations of the West to needy peoples, and to those suffering the temporary effects of famine, drought, and natural disaster.

These are deeds of peace. They speak more loudly than promises or protestations of peaceful intent.

But I do not wish to rest either upon the reiteration of past proposals or the restatement of past deeds. The gravity of the time is such that every new avenue of peace, no matter how dimly discernible, should be explored.

The Road to Disarmament

There is at least one new avenue of peace which has not yet been well explored—an avenue now laid out by the General Assembly of the United Nations.

In its resolution of November 18th, 1953, this General Assembly suggested—and I quote—"that the Disarmament Commission study the desirability of establishing a sub-committee consisting of representatives of the Powers principally involved, which should seek in private an acceptable solution . . . and report on such a solution to the General Assembly and to the Security Council not later than 1 September 1954."

The United States, heeding the suggestion of the General Assembly of the United Nations, is instantly prepared to meet privately with such other countries as may be "principally involved," to seek "an acceptable solution" to the atomic armaments race which overshadows not only the peace, but the very life, of the world.

We shall carry into these private or diplomatic talks a new conception.

The United States would seek more than the mere reduction or elimination of atomic materials for military purposes.

It is not enough to take this weapon out of the hands of the soldiers. It must be put into the hands of those who will know how to strip its military casing and adapt it to the arts of peace.

The United States knows that if the fearful trend of atomic military buildup can be reversed, this greatest of destructive forces can be developed into a great boon, for the benefit of all mankind.

The United States knows that peaceful power from atomic energy is no dream of the future. That capability, already proved, is here—now—today. Who can doubt, if the entire body of the world's scientists and engineers had adequate amounts of fissionable material with which to test and develop their ideas, that this capability would rapidly be transformed into universal, efficient, and economic usage.

To hasten the day when fear of the atom will begin to disappear from the minds of people, and the governments of the East and West, there are certain steps that can be taken now.

I therefore make the following proposals:

An Atomic Energy Agency

The Governments principally involved, to the extent permitted by elementary prudence, to begin now and continue to make joint contributions from their stockpiles of normal uranium and fissionable materials to an International Atomic Energy Agency. We would expect that such an agency would be set up under the aegis of the United Nations.

The ratios of contributions, the procedures and other details would properly be within the scope of the "private conversations" I have referred to earlier.

The United States is prepared to undertake these explorations in good faith. Any partner of the United States acting in the same good faith will find the United States a not unreasonable or ungenerous associate.

Undoubtedly initial and early contributions to this plan would be small in quantity. However, the proposal has the great virtue that it can be undertaken without the irritations and mutual suspicions incident to any attempt to set up a completely acceptable system of world-wide inspection and control.

The Atomic Energy Agency could be made responsible for the impounding, storage, and protection of the contributed fissionable and other materials. The ingenuity of our scientists will provide special, safe conditions under which such a bank of fissionable material can be made essentially immune to surprise seizure.

The more important responsibility of this Atomic Energy Agency would be to devise methods whereby this fissionable material would be allocated to serve the peaceful pursuits of mankind. Experts would be mobilized to apply atomic energy to the needs of agriculture, medicine, and other peaceful activities. A special purpose would be to provide abundant electrical energy in the power-starved areas of the world. Thus the contributing powers would be dedicating some of their strength to serve the needs rather than the fears of mankind.

The United States would be more than willing—it would be proud to take up with others "principally involved" the development of plans whereby such peaceful use of atomic energy would be expedited.

Of those "principally involved" the Soviet Union must, of course, be one.

Solving the Atomic Dilemma

I would be prepared to submit to the Congress of the United States, and with every expectation of approval, any such plan that would:

First—encourage world-wide investigation into the most effective peacetime uses of fissionable material, and with the certainty that they had all the material needed for the conduct of all experiments that were appropriate;

Second—begin to diminish the potential destructive power of the world's atomic stockpiles;

Third—allow all peoples of all nations to see that, in this enlightened age, the great powers of the earth, both of the East and of the West, are interested in human aspirations first, rather than in building up the armaments of war;

Fourth—open up a new channel for peaceful discussion, and initiate at least a new approach to the many difficult problems that must be solved in both private and public conversations, if the world is to shake off the inertia imposed by fear, and is to make positive progress toward peace.

Against the dark background of the atomic bomb, the United States does not wish merely to present strength, but also the desire and the hope for peace.

The coming months will be fraught with fateful decisions. In this Assembly; in the capitals and military head-quarters of the world; in the hearts of men everywhere, be they governors or governed, may they be the decisions which will lead this world out of fear and into peace.

To the making of these fateful decisions, the United States pledges before you—and therefore before the world—its determination to help solve the fearful atomic dilemma—to devote its entire heart and mind to find the way by which the miraculous inventiveness of man shall not be dedicated to his death, but consecrated to his life.

Nuclear Testing Must Be Stopped

Adlai Stevenson

Adlai Stevenson was the Democratic presidential candidate in 1952 and 1956, defeated in both elections by Dwight D. Eisenhower. Despite these defeats, Stevenson continued to have significant influence within the United States and abroad. When John F. Kennedy was elected president in 1960, Stevenson had hoped Kennedy would reward him with the office of secretary of state, but instead Kennedy appointed Stevenson ambassador to the United Nations (UN), a position he held until his death in 1965. Kennedy also made Stevenson's appointment a cabinet position to ensure Stevenson would have a voice in making policy and to emphasize the importance of the UN as a forum for foreign policy. While ambassador, Stevenson worked to strengthen the UN and to resist Soviet efforts to weaken the office of secretary general.

During his second campaign and while ambassador, Stevenson emphasized the importance of halting the arms race and putting an end to nuclear testing. In the following excerpt from a statement made to the Political Committee of the United Nations on October 19, 1961, Stevenson warns of the danger of nuclear weapons tests, and asks that these tests be banned as a first step toward the ultimate goal—an end to thermonuclear weapons. He explains, however, that the United States also has a right to protect itself and, if other nations do not halt nuclear weapons tests, the United States reserves the right to prepare for atmospheric and underground testing.

On August 5, 1963, the Kennedy administration took

Adlai Stevenson, statement before the Political Committee of the United Nations, New York, October 19, 1961.

the step that Stevenson had so long advocated and signed the Limited Test Ban Treaty, which prohibited nuclear explosions in the atmosphere, in outer space, and under water. The treaty did not include underground nuclear tests since verification was not seen as adequate at that time. After extensive hearings and almost three weeks of floor debate, on September 24, the Senate ratified the treaty by a vote of 80 to 19.

An emergency confronts this committee and the world! The Soviet Union is now nearing the conclusion of a massive series of nuclear weapon tests. Unless something is done quickly, the Soviet testing will necessarily result in further testing by my country and perhaps by others.

Negotiating the First Step

There is still time to halt this drift toward the further refinement and multiplication of these weapons. Perhaps this will be the last clear chance to reverse this tragic trend. For if testing is stopped, the terrible pace of technological progress will be decisively retarded. A ban on tests is, of course, only the first step; and the control and destruction of nuclear and thermonuclear weapons is the ultimate goal. But it is an indispensable first step.

Accordingly, I must inform the committee that the United States is obliged in self-protection to reserve the right to make preparations to test in the atmosphere, as well as underground.

But the United States stands ready to resume negotiations for a treaty tomorrow. We will devote all our energies to the quickest possible conclusion of these negotiations, either here or in Geneva. If the Soviet Union will do the same and stop its tests, there is no reason why a treaty with effective controls cannot be signed in thirty days and this suicidal business ended before it ends us.

But, I repeat, unless a treaty can be signed, and signed promptly, the United States has no choice but to prepare and take the action necessary to protect its own security and that of the world community.

I trust that this expression of hope for the triumph of reason will convey some measure of the depth of our feeling about the subject and of our desire to do our share to save the human race from a greater menace than the plagues which once ravaged Europe. We believe we have done our share, and more, ever since the United States proposals of 1946.[1] I remind you that if those proposals had been accepted by the Soviet Union, no state would now have nuclear weapons; and we would not now be in such a perilous crisis.

I have claimed the privilege of making this declaration for the United States because few delegates, I dare say, feel more deeply about this matter than I do, in part, perhaps, because I proposed that nuclear tests be stopped almost six years ago—and lost a great many votes in the 1956 Presidential election as a result! Had the nuclear powers agreed even then, think how much safer and healthier the world would be today.

I pray we do not lose still another chance to meet the challenge of our times and stop this dance of death.

A Need for Action

I confess a feeling of futility when I consider the immensity of the problems which confront us and the feebleness of our efforts to deal properly with them. We have lived for sixteen years in the Atomic Age. During these years we have ingeniously and steadily improved man's capacity to blow up the planet. But we have done little to improve man's control over the means of his own destruction. Instead, we have worried and wrangled and talked and trifled while time trickles away and the hands of the clock creep toward midnight.

I would not imply that the problems of control are easy. Just as the nuclear bomb itself lays open the inner mysteries of science, so the attempt to control the nuclear bomb cuts to

---

1. The United States proposed an international control system and on-site inspections be put into place before disarmament could proceed; the Soviet Union believed this would result in inspection without disarmament and proposed instead an immediate ban on nuclear weapons without inspections.

the core of our political ideas and mechanisms. As the bomb itself represented a revolution in science, so the control of the bomb may, in the end, mean a revolution in politics.

But we must not let the very immensity of the problem dwarf our minds and our calculations. We must act—and we must take hold of the problem where we can. One obvious way is to tackle the question of nuclear testing.

No one would argue that the abolition of testing would itself solve all our problems. It would mean only a small beginning in the assault on the evil, ancient institution of war. But in a world of no beginnings, a small beginning shines forth like the morning sun on the distant horizon. We have talked long enough about the horror which hangs over us. Now is the time for us to get down to business—to fight this horror, not with soft words and wistful hopes, but with the hard weapon of effective international arrangements.

The American People Must Act to Prevent a Nuclear Holocaust

Edward J. Bloustein

Edward J. Bloustein was an educational administrator and advocate, who served as president of Rutgers University from 1971 until his death in 1989. Bloustein served in the U.S. Army during World War II and after the war entered New York University. He later studied at Oxford on a Fulbright scholarship. Bloustein was awarded a Ph.D. from Cornell University and continued his studies in law at Cornell, graduating in 1959.

As an educator, Bloustein's primary concern was the education of America's children, and he often spoke out on the state of America's public schools, particularly those in his state, New Jersey. According to Bloustein, the ever-present threat of a nuclear holocaust is part of the problem in America's schools. In the following commencement address delivered at the University of Connecticut, in Storrs, on May 23, 1982, Bloustein discusses the impact of the threat of a nuclear holocaust on the American people. Because people are paralyzed by fear of disaster and overwhelmed by the complexity of the problem, they feel powerless to take action. However, says Bloustein, individual and collective action can make a positive difference. He points out, for example, that even President Ronald Reagan changed his views in response to public reaction and offered to discuss disarmament with the Soviets.

Edward J. Bloustein, Commencement Address, Storrs, Connecticut, May 23, 1982. Copyright © 1982 by Edward J. Bloustein. Reproduced by permission of the University of Connecticut.

During the years following Bloustein's address, the leaders of the Soviet Union and the United States negotiated and signed several agreements calling for arms reduction. Since the dissolution of the Soviet Union, additional arms reduction treaties were negotiated and signed throughout the 1990s and into the new century. However, the fear of mass destruction persists, as many more nations have acquired or are close to developing nuclear weapons. The threat of an attack by a nuclear missile from a rogue or terrorist state has increased, and the potential for a nuclear holocaust remains.

These exercises bring to an end the first full century of education at the University of Connecticut; they also inaugurate the second century of this university's educational venture. The occasion provokes consideration of continuity; consideration which, with your indulgence, will take me beyond this campus and your time and mine, to continuity of the race of man on earth.

If you are shocked at this sharp transition from celebration of the end of your education at Storrs, Connecticut, to contemplation of the end of the race of man, that is fine, because that was my intention. For, as much as any other single factor, we are menaced with our extinction as a race, because we are insufficiently mindful of the threat to our lives and to our posterity which the nuclear arms race presents. We desperately require a national shock of recognition of that menace. Although I pretend to neither sufficient eloquence, nor wit, to provide it, perhaps today I can lay a bare framework for it.

A Cultural Condition

But first I owe you some explanation of why a teacher and educator, without any special training in world affairs or nuclear armament, should address himself publicly to the danger of a nuclear holocaust. The reason is instructive of, not merely my psychology—because, of itself, that would not be worth talking to you about—but of the general torpor which besets the national consciousness on this issue.

Of recent months in the State of New Jersey I have been speaking out on the deplorable state of our public schools. What I have been saying is remarkable only because it took so long for a president of a state university to say out loud what is so obvious. The fundamental reason so many of our children are being so poorly educated is, not because they lack discipline and shun the hard work of learning; nor because we lack a sufficient number of well trained and well motivated teachers—these are causes, but not the basic one. The root of our difficulty must be traced to the fact that the public school system is society in microcosm. It can teach effectively only those skills, it can inculcate effectively only those habits, which the society esteems. It cannot create its own moral and intellectual climate; it is rather the creature of the culture in which it finds itself.

Unfortunately, the condition of our contemporary culture is grievous: the supermarket is our cathedral; the television set our omnipresent baby-sitter-teacher-preacher; the soap opera our moral liturgy; while overhead there lurks the ever-present terror of mass nuclear destruction. My conclusion—one which leads me as an educator to share with you my views on nuclear disarmament—is that a society which hovers between moral ambivalence and decadence, and is under the ever-present terror of mass nuclear destruction, cannot really hope to educate its young to sound habits of mind and behavior.

I have elsewhere spoken about the other aspects of our contemporary condition which impinge on education, and what we can do about them. Today I address the issue of the impact of the nuclear peril.

The Consequences of Nuclear Disaster

The primary consequence of the threat of nuclear disaster on the consciousness of our students is one which is also apparent in the population at large. Students, all of us, are simply numbed by it. It befuddles and confounds us. We obliterate it from our conscious thought, but it remains behind working its insidious effects. Teachers in the classroom report that they teach their students through a barely noticeable fog of fear; as a result, they are difficult to reach and easily distracted. Politicians find their constituents passive and inert when confronted by the issue of nuclear disarmament. It is difficult to get them to think about the issue; even more difficult to get them to take any action about it.

Jonathon Schell, in three recent articles in *The New Yorker* magazine entitled, "The Fate of Earth"—articles comparable in their significance for alerting us to the perils of nuclear war to Rachel Carson's "Silent Spring" in warning us of environmental hazards—describes our condition in this fashion:

> . . . in spite of the immeasurable importance of nuclear weapons, the world has declined, on the whole, to think about them very much. We have thus far failed to fashion, or to discover within ourselves, an emotional or intellectual or political response to them. This peculiar failure of response, in which hundreds of millions of people acknowledge the presence of an immediate, unremitting threat to their existence and to the existence of the world they live in but do nothing about it—a failure in which both self-interest and fellow-feeling seems to have died—has itself been such a striking phenomenon that it has to be regarded as an extremely important part of the nuclear predicament as this has existed so far.

What are the causes of our passivity, of our failure of response? One is that mankind has never been faced before this nuclear era with a peril of such an apocalyptic character; the very magnitude of the disaster we face paralyzes us. A second cause—especially instructive of what course of action we must take in the matter—is that each of us, as an individual, feels impotent to deal with the terror we feel. The third ground of our inaction again an instructive one—is that the issue seems veiled behind impenetrable complexity, technical obscurity, and military secrecy.

Finding a Source of Power

The history of the last two decades should have taught us at least two things, however. The first is the power of public debate to enlighten us collectively on issues which were beyond the ken of most of us individually. The second is the power of democratic public opinion, when widely enough held, and persistently enough expressed, to affect the course of political events. These lessons of the recent past, seen in the context of our current sense of impotence, hold a plain message which should embolden us as we confront the nuclear peril: If we discuss and debate the issue collectively we will indeed be able to react to it intelligently and responsibly. Thereafter, by expressing our collective will, we can be certain of our power as a people to determine our own destiny, rather than having it determined for us.

The position of minorities, of women, and of our youth, are unquestionably improved today over what they were in the 1950's. These changes were not handed down from on high; they were wrought in the cauldron of public debate and democratic political action. They prove that we are a Nation where the emphatic and responsibly articulated concerns of large numbers of people, acting in concert, can alter the course of public affairs.

I do not mean to suggest that popular opinion is necessarily progressive, or that a mass movement is always on the side of the angels, or that it will always succeed. Still less do I mean to say that cherished goals, once partly attained, are immune to reversal or erosion when their supporters disperse or their opponents gather fresh energies. My intention is rather to urge that no individual of good conscience is entitled to withdraw from the arena of public concern over nuclear war, and that it is unworthy of a free people to abdicate their responsibility for public debate and social action when confronted by an unprecedentedly grave source of concern.

The Voices of Concern

We can all be thankful that the beginning of an end to our sense of impotence about the nuclear threat seems to be emerging at last. Not only have there been numerous protest demonstrations in western Europe in recent years, but expressions of acute concern have recently taken shape in this country as well. I allude to the efforts of the nuclear freeze

activist organizations. I allude as well to the numerous artic-
ulations of our plight, and of possible ways to remove ourselves from the brink of the abyss, by Jonathon Schell, and
other national spokesmen and leaders.

The illustrious historian Barbara Tuchman, who we are
honoring here today, has suggested, for instance, that our
fear itself, now that we have begun to admit to consciousness
the extent of it, may provide the motive power we need to
override humanity's warlike history. She recommends that
every political candidate this fall be asked to state his or her
position on the nuclear arms race. "When control of arms
becomes a goal of the mainstream, then it will prevail," she
has written.

We can also adduce the testimony of George F. Kennan,
former Ambassador to the Soviet Union, on receiving the Albert Einstein Peace Prize in May of last year [1981], when he
urged that an immediate 50 percent across-the-board reduction in American and Soviet nuclear weapons be undertaken.
"There is no issue at stake in our political relations with the
Soviet Union, no hope, no fear, nothing to which we aspire,
nothing we would like to avoid, which could conceivably be
worth a nuclear war," he said on that occasion.

We have as well the observations of retired Admiral Noel
Cayler, former commander-in-chief of United States forces in
the Pacific, former director of the National Security Agency,
taking the Kennan proposal a step farther with a suggestion
for implementing it. Cayler urges that we cut through the im-
passes of the negotiating table—the issues of verification, of
weapons classification, of what is "fair and equal"—by having each side simply turn in to a joint Soviet-American commission an equal number of explosive nuclear devices, each
side to choose which devices it will give up, each device to
count as one, and to be converted, under safeguard, to nuclear power for civilian purposes.

And, then, most recently, President [Ronald] Reagan has
responded to these evidences of the unease of the American
people about the possibility of nuclear war by changing his
own views. He earlier had expressed the conviction that it
would harm our national interest to even discuss disarmament until we had greatly strengthened our nuclear arsenal.

He has now abandoned this refusal to even talk to the Soviets about the issue, and has, instead, offered them a concrete proposal for disarmament, one, we must note that they turned down out of hand.

Whether the President's proposal was a debater's tactic in a world war of words with Chairman [Leonid] Brezhnev, or a realistic attempt to find accommodation is open to skeptical question—as is, indeed, the immediate, seemingly reflexive and unduly hasty, response of the Soviet Union to it. Nevertheless, the President has taken a distinct first step forward. He must be congratulated for it—and, of course—urged to continue down the same path, as speedily and as effectively as possible; a course of action which must also be urged upon the Soviet Union.

A Need for Commonsense Solutions

I mention only a sample of the recent outpouring of analysis and recommendations for dealing with nuclear weapons. There are other critiques and other strategies to be examined. Some commend themselves more to me than others, but it is not my intention here to persuade you of the merits of any particular proposal. I only want to emphasize that this issue is, above all, one that can be dealt with only by thinking about it; that, once we begin to bring the issue to consciousness and think rationally about it, solutions will suggest themselves even to men and women like those of us gathered here today who are of ordinary intelligence, without any special expertise in the netherland of nuclear armaments and the diplomacy of disarmament.

The reason this is so is because, although there are those who would have us believe otherwise, the politics of nuclear disarmament is at root a generalist's, and not a specialist's, intellectual conundrum. Once a critical mass and variety of weapons became available to both the Soviet Union and the United States—as it now has—disarmament cannot be achieved by building more weapons. That course involves an endless spiraling cycle in which each side expends more and more of its resources to achieve either parity or superiority over the other.

We learned in the 60's that simply throwing money at social problems does not cause them to go away. The same is true of the perils of the nuclear arms race; more money spent by each side only adds to the other side's sense of military insecurity. The consequence is that we come not one step closer to disarmament, while each side further impoverishes its people, whose real needs are more and more neglected.

Nor can disarmament be achieved by force, since the use of force—the kind of force we are discussing, the force that nuclear physics has placed at our disposal—can only extinguish the problem along with life itself. If the intelligence of the human species has presented us with the nuclear dilemma, it is only through the application of human intelligence that we can find a way out of it.

The Role of Education

Thus, it seems to me that universities have a special responsibility and a special role to play in this issue. The experience of the recent past has taught us that, though universities may not always be able to solve problems, they can and do perform the very, very useful function of bringing attention to them. In the process of debate and discussion thus engendered, a variety of policy imperatives are clarified, and new alternatives for action emerge to be considered.

In my own State I am currently attempting to organize a coalition of college and university presidents to initiate discussions of nuclear disarmament on their campuses this fall. I am also urging university presidents across the Nation to bring all their campuses, which have thus far been relatively inert on the issue, into this vital dialogue.

There is no clear answer, no demonstrably certain way to achieve nuclear disarmament; there is much to debate. But I am convinced that increasingly large expenditures for nuclear arms by both powers, constitutes acceptance of the status quo, a *de facto* resignation to a state of helpless waiting for the world as we know it to end, and that such a course of action is not worthy of us. The process of debate, however unsettling, is healthier than the passive acceptance of a world-wide death sentence.

The Possibility of Extinction

You graduates assembled here today have grown up under the shadow of the possibility of a nuclear death sentence. Your earliest conceptions of the future must in some sense have included the awesome possibility of there being no posterity to follow you, no future for the human race. Consciously or not, this prospect must have colored your serious thoughts and your frivolous ones, your beliefs about life's continuity and the worth of planning, your ethos of social responsibility.

Whether your early introduction to the possibility of extinction may make it easier or more difficult for you to confront it than it has been for those of us who came of age before Hiroshima, whether that possibility is more or less paralyzing for you than for us—that I do not know. I do know, however, that you have a new vantage point, a set of difficult insights, and that we badly need that new perspective today.

I will spare you a recital of the numbers of people here in Connecticut who would be killed or dismembered in a nuclear holocaust, or who would survive it, only to die later more tortuously, or to live out dismembered and disfigured lives. I will also spare you a recital of the names of towns familiar to you which would be destroyed in a hypothetical ground zero analysis.

But I hope *you* would not spare *yourselves*. I hope I have shocked you into recognition of our peril. I hope you will think about this issue, talk about it, act on it. It needs our best minds, our varied perspectives, our keenest insights, our deepest commitment. It needs them now, before it is too late for thought and united action to work their wondrous ways in avoiding a nuclear holocaust.

GREAT
SPEECHES
IN
HISTORY

The Struggle
for Peace

A Message to the People of the Soviet Union

Richard M. Nixon

Richard M. Nixon, the thirty-seventh President of the United States, is remembered both for his achievement in foreign policy and the Watergate scandal, which forced him to resign on August 9, 1974. Many authorities agree that Nixon had a broad understanding of foreign affairs and was a skilled negotiator. One of his major successes during his first term was improving relations with the Soviet Union and reopening the door to mainland China. In 1968, the United States and the Soviet Union began talks on the limitation of strategic arms. These talks were completed during his visit to Russia in May 1972.

During his stay, Nixon addressed the Russian people. In his radio and television address, delivered on the evening of May 28, 1972, Nixon expresses his desire to develop better relations with the Soviet Union by pursuing common goals, including joint ventures in space, expansion of trade, and the limitation of nuclear strategic arms. As great powers, says Nixon, both nations have a responsibility to allow the growing number of independent nations to conduct their own affairs as they see fit. Nixon describes the spirit and beliefs of the American people, which he says are not unlike those of the Russian people. As Russians and Americans get to know each other better, suggests Nixon, both nations can learn to work together to create a world free from fear and the threat of war.

Richard M. Nixon, address to the people of the Soviet Union, Moscow, USSR, May 28, 1972.

The United States and Soviet Union achieved some of the goals outlined in Nixon's speech. When Soviet leader Leonid Brezhnev visited the United States in 1973, he and Nixon signed a nuclear nonaggression pact. In addition, in July 1975, after Nixon's resignation, the crews of a U.S. Apollo spacecraft docked with a Russian Soyuz spacecraft, the result of a joint effort of Soviet and American scientists, astronauts, and cosmonauts.

*D*obryy vecher [Good evening]. I deeply appreciate this opportunity your Government has given me to speak directly with the people of the Soviet Union, to bring you a message of friendship from all the people of the United States and to share with you some of my thoughts about the relations between our two countries and about the way to peace and progress in the world.

This is my fourth visit to the Soviet Union. On these visits I have gained a great respect for the peoples of the Soviet Union, for your strength, your generosity, your determination, for the diversity and richness of your cultural heritage, for your many achievements.

A History of Cooperation

In the 3 years I have been in office, one of my principal aims has been to establish a better relationship between the United States and the Soviet Union. Our two countries have much in common. Most important of all, we have never fought one another in war. On the contrary, the memory of your soldiers and ours embracing at the Elbe, as allies, in 1945, remains strong in millions of hearts in both of our countries. It is my hope that that memory can serve as an inspiration for the renewal of Soviet-American cooperation in the 1970's.

As great powers, we shall sometimes be competitors, but we need never be enemies.

Thirteen years ago, when I visited your country as Vice President, I addressed the people of the Soviet Union on radio and television, as I am addressing you tonight. I said then, "Let us have peaceful competition, not only in producing the best factories, but in producing better lives for our people. Let us cooperate in our exploration of outer space. ... Let our aim be not victory over other peoples, but the victory of all mankind over hunger, want, misery, and disease, wherever it exists in the world."

In our meetings this week, we have begun to bring some of those hopes to fruition. Shortly after we arrived here on Monday afternoon [May 22, 1972], a brief rain fell on Moscow, of a kind that I am told is called a mushroom rain, a warm rain, with sunshine breaking through, that makes the mushrooms grow and is therefore considered a good omen. The month of May is early for mushrooms, but as our talks progressed this week, what did grow was even better. A far-reaching set of agreements that can lead to a better life for both of our peoples, to a better chance for peace in the world.

We have agreed on joint ventures in space. We have agreed on ways of working together to protect the environment, to advance health, to cooperate in science and technology. We have agreed on means of preventing incidents at sea. We have established a commission to expand trade between our two nations.

Most important, we have taken an historic first step in the limitation of nuclear strategic arms. This arms control agreement is not for the purpose of giving either side an advantage over the other. Both of our nations are strong, each respects the strength of the other, each will maintain the strength necessary to defend its independence.

But in an unchecked arms race between two great nations, there would be no winners, only losers. By setting this limitation together, the people of both of our nations, and of all nations, can be winners. If we continue in the spirit of serious purpose that has marked our discussions this week, these agreements can start us on a new road of cooperation for the benefit of our people, for the benefit of all peoples.

There is an old proverb that says, "Make peace with man and quarrel with your sins." The hardships and evils that beset all men and all nations, these and these alone are what we should make war upon.

The Responsibility of Great Powers

As we look at the prospects for peace, we see that we have made significant progress at reducing the possible sources of direct conflict between us. But history tells us that great nations have often been dragged into war without intending it, by conflicts between smaller nations. As great powers, we can and should use our influence to prevent this from happening. Our goal should be to discourage aggression in other parts of the world and particularly among those smaller nations that look to us for leadership and example.

With great power goes great responsibility. When a man walks with a giant tread, he must be careful where he sets his feet. There can be true peace only when the weak are as safe as the strong. The wealthier and more powerful our own nations become, the more we have to lose from war and the threat of war, anywhere in the world.

Speaking for the United States, I can say this: We cover no one else's territory, we seek no dominion over any other people, we seek the right to live in peace, not only for ourselves, but for all the peoples of this earth. Our power will only be used to keep the peace, never to break it, only to defend freedom, never to destroy it. No nation that does not threaten its neighbors has anything to fear from the United States.

Soviet citizens have often asked me, "Does America truly want peace?"

I believe that our actions answer that question far better than any words could do. If we did not want peace, we would not have reduced the size of our armed forces by a million men, by almost one-third, during the past 3 years. If we did not want peace, we would not have worked so hard at reaching an agreement on the limitation of nuclear arms, at achieving a settlement of Berlin, at maintaining peace in the Middle East, at establishing better relations with the Soviet Union, with the People's Republic of China, with other nations of the world.

The American Point of View

Mrs. [Pat] Nixon and I feel very fortunate to have had the opportunity to visit the Soviet Union, to get to know the people of the Soviet Union, friendly and hospitable, courageous and strong. Most Americans will never have a chance to visit the Soviet Union and most Soviet citizens will never have a chance to visit America. Most of you know our country only through what you read in your newspapers and what you hear and see on radio and television and motion pictures. This is only a part of the real America.

I would like to take this opportunity to try to convey to you something of what America is really like, not in terms of its scenic beauties, its great cities, its factories, its farms, or its highways, but in terms of its people.

In many ways, the people of our two countries are very much alike. Like the Soviet Union, ours is a large and diverse nation. Our people, like yours, are hard-working. Like you, we Americans have a strong spirit of competition, but we also have a great love of music and poetry, of sports, and of humor. Above all, we, like you, are an open, natural, and friendly people. We love our country. We love our children. And we want for you and for your children the same peace and abundance that we want for ourselves and for our children.

Richard M. Nixon

We Americans are idealists. We believe deeply in our system of government. We cherish our personal liberty. We would fight to defend it, if necessary, as we have done before. But we also believe deeply in the right of each nation to choose its own system. Therefore, however much we like our own system for ourselves, we have no desire to impose it on anyone else.

As we conclude this week of talks, there are certain fundamental premises of the American point of view which I believe deserve emphasis. In conducting these talks, it has not been our aim to divide up the world into spheres of influence, to establish a condominium, or in any way to conspire together against the interests of any other nation. Rather we have sought to construct a better framework of understanding between our two nations, to make progress in our bilateral relationships, to find ways of ensuring that future frictions between us would never embroil our two nations, and therefore, the world, in war.

While ours are both great and powerful nations, the world is no longer dominated by two superpowers. The world is a better and safer place because its power and resources are more widely distributed.

Beyond this, since World War II, more than 70 new nations have come into being. We cannot have true peace unless they, and all nations, can feel that they share it.

America seeks better relations, not only with the Soviet Union, but with all nations. The only sound basis for a peaceful and progressive international order is sovereign equality and mutual respect. We believe in the right of each nation to chart its own course, to choose its own system, to go its own way, without interference from other nations.

As we look to the longer term, peace depends also on continued progress in the developing nations. Together with other advanced industrial countries, the United States and the Soviet Union share a twofold responsibility in this regard.

On the one hand, to practice restraint in those activities, such as the supply of arms, that might endanger the peace of developing nations. And second, to assist them in their orderly economic and social development, without political interference.

Getting to Know One Another

Some of you may have heard an old story told in Russia of a traveler who was walking to another village. He knew the way, but not the distance. Finally he came upon a woodsman chopping wood by the side of the road and he asked the woodsman, "How long will it take to reach the village?"

The woodsman replied, "I don't know."

The traveler was angry, because he was sure the woodsman was from the village and therefore knew how far it was. And so he started off down the road again. After he had gone a few steps, the woodsman called out, "Stop. It will take you about 15 minutes."

The traveler turned and demanded, "Why didn't you tell me that in the first place?"

The woodsman replied, "Because then I didn't know the length of your stride."

In our talks this week with the leaders of the Soviet Union, both sides have had a chance to measure the length of our strides toward peace and security. I believe that those strides have been substantial and that now we have well begun the long journey which will lead us to a new age in the relations between our two countries. It is important to both of our peoples that we continue those strides.

As our two countries learn to work together, our people will be able to get to know one another better. Greater cooperation can also mean a great deal in our daily lives. As we learn to cooperate in space, in health and the environment, in science and technology, our cooperation can help sick people get well. It can help industries produce more consumer goods. It can help all of us enjoy cleaner air and water. It can increase our knowledge of the world around us.

As we expand our trade, each of our countries can buy more of the other's goods and market more of our own. As we gain experience with arms control, we can bring closer the day when further agreements can lessen the arms burden of our two nations and lessen the threat of war in the world.

A World Free of Fear

Through all the pages of history, through all the centuries, the world's people have struggled to be free from fear, whether fear of the elements or fear of hunger or fear of their own rulers or fear of their neighbors in other countries. And yet, time and again, people have vanquished the source of one fear only to fall prey to another.

Let our goal now be a world free of fear. A world in which nation will no longer prey upon nation, in which human energies will be turned away from production for war and toward more production for peace, away from conquest and toward invention, development, creation. A world in which together we can establish that peace which is more than the absence of war, which enables man to pursue those higher goals that the spirit yearns for.

Yesterday, I laid a wreath at the cemetery which com-
memorates the brave people who died during the siege of
Leningrad in World War II. At the cemetery, I saw the picture
of a 12-year-old girl. She was a beautiful child. Her name
was Tanya. The pages of her diary tell the terrible story of
war. In the simple words of a child, she wrote of the deaths
of the members of her family: Zhenya in December. Grannie
in January. Leka then next. Then Uncle Vasya. Then Uncle
Lyosha. Then Mama. And then the Savichevs. And then finally, these words, the last words in her diary, "All are dead.
Only Tanya is left."

As we work toward a more peaceful world, let us think
of Tanya and of the other Tanyas and their brothers and sisters everywhere. Let us do all that we can to insure that no
other children will have to endure what Tanya did and that
your children and ours, all the children of the world can live
their full lives together in friendship and in peace.

Spasibo y do svidaniye [Thank you and goodbye].

Meeting New Global Challenges

Henry Kissinger

Henry Kissinger is an American political scientist who
served as U.S. secretary of state from 1973 to 1977 and
as national security advisor from 1969 to 1975. Kissinger
was born in Fuerth, Germany, on May 27, 1923, but
came to the United States in 1938, becoming a naturalized citizen in 1943. He studied at Harvard University,
receiving a Ph.D. in 1954, and was a member of the Harvard University faculty between 1954 and 1971. During
the 1960s, Kissinger served as a consultant to the Department of State, National Security Council, and the United
States Arms Control and Disarmament Agency. During
the Cold War, Kissinger played a significant role in formulating U.S. foreign policy and helped initiate the
Strategic Arms Limitation Talks (SALT) and détente with
the Soviet Union. He arranged former president Richard
M. Nixon's visit to the People's Republic of China and
won the Nobel Peace Prize for negotiating a cease-fire
with North Vietnam during the Vietnam War. Kissinger
continues to lecture and serve as a consultant on international affairs.

In the following speech, delivered on September 7,
1973, during his confirmation hearings before the Senate
Foreign Relations Committee, Kissinger explains his foreign policy approach. Kissinger claims that to overcome
the nation's internal division, foreign policy must be
based upon the shared values of all Americans. To restore
the nation's confidence in its government, he suggests that
all branches of the government be more open and honest

Henry Kissinger, statement before the Senate Foreign Relations Committee, Washington, DC, September 7, 1973.

with the American people about their foreign policy decisions. According to Kissinger, the United States faces issues such as limited energy supplies and environmental problems that can no longer be handled in isolation. To meet these global challenges, the United States must continue to turn from confrontation to cooperation.

We have come to experience in recent years that peace at home and peace abroad are closely related. How well we perform in foreign policy depends importantly on how purposeful we are at home. America has passed through a decade of domestic turbulence which has deepened divisions and even shaken our national self-confidence in some measure. At the same time, profound changes have occurred in the world around us, a generation after World War II. Our era is marked by both the anxieties of a transitional period and the opportunities of fresh creation.

A Foreign Policy Based on Shared Values

These challenges, though they appear as practical issues, cannot be solved in technical terms; they closely reflect our view of ourselves. They require a sense of identity and purpose as much as a sense of policy. Throughout our history we have thought of what we did as growing out of deeper moral values. America was not true to itself unless it had a meaning beyond itself. In this spiritual sense, America was never isolationist.

This must remain our attitude.

This is why our international policies must enlist the contributions of our best people regardless of political persuasion. Our task is to define—together—the contours of a new world and to shape America's contribution to it. Our foreign policy cannot be effective if it reflects only the sporadic and esoteric initiatives of a small group of specialists. It must rest on a broad national base and reflect a shared community of values.

With good will on all sides, I deeply believe we can reach this goal. There is no dispute about many of the fundamental objectives of national policy. We are at a crucial point of transition in the international order, with major changes in the global structure promising a more peaceful world.

Reducing Tension

Successful postwar policies have helped our friends to new strength and responsibilities. We shall work constructively and openly with our partners in Europe and Japan to give new impetus to associations based on shared purposes and ideals. We shall always remember that the vitality of our friendships is the necessary condition for the lowering of tensions with our opponents.

We have developed fresh relationships with adversaries that can ease us away from confrontation toward cooperation. Tensions have been reduced in many areas. For the first time since the end of World War II, all great nations have become full participants in the international system. There is the hope that the arms race can be arrested and the burden of armaments reduced.

Our most anguishing and divisive problem, the Vietnam War, is behind us. We achieved a negotiated settlement last January [1973]. The Congress has since expressed its view on how to terminate our military participation in the last area of conflict—Cambodia. As you gentlemen know, the administration differs with that view. But it will not attempt to circumvent it.

The Challenges of a Global Society

We face unprecedented issues, which transcend borders and ideologies and beckon global cooperation. Many traditional assumptions need adjustment. We have viewed ourselves as blessed with unlimited agricultural surpluses; today we must contemplate scarcity in relation to world needs. We have assumed self-sufficiency in energy; now we face increasing needs for external supply at least for an interim period. Environmental problems used to be considered national issues, if they were considered at all; now many must be met internationally if they are going to be met at all. We need to explore new conceptual frontiers to reflect the new reality produced by both technology and human aspirations: that our planet has become a truly global society.

This administration will continue to adapt America's role to these new conditions. But we cannot take for granted what has been begun. We cannot let irretrievable opportunities slip from our grasp. Just as we have benefited from the efforts of our predecessors, so must we build for our successors. What matters to other countries—and to the world—is not so much the work of one administration as the steadiness of America. So the nation is challenged to render our purposes durable and our performance reliable. This we achieved during most of a generation after the Second World War. We need to continue to do so. . . .

A Closer Relationship with Congress

As you know, the president [Richard Nixon] has asked me to retain my position as assistant to the president [for national security affairs] if I am confirmed as secretary of state. I believe this will benefit the coherence and effectiveness of our foreign policy. The secretary of state will be clearly the principal foreign policy adviser to the president. The locus of authority and the chain of authority will be unambiguous. Bureaucratic friction will be minimized. As the president said in announcing my appointment, the unity of position will underline the traditional principal role of the Department of State in the policy-making process.

There must be, as well, a closer relationship between the executive and legislative branches. It is the president's objective to make policy more accessible to the scrutiny and the views of the Congress. This is the fundamental answer to the question of executive privilege. As you gentlemen know, over an extended period of time when I was fully covered by this principle, I met regularly with the members of this committee, both individually and as a group, and most frequently with the chairman.

In my new capacity, I shall be prepared to testify formally on all my activities. In other words, I shall testify with respect to all matters traditionally covered by secretaries of state and on my duties as assistant to the president concerning inter-departmental issues. I will not claim executive privilege in ei-ther capacity except for the one area customarily invoked by Cabinet officers, that is, direct communications with the president or the actual deliberations of the National Security Council. . . .

This process of greater cooperation will not be confined to formal testimony. If confirmed, I will propose to meet im-mediately with the chairman and the ranking member to work out procedures for enabling the committee to share more fully in the design of our foreign policy. . . .

A Partnership with the People

If our foreign policy is to be truly national, we must deepen our partnership with the American people. This means an open articulation of our philosophy, our purposes, and our actions. We have sought to do this in the president's annual reports to the Congress on foreign policy. Equally, we must listen to the hopes and aspirations of our fellow countrymen. I plan, therefore, on a regular basis, to elicit the views of America's opinion leaders and to share our perspectives freely. . . .

Americans have recently endured the turmoil of assassi-nations and riots, racial and generational confrontations, and a bitter, costly war. Just as we were emerging from that conflict, we were plunged into still another ordeal.

These traumatic events have cast lengthening shadows on our traditional optimism and self-esteem. A loss of confi-dence in our own country would inevitably be mirrored in our international relations. Where once we ran the risk of thinking we were too good for the world, we might now swing to believing we are not good enough. Where once a soaring optimism tempted us to dare too much, a shrinking spirit could lead us to attempt too little. Such an attitude—and the foreign policy it would produce—would deal a sav-age blow to global stability.

But I am hopeful about our prospects. America is re-silient. The dynamism of this country is irrepressible. What-ever our divisions, we can rally to the prospects of building a world at peace and responsive to humane aspirations. In so doing, we can replenish our reservoir of faith.

The Creation of a New Era

This is our common challenge:

To distinguish the fundamental from the ephemeral.

To seek out what unites us, without stifling the healthy debate that is the lifeblood of democracy.

To promote the positive trends that are the achievements not just of this administration but also of those who came before.

To shape new initiatives that will serve not just the next forty months but also the decades to follow.

A few years before he died, one of our most distinguished secretaries of state, Dean Acheson, entitled his memoirs *Present at the Creation*. He chose that title because he was one of the leading participants in the creation of the postwar international system. The challenge before our country now is whether our generation has the vision—as Dean Acheson's did more than two decades ago—to turn into dynamic reality the hopeful beginnings we have made toward a more durable peace and a more benevolent planet.

Mr. Chairman and gentlemen of the committee, I am confident that working together we can speed the day when all of us will be able to say that we were "present at the creation" of a new era of peace, justice, and humanity.

Building a Relationship with China

Walter F. Mondale

Walter F. Mondale served as Jimmy Carter's vice president from 1976 to 1980 and was the Democratic presidential nominee in 1984, losing the election to Ronald Reagan. During his tenure as vice president, Mondale was an influential foreign affairs adviser to the president and acted as his emissary abroad.

Mondale made a historic trip to the People's Republic of China on August 13, 1979. During his visit, he met with Deputy Premier Deng Xiaoping and Communist Party chairman Hua Kuofeng, discussing trade agreements, establishing credit to China, organizing cultural and technical exchanges, and preparing for U.S. assistance in developing China's hydroelectric power. On August 27, Mondale delivered a message from President Jimmy Carter to a standing audience of eight hundred at Beijing University, Bei-Da, and to a radio and televison audience. He was the first American political figure to speak to the citizens of the People's Republic of China. Authorities point out that the speech was, of course, a gesture of goodwill and an official statement on U.S. foreign policy, most likely crafted by members of both Mondale's staff and the U.S. State Department.

In his address, Mondale describes the success of Chinese development and the nation's importance in promoting stability in world affairs. He explains that in order to protect the security of China and ensure world peace, the

Walter F. Mondale, speech before the students at Beijing University (Bei-Da), August 27, 1979.

United States and China must develop strong economic, cultural, and political ties. Sino-American relations, he says, have already born fruit—a trade agreement has been developed and scientific and cultural exchanges established. Despite ideological differences, Mondale explains, the United States and China share many interests. As a nation that values diversity, tolerance, and mutual respect, the United States hopes to develop Sino-American relations not to increase its power but to foster a world of independent nations.

After losing the 1984 presidential election, Mondale remained involved in international affairs. In the spring of 1993, he was elected director of the Council on Foreign Relations, and on August 13, 1993, was appointed U.S. ambassador to Japan. In March 1998, Mondale traveled to Jakarta as President Bill Clinton's personal representative in discussions with President Suharto and other Indonesian officials.

I am honored to appear before you. And I bring you the warm greetings and the friendship of the President of the United States [Jimmy Carter] and the American people.

For an American of my generation to visit the People's Republic of China is to touch the pulse of modern political history. For nearly three decades our nations stood separate and apart. But the ancient hunger for community unites humanity. It urges us to find common ground.

As one of your poets wrote over a thousand years ago, "We widen our view three hundred miles by ascending one flight of stairs." We are ascending that flight of stairs together.

Each day we take another step. This afternoon, I am privileged to be the first American political figure to speak directly to the citizens of the People's Republic of China.

A Place of New Beginnings

And no setting for that speech could be more symbolic of our relationship than this place of new beginnings. The history of modern China is crystallized in the story of Beijing University and the other distinguished institutions you represent. At virtually every turning point in 20th-century China, Bei-Da has been the fulcrum.

Sixty years ago [1919], it was at Bei-Da that the May 4th movement began, launching an era of unprecedented intellectual ferment. It inaugurated an effort to modernize Chinese culture and society. It established a new meeting ground for eastern and western cultures. And its framework of mutual respect sustains our own cultural cooperation today.

Forty-four years ago, Bei-Da was where the December 9th movement galvanized a student generation to resist external aggression. And its message of sovereignty and nonaggression underpins our own political cooperation today.

As China looks to the future, once again it is Bei-Da and your other research centers which are leading the drive toward "the four modernizations" [agriculture, science and technology, industry, and defense]. And the closeness of your development goals to our own interests will provide the basis for our continuing economic cooperation.

Today, we find our two nations at a pivotal moment. We have normalized our relations. The curtain has parted; the mystery is being dispelled. We are eager to know more about one another, to share the texture of our daily lives, to forge the human bonds of friendship.

That is a rich beginning. But it is only a beginning.

A modern China taking its place in the family of nations is engaged in a search not only for friendship, but also for security and development. An America deepening its relations with China does so not only out of genuine sentiment, and not only out of natural curiosity. It does so out of the same combination of principle and self-interest that is the engine of mature relations among all modern states.

Our job today is to establish the basis for an enduring relationship tomorrow. We could not have set that task without our friendship. But we cannot accomplish it with friendship alone.

On behalf of President Carter, this is the message I carry to the people of China—a message about America, its purposes in the world, and our hopes for our relations with you.

The Americans are historically confident people. Our politics are rooted in our values. We cherish our fundamental beliefs in human rights, and compassion, and social justice. We believe that our democratic system institutionalizes those values. The opportunities available to our citizens are incomparable. Our debates are vigorous and open. And the differences we air among ourselves—whether on strategic nuclear policy or on energy—are signs of our society's enduring strength.

My country is blessed with unsurpassed natural resources. Moreover, we also have unparalleled human resources—workers and farmers and scientists and engineers and industrialists and financiers. With their genius we are able to transform our natural assets into abundance—not only for ourselves, but for the world.

Of course we face unsolved problems. But the high goals we set for ourselves—and our determination to meet them— are measures of our national spirit. In that striving, in that restless pursuit of a better life, we feel a special affinity for the people of modern China.

In the world community, the United States seeks international stability and peace. But we have no illusions about the obstacles we face. We know that we live in a dangerous world. And we are determined to remain militarily prepared. We are fashioning our defenses from the most advanced technology anywhere. We have forged alliances in Europe and Asia which grow stronger every year. Together with our Japanese and Western allies, we will ensure that our investment in security is equal to the task of ensuring peace—as we have for thirty years.

Advancing Shared Interests

But we want to be more than a firm and reliable partner in world affairs. We also believe in a world of diversity. For Sino-American relations, that means that we respect the distinctive qualities which the great Chinese people contribute to our relationship. And despite the sometimes profound differences between our two systems, we are committed to joining with you to advance our many parallel strategic and bilateral interests.

Thus any nation which seeks to weaken or isolate you in world affairs assumes a stance counter to American interests. This is why the United States normalized relations with your country, and that is why we must work to broaden and strengthen our new friendship.

We must press forward now to widen and give specificity to our relations. The fundamental challenges we face are to build concrete political ties in the context of mutual security . . . to establish broad cultural relations in a framework of genuine equality . . . and to forge practical economic bonds with the goal of common benefit.

As we give substance to our shared interests, we are investing in the future of our relationship. The more effectively we advance our agenda, the more bonds we build between us—the more confident we can be that our relationship will endure.

And so what we accomplish today lays the groundwork for the decade ahead. The 1980s can find us working together—and working with other nations—to meet world problems. Enriching the global economy, containing international conflicts, protecting the independence of nations: these goals must also be pursued from the perspective of our bilateral relationship. The deeper the relationship, the more successful that world-wide pursuit will be.

That is the agenda President Carter has asked me to come to the People's Republic of China to pursue. That is the principal message President Carter has asked me to bring to you. It is the agenda we share for the future.

Strengthening Sino-American Relations

In the eight months since normalization, we have witnessed the rapid expansion of Sino-American relations.

We have reached a settlement on claims/assets and signed the trade agreement. Trade between our countries is expanding. American oil companies are helping you explore China's offshore oil reserves. Joint commissions on Sino-American economic relations and on scientific and technical exchange have been established. We have exchanged numerous governmental delegations, including the visits of many heads of our respective ministries and departments. And the flow of people between our two countries is reaching new heights.

We have gained a cooperative momentum. Together let us sustain and strengthen it.

For a strong and secure and modernizing China is also in the American interest in the decade ahead.

In agriculture, your continued development not only provides a better life for the Chinese people, it also serves our interests—for your gains in agriculture will increase limited world food supplies.

In trade, our interests are served by your expanding exports of natural resources and industrial products. And at the same time your interests are served by the purchases you can finance through those exports.

As you industrialize, you provide a higher standard of living for your people. And at the same time our interests are served—for this will increase the flow of trade, narrow the wealth gap between the developed and the developing world, and thus help alleviate a major source of global instability.

Above all, both our political interests are served by your growing strength in all fields—for it helps deter others who might seek to impose themselves on you.

Efforts in the 1920s and 1930s to keep China weak destabilized the entire world. For many years, China was a flash point of great power competition. But a confident China can contribute to the maintenance of peace in the region. Today, the unprecedented and friendly relations among China, Japan, and the United States bring international stability to Northeast Asia.

That is why deepening our economic, cultural, and political relations is so strategically important—not only for your security, but for the peace of the world community.

Promoting Economic Ties

We are taking crucial steps to advance our economic relationship.

First, before the end of the year, President Carter will submit for the approval of the US Congress the trade agreement we reached with you. This agreement will extend "most favored nation" treatment to China. And its submission is not linked to any other issue.

Second, I will be signing an agreement on development of hydroelectric energy in the People's Republic of China. US Government agencies are now ready to help develop China's hydroelectric power on a compensatory basis.

Third, the United States is prepared to establish Export-Import Bank credit arrangements for the PRC [People's Republic of China] on a case-by-case basis, up to a total of 2 billion (two thousand million) dollars over a five-year period. If the pace of development warrants it, we are prepared to consider additional credit arrangements. We have begun discussions toward this end.

Fourth, the Carter Administration this year will seek congressional authority to encourage American businesses to invest in China—by providing the guarantees and insurance of the Overseas Private Investment Corporation.

We also stand ready to work with the Chinese Government to reach textile, maritime, and civil aviation agreements in the shortest possible time.

As we advance our cultural relationship, universities will again be a crucial meeting-ground between Chinese and Americans, just as they were in an earlier era.

Sharing Knowledge

Today, gifted Chinese scholars study in America, and American scholars—many of whom I am delighted to see here today—study in China. That exchange inherits a distinguished tradition. On campuses all across the United States, Americans who lectured and studied in China in the 1930s and 1940s today are invigorating our own intellectual life—none of them with greater distinction than Professor John K. Fairbank, who honors us by joining my traveling party. At the same time, we are proud that Chinese scholars who studied American agronomy, engineering, and medicine have been able to contribute the skills they gained in our country to the progress of Chinese society.

It is a mutual relationship—a true reciprocity—we are now engaged in building. From us, you will learn aspects of science and technology. Our anthropologists and archeologists have tools to share with you as you explore your own past. American and Chinese social scientists and humanists have insights to offer each other—a fuller understanding of our respective institutions and values.

And so with your help, we intend to broaden our horizons. Chinese researchers pioneer in key areas, from medical burn therapy to earthquake prediction—and we want to learn these skills from you. Where the progress of science requires global cooperation—in astronomy, in oceanography, in meteorology—our common efforts can benefit the world. And our social scientists and humanists have hardly begun to share your understanding of history, of social change, and of human potential.

Strong bilateral relations serve our strategic interests. Through them, both of us can foster the world community we seek—a world that respects diversity and welcomes constructive change.

The Struggle Against Totalitarianism

Ronald Reagan

One of the accomplishments for which President Ronald Reagan will be remembered is negotiating the short- and intermediate-range missile treaty with the Soviet Union. Reagan's warm relationship with the Soviet Union, however, did not develop until his second term. Prior to the 1985 meeting between Reagan and Soviet leader Mikhail Gorbachev in Geneva, Switzerland, Reagan identified the Soviet Union as an "evil empire" in a speech before an annual convention of the National Association of Evangelicals. Reagan later defended his remarks, but also claimed that as a result of the changes instituted by his friend, Mikhail Gorbachev, the Soviet Union was no longer "evil." However, despite efforts at détente during the Nixon and Ford administrations, tension increased as a result of actions by both nations: The Soviet invasion of Afghanistan, the 1983 downing of a South Korean airliner by a Soviet military plane, the U.S. deployment of intermediate-range missiles in Western Europe, and Reagan's proposed Strategic Defense Initiative, the technological pursuit of defensive weapons in space.

Reagan's distrust of the Soviet Union at this time is clearly stated in an address to members of the British Parliament in Westminster, on June 8, 1982. In his speech, Reagan examines the success of democracy and the failure of the Soviet system. Because communism oppresses rather than liberates people, says Reagan, more and more

Ronald Reagan, address before the British Parliament, London, England, June 8, 1982.

people are hoping to renew the struggle against totalitarian police states. The free nations of the world must support not only those who struggle against dictatorships, but those who struggle against Communist regimes. To do so, however, free nations must strengthen their military alliances, reasons Reagan. Although the hope is that nuclear weapons will never be used, according to Reagan, maintaining military strength is essential to ensure peace.

Political analysts claim that this speech led to the Reagan Doctrine, an often controversial policy of supporting those fighting for freedom against communism. For example, during Reagan's administration, the United States assisted anti-Communist guerrillas, known as Contras, in Nicaragua and pressured the Sandinista government to hold free elections. As a result of this policy, late in 1986, the administration admitted it had been secretly selling arms to Iran, using the profits to support the Contras in Nicaragua. Reagan's role in the affair was never determined, and despite what some believed was his inability to control the actions of his subordinates, Reagan remained one of the most popular presidents in American history.

We're approaching the end of a bloody century plagued by a terrible political invention—totalitarianism. Optimism comes less easily today, not because democracy is less vigorous, but because democracy's enemies have refined their instruments of repression. Yet optimism is in order, because day by day democracy is proving itself to be a not-at-all-fragile flower. From Stettin on the Baltic to Varna on the Black Sea, the regimes planted by totalitarianism have had more than thirty years to establish their legitimacy. But none—not one regime—has yet been able to risk free elections. Regimes planted by bayonets do not take root. . . .

Historians looking back at our time will note the consistent restraint and peaceful intentions of the West. They will note that it was the democracies who refused to use the threat of their nuclear monopoly in the forties and early fifties for territorial or imperial gain. Had that nuclear monopoly been in the hands of the Communist world, the map of Europe—indeed, the world—would look very different today. And certainly they will note it was not the democracies [but the Soviet Union] that invaded Afghanistan or suppressed Polish Solidarity or used chemical and toxic warfare in Afghanistan and Southeast Asia.

Choosing to Preserve Freedom

If history teaches anything, it teaches self-delusion in the face of unpleasant facts is folly. We see around us today the marks of our terrible dilemma—predictions of doomsday, antinuclear demonstrations, an arms race in which the West must, for its own protection, be an unwilling participant. At the same time we see totalitarian forces in the world who seek subversion and conflict around the globe to further their barbarous assault on the human spirit. What, then, is our course? Must civilization perish in a hail of fiery atoms? Must freedom wither in a quiet, deadening accommodation with totalitarian evil?

Sir Winston Churchill refused to accept the inevitability of war or even that it was imminent. He said, "I do not believe that Soviet Russia desires war. What they desire is the fruits of war and the indefinite expansion of their power and doctrines. But what we have to consider here today while time remains is the permanent prevention of war and the establishment of conditions of freedom and democracy as rapidly as possible in all countries."

Well, this is precisely our mission today: to preserve freedom as well as peace. It may not be easy to see; but I believe we live now at a turning point.

The Failure of the Soviet System

In an ironic sense Karl Marx [a German political philosopher and author of the *Communist Manifesto*] was right. We are witnessing today a great revolutionary crisis, a crisis where the demands of the economic order are conflicting directly with those of the political order. But the crisis is happening not in the free, non-Marxist West, but in the home of Marxist-Leninism, the Soviet Union. It is the Soviet Union that runs against the tide of history by denying human freedom and human dignity to its citizens. It also is in deep economic difficulty. The rate of growth in the national product has been steadily declining since the fifties and is less than half of what it was then.

The dimensions of this failure are astounding: A country which employs one-fifth of its population in agriculture is unable to feed its own people. Were it not for the private sector, the tiny private sector tolerated in Soviet agriculture, the country might be on the brink of famine. These private plots occupy a bare 3 percent of the arable land but account for nearly one-quarter of Soviet farm output and nearly one-third of meat products and vegetables. Overcentralized, with little or no incentives, year after year the Soviet system pours its best resources into the making of instruments of destruction. The constant shrinkage of economic growth combined with the growth of military production is putting a heavy strain on the Soviet people. What we see here is a political structure that no longer corresponds to its economic base, a society where productive forces are hampered by political ones.

The decay of the Soviet experiment should come as no surprise to us. Wherever the comparisons have been made between free and closed societies—West Germany and East Germany, Austria and Czechoslovakia, Malaysia and Vietnam—it is the democratic countries that are prosperous and responsive to the needs of their people. And one of the simple but overwhelming facts of our time is this: Of all the millions of refugees we've seen in the modern world, their flight is always away from, not toward the Communist world. Today on the NATO line, our military forces face east to prevent a possible invasion. On the other side of the line, the Soviet forces also face east to prevent their people from leaving.

An Uprising Against Totalitarianism

The hard evidence of totalitarian rule has caused in mankind an uprising of the intellect and will. Whether it is the growth of the new schools of economics in America or England or the appearance of the so-called new philosophers in France, there is one unifying thread running through the intellectual work of these groups—rejection of the arbitrary power of the state, the refusal to subordinate the rights of the individual to the super-state, the realization that collectivism stifles all the best human impulses. . . .

In the Communist world as well, man's instinctive desire for freedom and self-determination surfaces again and again. To be sure, there are grim reminders of how brutally the police state attempts to snuff out this quest for self-rule—1953 in East Germany, 1956 in Hungary, 1968 in Czechoslovakia, 1981 in Poland. But the struggle continues in Poland. And we know that there are even those who strive and suffer for freedom within the confines of the Soviet Union itself. How we conduct ourselves here in the Western democracies will determine whether this trend continues.

No, democracy is not a fragile flower. Still it needs cultivating. If the rest of this century is to witness the gradual growth of freedom and democratic ideals, we must take actions to assist the campaign for democracy.

Some argue that we should encourage democratic change in right-wing dictatorships, but not in Communist regimes. Well, to accept this preposterous notion—as some well-meaning people have—is to invite the argument that once countries achieve a nuclear capability, they should be allowed an undisturbed reign of terror over their own citizens. We reject this course.

As for the Soviet view, Chairman [Leonid] Brezhnev repeatedly has stressed that the competition of ideas and systems must continue and that this is entirely consistent with relaxation of tensions and peace.

Well, we ask only that these systems begin by living up to their own constitutions, abiding by their own laws, and complying with the international obligations they have undertaken. We ask only for a process, a direction, a basic code of decency, not for an instant transformation.

We cannot ignore the fact that even without our encouragement there has been and will continue to be repeated explosions against repression and dictatorships. The Soviet

Union itself is not immune to this reality. Any system is inherently unstable that has no peaceful means to legitimize its leaders. In such cases, the very repressiveness of the state ultimately drives people to resist it, if necessary, by force.

Strengthening Democracy

While we must be cautious about forcing the pace of change, we must not hesitate to declare our ultimate objectives and to take concrete actions to move toward them. We must be staunch in our conviction that freedom is not the sole prerogative of a lucky few, but the inalienable and universal right of all human beings. So states the United Nations Universal Declaration of Human Rights, which, among other things, guarantees free elections.

The objective I propose is quite simple to state: to foster the infrastructure of democracy, the system of a free press, unions, political parties, universities, which allows a people to choose their own way to develop their own culture, to reconcile their own differences through peaceful means.

This is not cultural imperialism, it is providing the means for genuine self-determination and protection for diversity. Democracy already flourishes in countries with very different cultures and historical experiences. It would be cultural condescension, or worse, to say that any people prefer dictatorship to democracy. Who would voluntarily choose not to have the right to vote, decide to purchase government propaganda handouts instead of independent newspapers, prefer government- to worker-controlled unions, opt for land to be owned by the state instead of those who till it, want government repression of religious liberty, a single political party instead of a free choice, a rigid cultural orthodoxy instead of democratic tolerance and diversity?

Since 1917 the Soviet Union has given covert political training and assistance to Marxist-Leninists in many countries. Of course, it also has promoted the use of violence and subversion by these same forces. Over the past several decades, West European and other Social Democrats, Christian Democrats, and leaders have offered open assistance to fraternal, political, and social institutions to bring about peaceful and democratic progress. Appropriately, for a vigorous new democracy, the Federal Republic of Germany's political foundations have become a major force in this effort.

A Global Campaign

We in America now intend to take additional steps, as many of our allies have already done, toward realizing this same goal. The chairmen and other leaders of the national Republican and Democratic party organizations are initiating a study with the bipartisan American Political Foundation to determine how the United States can best contribute as a nation to the global campaign for democracy now gathering force. They will have the cooperation of congressional leaders of both parties, along with representatives of business, labor, and other major institutions in our society. I look forward to receiving their recommendations and to working with these institutions and the Congress in the common task of strengthening democracy throughout the world.

It is time that we committed ourselves as a nation—in both the public and private sectors—to assisting democratic development. . . .

I've often wondered about the shyness of some of us in the West about standing for these ideals that have done so much to ease the plight of man and the hardships of our imperfect world. This reluctance to use those vast resources at our command reminds me of the elderly lady whose home was bombed in the Blitz. As the rescuers moved about, they found a bottle of brandy she'd stored behind the staircase, which was all that was left standing. And since she was barely conscious, one of the workers pulled the cork to give her a taste of it. She came around immediately and said, "Here now—there now, put it back. That's for emergencies."

Well, the emergency is upon us. Let us be shy no longer. Let us go to our strength. Let us offer hope. Let us tell the world that a new age is not only possible but probable.

Transforming the Soviet Union

Mikhail Gorbachev

Mikhail Gorbachev was born on March 2, 1931, in Privolnoye, a city in the Stavropol province of the Soviet
Union. After studying law at Moscow University, he
joined the Communist Party, gradually increasing his influence. Following the death of Konstantin Chernenko in
1985, Mikhail Gorbachev became the leader of the Soviet
Union and began a political, economic, and social program that radically altered the Soviet government and,
some authorities claim, effectively ended the Cold War.
For his contribution to reducing tension between the East
and West, Gorbachev was awarded the Nobel Peace Prize
in 1990.

In the following excerpts from his speech before the
UN General Assembly on December 7, 1988, Gorbachev
outlines some of the principles of the Soviet restructuring
program known as *perestroika* and discusses his foreign
policy. Gorbachev explains the process of constructing a
socialist state based on law. He describes some of the new
laws, including those establishing *glasnost* (openness),
freedom of association, and revision of the criminal code.
Gorbachev discusses proposed demilitarization in Eastern
Europe and the joint undertaking with the United States
toward nuclear disarmament. According to Gorbachev,
nations are no longer isolated, but mutually dependent.
Improving people's lives worldwide and protecting the
environment should be higher priorities than developing
military strength. In addition, he says that international
relationships should be based not on confrontational

Mikhail Gorbachev, address before the General Assembly of the United Nations,
New York, December 7, 1988.

rivalries but on reasonable competition, and that ideological differences should be used to improve the world.

Gorbachev's reforms were not without strong opposition in the Soviet Union, and the elimination of political and social control led to ethnic and national tension in the Baltic states of Armenia, Georgia, Ukraine, and Moldova. However, in 1990, the newly created Congress of People's Deputies ended the Communist Party's control over the government and elected Gorbachev president. He dissolved the Communist Party, granted independence to the Baltic states, and proposed an economic federation among the remaining republics, the Commonwealth of Independent States, which effectively ended the central power of the Soviet Union. Gorbachev resigned as president on December 25, 1991.

Two great revolutions, the French revolution of 1789 and the Russian revolution of 1917, have exerted a powerful influence on the actual nature of the historical process and radically changed the course of world events. Both of them, each in its own way, have given a gigantic impetus to man's progress. They are also the ones that have formed in many respects the way of thinking which is still prevailing in the public consciousness.

That is a very great spiritual wealth, but there emerges before us today a different world, for which it is necessary to seek different roads toward the future, to seek—relying, of course, on accumulated experience—but also seeing the radical differences between that which was yesterday and that which is taking place today.

A Mutually Connected World

The newness of the tasks, and at the same time their difficulty, are not limited to this. Today we have entered an era when progress will be based on the interests of all mankind. Consciousness of this requires that world policy, too, should be determined by the priority of the values of all mankind.

The history of the past centuries and millennia has been a history of almost ubiquitous wars, and sometimes desperate battles, leading to mutual destruction. They occurred in the clash of social and political interests and national hostility, be it from ideological or religious incompatibility. All that was the case, and even now many still claim that this past—which has not been overcome—is an immutable pattern. However, parallel with the process of wars, hostility, and alienation of peoples and countries, another process, just as objectively conditioned, was in motion and gaining force: The process of the emergence of a mutually connected and integral world.

Further world progress is now possible only through the search for a consensus of all mankind, in movement toward a new world order. We have arrived at a frontier at which controlled spontaneity leads to a dead end. The world community must learn to shape and direct the process in such a way as to preserve civilization, to make it safe for all and more pleasant for normal life. It is a question of cooperation that could be more accurately called "co-creation" and "co-development." The formula of development "at another's expense" is becoming outdated. In light of present realities, genuine progress by infringing upon the rights and liberties of man and peoples, or at the expense of nature, is impossible.

The very tackling of global problems requires a new "volume" and "quality" of cooperation by states and sociopolitical currents regardless of ideological and other differences. . . .

The de-ideologization of interstate relations has become a demand of the new stage. We are not giving up our convictions, philosophy, or traditions. Neither are we calling on anyone else to give up theirs. Yet we are not going to shut ourselves up within the range of our values. That would lead to spiritual impoverishment, for it would mean renouncing so powerful a source of development as sharing all the original things created independently by each nation. In the course of such sharing, each should prove the advantages of his own system, his own way of life and values, but not through words or propaganda alone, but through real deeds as well. That is, indeed, an honest struggle of ideology, but it must not be carried over into mutual relations between states. Otherwise we simply will not be able to solve a single world problem; arrange broad, mutually advantageous and equitable cooperation between peoples; manage rationally the achievements of the scientific and technical revolution; transform world economic relations; protect the environment; overcome underdevelopment; or put an end to hunger, disease, illiteracy, and other mass ills. Finally, in that case, we will not manage to eliminate the nuclear threat and militarism. . . .

Restructuring in the Soviet Union

Our country is undergoing a truly revolutionary upsurge. The process of restructuring is gaining pace. We started by elaborating the theoretical concepts of restructuring; we had to assess the nature and scope of the problems, to interpret the lessons of the past, and to express this in the form of political conclusions and programs. This was done. The theoretical work, the re-interpretation of what had happened, the final elaboration, enrichment, and correction of political stances have not ended. They continue. However, it was fundamentally important to start from an overall concept, which is already now being confirmed by the experience of past years, which has turned out to be generally correct and to which there is no alternative.

In order to involve society in implementing the plans for restructuring it had to be made more truly democratic. Under the badge of democratization, restructuring has now encompassed politics, the economy, spiritual life, and ideology. We have unfolded a radical economic reform, we have accumulated experience, and from the new year we are transferring the entire national economy to new forms and work methods. Moreover, this means a profound reorganization of production relations and the realization of the immense potential of socialist property.

In moving toward such bold revolutionary transformations, we understood that there would be errors, that there would be resistance, that the novelty would bring new problems. We foresaw the possibility of breaking in individual sections. However, the profound democratic reform of the entire system of power and government is the guarantee that the overall process of restructuring will move steadily forward and gather strength.

We completed the first stage of the process of political reform with the recent decisions by the U.S.S.R. Supreme Soviet on amendments to the Constitution and the adoption of the Law on Elections. Without stopping, we embarked upon the second stage of this. At which the most important task will be working on the interaction between the central government and the republics, settling relations between nationalities on the principles of Leninist internationalism bequeathed to us by the great revolution and, at the same time, reorganizing the power of the Soviets locally. We are faced with immense work. At the same time we must resolve major problems.

We are more than fully confident. We have both the theory, the policy and the vanguard force of restructuring a party which is also restructuring itself in accordance with the new tasks and the radical changes throughout society. And

the most important thing: all peoples and all generations of citizens in our great country are in favor of restructuring.

Adopting New Laws

We have gone substantially and deeply into the business of constructing a socialist state based on the rule of law. A whole series of new laws has been prepared or is at a completion stage. Many of them come into force as early as 1989, and we trust that they will correspond to the highest standards from the point of view of ensuring the rights of the individual. Soviet democracy is to acquire a firm, normative base. This means such acts as the Law on Freedom of Conscience, on glasnost, on public associations and organizations, and on much else. There are now no people in places of imprisonment in the country who have been sentenced for their political or religious convictions. It is proposed to include in the drafts of the new laws additional guarantees ruling out any form or persecution on these bases. Of course, this does not apply to those who have committed real criminal or state offenses: espionage, sabotage, terrorism, and so on, whatever political or philosophical views they may hold.

The draft amendments to the criminal code are ready and waiting their turn. In particular, those articles relating to the use of the supreme measure of punishment are being reviewed. The problem of exit and entry is also being resolved in a humane spirit, including the case of leaving the country in order to be reunited with relatives. As you know, one of the reasons for refusal of visas is citizens' possession of secrets. Strictly substantiated terms for the length of time for possessing secrets are being introduced in advance. On starting work at a relevant institution or enterprise, everyone will be made aware of this regulation. Disputes that arise can be appealed under the law. Thus the problem of the so-called "refuseniks" is being removed.

We intend to expand the Soviet Union's participation in the monitoring mechanism on human rights in the United Nations and within the framework of the pan-European process. We consider that the jurisdiction of the International Court in The Hague with respect to interpreting and applying agreements in the field of human rights should be obligatory for all states. . . .

The Process of Demilitarization

Today I can inform you of the following: The Soviet Union has made a decision on reducing its armed forces. In the next two years, their numerical strength will be reduced by 500,000 persons, and the volume of conventional arms will also be cut considerably. These reductions will be made on a unilateral basis, unconnected with negotiations on the mandate for the Vienna meeting. By agreement with our allies in the Warsaw Pact, we have made the decision to withdraw six tank divisions from the GDR [German Democratic Republic (East Germany)], Czechoslovakia, and Hungary, and to disband them by 1991. Assault landing formations and units, and a number of others, including assault river-crossing forces, with their armaments and combat equipment, will also be withdrawn from the groups of Soviet forces situated in those countries. The Soviet forces situated in those countries will be cut by 50,000 persons, and their arms by 5,000 tanks. All remaining Soviet divisions on the territory of our allies will be reorganized. They will be given a different structure from today's which will become unambiguously defensive, after the removal of a large number of their tanks. . . .

By this act, just as by all our actions aimed at the demilitarization of international relations, we would also like to draw the attention of the world community to another topical problem, the problem of changing over from an economy of armament to an economy of disarmament. Is the conversion of military production realistic? I have already had occasion to speak about this. We believe that it is, indeed, realistic. For its part, the Soviet Union is ready to do the following. Within the framework of the economic reform we are ready to draw up and submit our internal plan for conversion, to prepare in the course of 1989, as an experiment, the plans for the conversion of two or three defense enterprises, to publish our experience of job relocation of specialists from the military industry, and also of using its equipment, buildings, and works in civilian industry. It is desirable that all states, primarily the major military powers, submit their national plans on this issue to the United Nations.

It would be useful to form a group of scientists, entrusting it with a comprehensive analysis of problems of conversion as a whole and as applied to individual countries and regions, to be reported to the U.N. secretary-general, and later to examine this matter at a General Assembly session.

A New Relationship with the United States

Finally, being on U.S. soil, but also for other, understandable reasons, I cannot but turn to the subject of our relations with this great country. . . . Relations between the Soviet Union and the United States of America span 5½ decades. The world has changed, and so have the nature, role, and place of these relations in world politics. For too long they were built under the banner of confrontation, and sometimes of hostility, either open or concealed. But in the last few years, throughout the world people were able to heave a sigh of relief, thanks to the changes for the better in the substance and atmosphere of the relations between Moscow and Washington.

No one intends to underestimate the serious nature of the disagreements, and the difficulties of the problems which have not been settled. However, we have already graduated from the primary school of instruction in mutual understanding and in searching for solutions in our and in the common interests. The U.S.S.R. and the United States created the biggest nuclear missile arsenals, but after objectively recognizing their responsibility, they were able to be the first to conclude an agreement on the reduction and physical destruction of a proportion of these weapons, which threatened both themselves and everyone else.

Both sides possess the biggest and the most refined military secrets. But it is they who have laid the basis for and are developing a system of mutual verification with regard to both the destruction and the limiting and banning of armaments production. It is they who are amassing experience for future bilateral and multilateral agreements. We value this.

We acknowledge and value the contribution of President

Ronald Reagan and the members of his administration, above all Mr. George Shultz. All this is capital that has been invested in a joint undertaking of historic importance. It must not be wasted or left out of circulation. The future U.S. administration headed by newly elected President George Bush [Senior] will find in us a partner, ready—without long pauses and backward movements—to continue the dialogue in a spirit of realism, openness, and goodwill, and with a striving for concrete results, over an agenda encompassing the key issues of Soviet-U.S. relations and international politics.

We are talking first and foremost about consistent progress toward concluding a treaty on a 50 percent reduction in strategic offensive weapons, while retaining the ABM [Anti-Ballistic Missile] Treaty; about elaborating a convention on the elimination of chemical weapons—here, it seems to us, we have the preconditions for making 1989 the decisive year; and about talks on reducing conventional weapons and armed forces in Europe. We are also talking about economic, ecological and humanitarian problems in the widest possible sense. . . .

A Need for Respect and Balance

We are not inclined to oversimplify the situation in the world. Yes, the tendency toward disarmament has received a strong impetus, and this process is gaining its own momentum, but it has not become irreversible. Yes, the striving to give up confrontation in favor of dialogue and cooperation has made itself strongly felt, but it has by no means secured its position forever in the practice of international relations. Yes, the movement toward a nuclear-free and nonviolent world is capable of fundamentally transforming the political and spiritual face of the planet, but only the very first steps have been taken. Moreover, in certain influential circles, they have been greeted with mistrust, and they are meeting resistance.

The inheritance of inertia of the past are continuing to operate. Profound contradictions and the roots of many conflicts have not disappeared. The fundamental fact remains that the formation of the peaceful period will take place in conditions of the existence and rivalry of various socioeconomic and political systems. However, the meaning of our international efforts, and one of the key tenets of the new thinking, is precisely to impart to this rivalry the quality of sensible competition in conditions of respect for freedom of choice and a balance of interests. In this case it will even become useful and productive from the viewpoint of general world development; otherwise; if the main component remains the arms race, as it has been till now, rivalry will be fatal. Indeed, an ever greater number of people throughout the world, from the man in the street to leaders, are beginning to understand this.

Esteemed Mr. Chairman, esteemed delegates: I finish my first speech at the United Nations with the same feeling with which I began it: a feeling of responsibility to my own people and to the world community. We have met at the end of a year that has been so significant for the United Nations, and on the threshold of a year from which all of us expect so much. One would like to believe that our joint efforts to put an end to the era of wars, confrontation and regional conflicts, aggression against nature, the terror of hunger and poverty, as well as political terrorism, will be comparable with our hopes. This is our common goal, and it is only by acting together that we may attain it.

GREAT
SPEECHES
IN
HISTORY

The Berlin Wall: Symbol of the Cold War

A Call for Action Against the Building of the Berlin Wall

Thomas J. Dodd

Thomas J. Dodd was born in Norwich, Connecticut, and received a law degree from Yale University in 1934. After serving in the FBI, Dodd became special assistant to the attorney general, prosecuting espionage and sabotage cases during World War II. After the war, Dodd was appointed vice-chairman of the review board and later executive trial counsel at the prosecution of war criminals in Nuremberg, Germany. On his return to the United States, Dodd became active in Democratic politics, serving as a U.S. congressman in 1952 and 1954 and as a senator from 1959 to 1970. As a member of the Senate Foreign Relations Committee, Dodd was a vigorous opponent of Soviet communism, considering it the moral equivalent of the National Socialism of Nazi Germany. He advocated strong action to free those oppressed by communism, particularly Eastern Europeans residing in nations such as Lithuania, Poland, and Hungary.

To offer a united front against Nazi Germany in World War II, the Soviet Union became an ally of the United States and Britain. Before the war's end, the leaders of the Allied nations met to discuss the organization of postwar Europe. The leaders agreed to divide occupation of Germany among Britain, France, the Soviet Union, and the United States. Democratic West Germany emerged from the territory occupied by the western nations; Communist East Germany emerged from the territory occupied by the Soviet Union, becoming a Soviet

Thomas J. Dodd, address before the U.S. Senate, Washington, DC, August 18, 1961.

satellite. The city of Berlin was located in the middle of East Germany and was also divided between the Communist East and democratic West so that Western nations could maintain access to the strategic European city. However, Soviet leader Nikita Khrushchev threatened to sign a treaty with East Germany that would limit access to Berlin if the United States did not remove its troops stationed in West Berlin. Moreover, those who opposed the new Communist government in East Germany hoped to flee to the West through Berlin, and East Germany built a wall to keep East Germans from escaping. The United States's reaction to the wall was moderate since its troops and access to West Berlin remained.

In the following address before the Senate, delivered on August 18, 1961, Dodd expresses his disappointment with the United States's weak response to the building of the wall in Berlin. Dodd argues that the administration's toothless protest against East Germany's actions is only one of the many times the United States has failed in its commitment to those struggling to oppose Communist expansion. Dodd cites, for example, the nation's failure to support the Freedom Fighters of Hungary, who opposed their Communist government; as a result of America's inaction, the Freedom Fighters were defeated by Soviet forces in 1956. By failing to take action, says Dodd, the United States invites further Soviet aggression. Rather than make weak protests against East Germany's use of force to permanently divide East and West Berlin, the United States must take action to show the Soviet Union that the West will not tolerate such flagrant violations of treaties and human rights.

Although Khrushchev never signed a treaty with East Germany, tension in Berlin remained throughout the Cold War until the wall fell on November 9, 1989.

We have been warned on every side that the Berlin crisis may lead to war. I am convinced that it will not lead to war if we can persuade Prime Minister

[Nikita] Khrushchev that we mean business when we say that we will fight, if necessary, to defend the freedom of Berlin.

On the other hand, there is a very serious chance of war by miscalculation if Khrushchev believes that the West will back down again, as it has in the past, that it is not irrevocably committed to the defense of Berlin.

Perhaps the most disturbing thing I learned during my recent visit to Europe is that Khrushchev apparently does not take our declarations on Berlin seriously. He is convinced that the United States is divided, that the NATO [North Atlantic Treaty Organization] alliance is divided, that the West talks big but acts little.

I report this to the Senate on the very highest authority.

It is from this standpoint that the Allied note on Berlin is particularly dangerous.

Every time we fail to live up to our commitments, every time we limit ourselves to oral protest when the situation calls imperatively for action, every time we give the impression of weakness or hesitation, we fortify Khrushchev's beliefs that the West will "chicken out" if he pushes things to the brink of a showdown.

An Opportunity Missed

Unfortunately, since the terrible days of the Hungarian Revolution, we have given Khrushchev far too many reasons for believing that we are incapable of decisive action.

The Hungarian Revolution was without question the greatest opportunity the West has had to force the Kremlin back to its pre-war frontiers and to reestablish a stable political balance in Europe. The satellite empire was seething with discontent. Poland and East Germany, in particular, stood on the very brink of explosion. The Red Army units stationed in Hungary had, in the first phase of the fighting, given indications of massive disaffection. Thousands of them, in fact, had gone over to the side of the Hungarian Freedom Fighters with their weapons. The Kremlin itself, as Khrushchev has publicly admitted, was aware of the gravity of the crisis and was divided on the course to be followed.

But instead of taking action to support the heroic Freedom Fighters of Hungary, we limited ourselves to pious declarations of sympathy.

We took no action to make it clear to the world that we accepted the Government of Imre Nagy as the legitimate government of Hungary. . . .

In the Berlin crisis we are paying, too, for our inaction in Laos. In the early days of the Laos crisis, Khrushchev apparently was still uncertain about our reaction. He felt his way gingerly because he apparently believed that we might take the action we had committed ourselves to take through our membership in Southeast Asia Treaty Organization (SEATO) and through our repeated declarations that we would defend Laos.

The Price of Inaction

The first Soviet planes that flew into Laos brought only benzene. We did nothing.

The next group of planes that flew in brought small arms munitions. Still we did nothing.

The next group of planes brought artillery and artillery ammunition; and still we did nothing.

Finally, when they were convinced that we would take no action no matter how great the provocation, the Soviet airlift to Laos brought in Communist military personnel. At this point they knew that Laos was theirs for the taking.

Our failure to back up the Cuban Freedom Fighters was inevitably construed by Khrushchev as another evidence of weakness and indecision. Khrushchev must have compared our inaction in this case with the action he himself would certainly have taken had he been confronted with a situation in reverse on his own frontier.

The nuclear test ban moratorium is another instance where we have been long on words and short on action.

On December 29, 1959, President Dwight Eisenhower announced that, in view of the lack of progress at Geneva, the United States would not renew the moratorium but would reserve the right to resume testing, with proper notice to the international community. Since that time, we have declared on at least three or four occasions that we would make a final effort to reach an agreement at Geneva and that, if this effort

Germany During the Cold War

Berlin

Potsdam

EAST GERMANY

Bonn

BELGIUM

LUXEMBOURG

WEST GERMANY

FRANCE

BRITAIN

POLAND

CZECHOSLOVAKIA

AUSTRIA

failed, we would have no alternative but to resume testing. . . .

If war should erupt over Berlin, it will be a war of miscalculation, a war that neither we nor the Soviets want. But, to a far greater extent than we realize, such a war would be the consequence of our failure to act in Hungary and Laos and Cuba, of our failure to act on the nuclear test ban moratorium, and, more immediately, of our failure to take any action in response to Khrushchev's monstrous action in Berlin.

Convincing Khrushchev

I am convinced that we will not back down on Berlin. I know that this conviction is shared by Chancellor [Konrad] Adenauer and the leaders of the West German Government. I have every reason to believe that it is also shared by our other NATO allies.

This is all to the good. But it is not enough. It is just as important to convince Khrushchev that we mean business as it is to convince our allies. And it is here that we have failed.

In the months that remain to us before the Berlin crisis comes to a head, it is essential that we do everything in our power to convince Prime Minister Khrushchev that we mean it when we say that we are prepared to fight over Berlin, to convince him that we have the capacity for decision and the capacity for action, if need be.

The flabbiness of our protest over the sealing off of East Berlin, the serious delay in issuing it, the total avoidance of action, will have precisely the contrary effect.

Mr. President, to illustrate my point, I ask unanimous consent to insert into the Record at this point the brief text of the allied protest note of August 15th:

The Commandants' Protest

Berlin, Aug. 15 [1961] (Reuters)—Following is the text of a note sent today by the United States, British and French commandants in Berlin to the Soviet commandant:

During the night of Aug. 12–13 the East German authorities put into effect illegal measures designed to turn the boundaries between the West sectors of Berlin and the Soviet sector into an arbitrary barrier to movement of German citizens resident in East Berlin and East Germany.

Not since the imposition of the Berlin blockade has there been such a flagrant violation of the four-power agreements concerning Berlin. The agreement of June 20, 1949, in which the U.S.S.R. pledged itself to facilitate freedom of movement within Berlin and between Berlin and the rest of Germany, has also been violated.

In disregard of these agreements and of the wishes of the population of this city, for the welfare of which the four powers are jointly responsible, freedom of circulation throughout Berlin has been severely curtailed.

Traffic between the East sector and the Western sectors of Berlin has been disrupted by the cutting of S-bahn (elevated) and U-bahn (subway) service, the tearing up of streets, the erection of road blocks and the stringing of barbed wire.

In carrying out these illegal actions, military and paramilitary units, which were formed in violation of four-power agreements and whose very presence in East Berlin is illegal, turned the Soviet sector of Berlin into an armed camp.

Moreover, the East German authorities have now prohibited the many inhabitants of East Berlin and East Germany who were employed in West Berlin from continuing to pursue their occupations in West Berlin. They have thus denied to the working population under their control the elementary right of free choice of place of employment.

It is obvious that the East German authorities have taken these repressive measures because the people under their control, deeply perturbed by the threats on Berlin recently launched by Communist leaders, were fleeing in large numbers to the West.

We must protest against the illegal measures introduced on Aug. 13 and hold you responsible for the carrying out of the relevant agreements.

Gaston Coblentz, in his article in the *Herald Tribune*, quoted a typical Berlin reaction as follows:

"Well, the first five paragraphs tell the Communists what they already know—that they have sealed off East Berlin. The last paragraph says rather politely that they really should not have done it."

I am in complete agreement with this evaluation. There are those who say that we *can* take no action, and others who say that we *should* take no action in reply to this new Communist provocation, because any action we took would increase the tensions and increase the danger of war.

But there are many measures we can take and should take which would in no way increase the danger of a military confrontation. . . .

A Plan of Action

I believe there are five actions we can take to persuade the Kremlin that we do have the will and the capacity for decisive action.

First, I propose that we organize a massive airlift to Berlin of thousands of journalists and correspondents from all over the world. We might call this the "Truth Airlift".

Second, I propose that we immediately suspend shipment of all machine tools and chemical processing equipment to the Soviet bloc, and warn them that further aggression will result in further economic sanctions.

Third, I propose that we recall our Ambassadors from the satellite countries for an indefinite period, and warn them that further complicity in the Kremlin's aggression will result in further diplomatic sanctions.

Fourth, I propose that we raise the issue in the United Nations, and demand that a special commission be set up to examine into the question of self-determination for the German people and the reasons for the mass influx of refugees from East Germany.

Fifth, I propose that we resume testing forthwith if the impending meeting between Ambassadors Arthur H. Dean [of the United States] and Semyon K. Tsarapkin [of the Soviet Union] fails to budge the Kremlin from its insistence on the veto.

There are bound to be negotiations with the Kremlin. If we fail to take action of any kind, if we confine ourselves to verbal protests over each Soviet provocation, we shall go to the conference table gravely handicapped, because we shall have no *quid pro quo* to offer in demanding that the Soviets retreat from all those actions they have taken that are in violation of the occupation statute and the Four Power agreement on Berlin. From such a conference we shall inevitably emerge the loser.

But worse still, if we fail to take action, we greatly increase the chances of war by miscalculation.

I believe the proposals I have presented here are realistic.

I believe they would in no way increase the danger of a military clash.

I believe that, taken in concert, they would persuade the Kremlin that we mean business about Berlin, and that the democracies are not effete and incapable of action.

I believe that, in the long run, a course of action such as I have outlined is the one sure way to defend Berlin and the one sure way to preserve the peace.

Mr. President, we cannot escape the fact that Khrushchev judges us not by our words but by our actions.

We must draw the necessary conclusions from this. Because history, too, will judge us by our deeds rather than by our words.

Berlin Reflects the Struggle Between Freedom and Oppression

John F. Kennedy

The city of Berlin, which was located within the borders of East Germany, had been divided between the Western Allies and the Communists since World War II: East Berlin was Communist and West Berlin was non-Communist. In June 1948, Soviet troops blocked all road, rail, and water traffic between East and West Berlin. In response to efforts to seal off Berlin from the West, the United States, Great Britain, and France airlifted 2.3 million tons of food and supplies to the city for fifteen months until the Soviets lifted the blockade on May 12, 1949.

Thirteen years later, Soviet leader Nikita Khrushchev threatened to sign a treaty with East Germany that would give the East Germans control over access to Berlin. In June 1961, President John F. Kennedy spent two days with Khrushchev, making it clear to him that the United States was determined to ensure that the West had access to Berlin. Despite these threats, East Germany began efforts to prevent access to West Berlin, which culminated in the building of the Berlin Wall on August 13. The Wall was erected to keep East Germans from escaping their country through West Berlin. Kennedy responded by appropriating money for armaments and ordering National Guard and reserve units into active service in the event the crisis led to war with the Soviet Union. Khrushchev

John F. Kennedy, address to the people of Berlin, West Berlin, Germany, June 26, 1963.

did not sign a treaty with East Germany, but the wall remained, a symbol of the tension between East and West.

Kennedy returned to Berlin in 1963. On June 26, Kennedy spoke to the people of Berlin in the Rudolf Wilde Platz, explaining that the struggle of the people of Berlin represents the battle between the free world and the Communist world. The erection of a wall to keep a people from escaping, says Kennedy, reflects the failure of communism. Although West Berlin remains free, others remain enslaved, and people must continue to work toward freedom for all men. Kennedy begins and ends his speech with the now famous proclamation he says represents the world of freedom, *Ich bin ein Berliner*—I am a citizen of Berlin. Although legend has it Kennedy had misspoken, actually saying "I am a jelly doughnut," most authorities claim his audience understood his meaning and cheered in response.

The wall remained a symbol of the struggle between East and West—democracy and communism—until it was dismantled on November 9, 1989. To many, the destruction of the Berlin Wall represented an end to the Cold War.

Two thousand years ago the proudest boast was "*civis Romanus sum* [I am a Roman Citizen]." Today, in the world of freedom, the proudest boast is "*Ich bin ein Berliner* [I am a citizen of Berlin]."

I appreciate my interpreter translating my German!

There are many people in the world who really don't understand, or say they don't, what is the great issue between the free world and the Communist world. Let them come to Berlin. There are some who say that communism is the wave of the future. Let them come to Berlin. And there are some who say in Europe and elsewhere we can work with the Communists. Let them come to Berlin. And there are even a few who say that it is true that communism is an evil system, but it permits us to make economic progress. *Lass' sie nach Berlin kommen*. Let them come to Berlin.

Freedom has many difficulties and democracy is not perfect, but we have never had to put a wall up to keep our people in, to prevent them from leaving us. I want to say, on behalf of my countrymen, who live many miles away on the other side of the Atlantic, who are far distant from you, that they take the greatest pride that they have been able to share with you, even from a distance, the story of the last 18 years. I know of no town, no city, that has been besieged for 18 years that still lives with the vitality and the force, and the hope and the determination of the city of West Berlin. While the wall is the most obvious and vivid demonstration of the failures of the Communist system, for all the world to see, we take no satisfaction in it, for it is, as your Mayor has said, an offense not only against history but an offense against humanity, separating families, dividing husbands and wives and brothers and sisters, and dividing a people who wish to be joined together.

What is true of this city is true of Germany—real, lasting peace in Europe can never be assured as long as one German out of four is denied the elementary right of free men, and that is to make a free choice. In 18 years of peace and good faith, this generation of Germans has earned the right to be free, including the right to unite their families and their nation in lasting peace, with good will to all people. You live in a defended island of freedom, but your life is part of the main. So let me ask you as I close, to lift your eyes beyond the dangers of today, to the hopes of tomorrow, beyond the freedom merely of this city of Berlin, or your country of Germany, to the advance of freedom everywhere, beyond the wall to the day of peace with justice, beyond yourselves and ourselves to all mankind.

Freedom is indivisible, and when one man is enslaved, all are not free. When all are free, then we can look forward to that day when this city will be joined as one and this country and this great Continent of Europe in a peaceful and hopeful globe. When that day finally comes, as it will, the people of West Berlin can take sober satisfaction in the fact that they were in the front lines for almost two decades.

All free men, wherever they may live, are citizens of Berlin, and, therefore, as a free man, I take pride in the words "Ich bin ein Berliner."

Tear Down This Wall

Ronald Reagan

In the early years of President Ronald Reagan's administration, relations between the Soviet Union and the United States were strained. Years of détente during the Nixon and Ford administrations appeared to end with the Soviet invasion of Afghanistan in December 1979, between Reagan's election and inauguration. Moreover, Reagan believed in a stronger stand against communism; in 1983, the United States began to deploy intermediate-range missiles in Western Europe, and in 1985, Reagan proposed the Strategic Defense Initiative, the technological pursuit of defensive weapons in space.

However, in March 1985, Mikhail Gorbachev became the leader of the Soviet Union, and a skeptical Reagan met with Gorbachev in Geneva, Switzerland, in November 1985. In his 1989 book *Speaking My Mind*, Reagan says, "I did not know when I left for that meeting in Geneva, I would eventually call Mikhail Gorbachev a friend." As a result of meetings with Gorbachev and the implementation of Gorbachev's restructuring plan within the Soviet Union, East-West relations did indeed begin to change.

A little more than two years before the Berlin Wall fell, on June 12, 1987, Reagan spoke at the Brandenburg Gate that separated East and West Berlin. In August 1961 a wall was erected in Berlin to prevent East Germans who rejected communism from escaping to West Germany through West Berlin. Although Reagan's attitude toward the Soviet Union was warming, his speech reflects

Ronald Reagan, speech at the Brandenburg Gate, West Berlin, Germany, June 12, 1987.

his continuing opposition to communism's restrictions on human freedom. According to Reagan, the Berlin Wall represents a scar across the face of Europe, but also the triumph of West Berlin. Reagan compares the economic success of West Berlin with the economic failure of communism. If Gorbachev seeks peace and prosperity, says Reagan, he must come to Berlin and tear down the wall. To open the Brandenburg Gate, Reagan reasons, represents an opportunity to develop economic, cultural, and political ties between East and West. According to Reagan, the State Department and the National Security Council thought his lines about tearing down the wall and opening the gate were too provocative, but he decided to keep them in his address. The lines, says Reagan, "got quite a reaction from the crowd."

Twenty-four years ago, President John F. Kennedy visited Berlin, speaking to the people of this city and the world at the City Hall. Well, since then two other presidents have come, each in his turn, to Berlin. And today I, myself, make my second visit to your city.

We come to Berlin, we American presidents, because it's our duty to speak, in this place, of freedom. But I must confess, we're drawn here by other things as well: by the feeling of history in this city, more than five hundred years older than our own nation; by the beauty of the Grünewald and the Tiergarten; most of all, by your courage and determination.

Perhaps the composer Paul Lincke understood something about American presidents. You see, like so many presidents before me, I come here today because wherever I go, whatever I do: *Ich hab noch einen Koffer in Berlin.* [I still have a suitcase in Berlin.]

Our gathering today is being broadcast throughout Western Europe and North America. I understand that it is being seen and heard as well in the East. To those listening throughout Eastern Europe, I extend my warmest greetings and the goodwill of the American people. To those listening in East Berlin, a special word: Although I cannot be with you, I address my remarks to you just as surely as to those standing here before me. For I join you, as I join your fellow countrymen in the West, in this firm, this unalterable belief: *Es gibt nur ein Berlin.* [There is only one Berlin.]

A Symbol of Division

Behind me stands a wall that encircles the free sectors of this city, part of a vast system of barriers that divides the entire continent of Europe. From the Baltic, south, those barriers cut across Germany in a gash of barbed wire, concrete, dog runs, and guard towers. Farther south, there may be no visible, no obvious wall. But there remain armed guards and checkpoints all the same—still a restriction on the right to travel, still an instrument to impose upon ordinary men and women the will of a totalitarian state. Yet it is here in Berlin where the wall emerges most clearly; here, cutting across your city, where the news photo and the television screen have imprinted this brutal division of a continent upon the mind of the world. Standing before the Brandenburg Gate, every man is a German, separated from his fellow men. Every man is a Berliner, forced to look upon a scar.

President [Richard] von Weizsäcker has said, "The German question is open as long as the Brandenburg Gate is closed." Today I say: As long as this gate is closed, as long as this scar of a wall is permitted to stand, it is not the German question alone that remains open, but the question of freedom for all mankind. Yet I do not come here to lament. For I find in Berlin a message of hope, even in the shadow of this wall, a message of triumph.

In this season of spring in 1945, the people of Berlin emerged from their air-raid shelters to find devastation. Thousands of miles away, the people of the United States reached out to help. And in 1947 Secretary of State—as you've been told—George Marshall announced the creation of what would become known as the Marshall Plan. Speaking precisely forty years ago this month, he said: "Our policy is directed not against any country or doctrine, but against hunger, poverty, desperation, and chaos."

In the Reichstag a few moments ago, I saw a display commemorating this fortieth anniversary of the Marshall Plan. I was struck by the sign on a burnt-out, gutted structure that was being rebuilt. I understand that Berliners of my own generation can remember seeing signs like it dotted throughout the western sectors of the city. The sign read simply: "The Marshall Plan is helping here to strengthen the free world." A strong, free world in the West, that dream became real. Japan rose from ruin to become an economic giant. Italy, France, Belgium—virtually every nation in Western Europe saw political and economic rebirth; the European Community was founded.

A Story of Economic Success

In West Germany and here in Berlin, there took place an economic miracle, the *Wirtschaftswunder*. [Konrad] Adenauer [West German chancellor, 1949–63], [Ludwig] Erhard [West German chancellor, 1963–66], [Ernst] Reuter, [mayor of West Berlin during the blockade, 1948–49], and other leaders understood the practical importance of liberty,—that just as truth can flourish only when the journalist is given freedom of speech, so prosperity can come about only when the farmer and businessman enjoy economic freedom. The German leaders reduced tariffs, expanded free trade, lowered taxes. From 1950 to 1960 alone, the standard of living in West Germany and Berlin doubled.

Where four decades ago there was rubble, today in West Berlin there is the greatest industrial output of any city in Germany—busy office blocks, fine homes and apartments, proud avenues, and the spreading lawns of parkland. Where a city's culture seemed to have been destroyed, today there are two great universities, orchestras and an opera, countless theaters, and museums. Where there was want, today there's abundance—food, clothing, automobiles—the wonderful goods of the Ku'damm. From devastation, from utter ruin, you Berliners have, in freedom, rebuilt a city that once again ranks as one of the greatest on earth. The Soviets may have had other plans. But my friends, there were a few things the Soviets didn't count on—*Berliner Herz, Berliner Humor, ja, und Berliner Schnauze*. [Berliner heart, Berliner humor, yes, and a Berliner Schnauze.]

The Value of Freedom

In the 1950s, Soviet leader [Nikita] Khrushchev predicted: "We will bury you." But in the West today, we see a free world that has achieved a level of prosperity and well-being unprecedented in all human history. In the Communist world, we see failure, technological backwardness, declining standards of health, even want of the most basic kind—too little food. Even today, the Soviet Union still cannot feed itself. After these four decades, then, there stands before the entire world one great and inescapable conclusion: Freedom leads to prosperity. Freedom replaces the ancient hatreds among the nations with comity and peace. Freedom is the victor.

And now the Soviets themselves may, in a limited way, be coming to understand the importance of freedom. We hear much from Moscow about a new policy of reform and openness. Some political prisoners have been released. Certain foreign news broadcasts are no longer being jammed. Some economic enterprises have been permitted to operate with greater freedom from state control.

Are these the beginnings of profound changes in the Soviet state? Or are they token gestures, intended to raise false hopes in the West, or to strengthen the Soviet system without changing it? We welcome change and openness; for we believe that freedom and security go together, that the advance of human liberty can only strengthen the cause of world peace. There is one sign the Soviets can make that would be unmistakable, that would advance dramatically the cause of freedom and peace.

General Secretary Gorbachev, if you seek peace, if you seek prosperity for the Soviet Union and Eastern Europe, if you seek liberalization: Come here to this gate! Mr. Gorbachev, open this gate! Mr. Gorbachev, tear down this wall!

The Struggle for Arms Reduction

I understand the fear of war and the pain of division that afflict this continent—and I pledge to you my country's efforts to help overcome these burdens. To be sure, we in the West must resist Soviet expansion. So we must maintain defenses of unassailable strength. Yet we seek peace; so we must strive to reduce arms on both sides. . . .

While we pursue these arms reductions, I pledge to you that we will maintain the capacity to deter Soviet aggression at any level at which it might occur. And in cooperation with many of our allies, the United States is pursuing the Strategic Defense Initiative—research to base deterrence not on the threat of offensive retaliation, but on defenses that truly defend; on systems, in short, that will not target populations, but shield them. By these means we seek to increase the safety of Europe and all the world. But we must remember a crucial fact: East and West do not mistrust each other because we are armed; we are armed because we mistrust each other. And our differences are not about weapons but about liberty. When President Kennedy spoke at the City Hall those twenty-four years ago, freedom was encircled, Berlin was under siege. And today, despite all the pressures upon this city, Berlin stands secure in its liberty. And freedom itself is transforming the globe. . . .

Bringing East and West Together

Today thus represents a moment of hope. We in the West stand ready to cooperate with the East to promote true openness, to break down barriers that separate people, to create a safer, freer world. And surely there is no better place than Berlin, the meeting place of East and West, to make a start. Free people of Berlin: Today, as in the past, the United States stands for the strict observance and full implementation of all parts of the Four Power Agreement of 1971. Let us use this occasion, the 750th anniversary of this city, to usher in a new era, to seek a still fuller, richer life for the Berlin of the future. Together, let us maintain and develop the ties between the Federal Republic and the Western sectors of Berlin, which is permitted by the 1971 agreement.

And I invite Mr. Gorbachev: Let us work to bring the Eastern and Western parts of the city closer together, so that all the inhabitants of all Berlin can enjoy the benefits that come with life in one of the great cities of the world.

To open Berlin still further to all Europe, East and West,

let us expand the vital air access to this city, finding ways of making commercial air service to Berlin more convenient, more comfortable, and more economical. We look to the day when West Berlin can become one of the chief aviation hubs in all central Europe.

With our French and British partners, the United States is prepared to help bring international meetings to Berlin. It would be only fitting for Berlin to serve as the site of United Nations meetings, or world conferences on human rights and arms control or other issues that call for international cooperation.

There is no better way to establish hope for the future than to enlighten young minds, and we would be honored to sponsor summer youth exchanges, cultural events, and other programs for young Berliners from the East. Our French and British friends, I'm certain, will do the same. And it's my hope that an authority can be found in East Berlin to sponsor visits from young people of the Western sectors.

One final proposal, one close to my heart: Sport represents a source of enjoyment and ennoblement, and you may have noted that the Republic of Korea—South Korea—has offered to permit certain events of the 1988 Olympics to take place in the North. International sports competitions of all kinds could take place in both parts of this city. And what better way to demonstrate to the world the openness of this city than to offer in some future year to hold the Olympic games here in Berlin, East and West?

The Spirit of Berlin

In these four decades, as I have said, you Berliners have built a great city. You've done so in spite of threats—the Soviet attempts to impose the East-mark, the blockade. Today the city thrives in spite of the challenges implicit in the very presence of this wall. What keeps you here? Certainly there's a great deal to be said for your fortitude, for your defiant courage. But I believe there's something deeper, something that involves Berlin's whole look and feel and way of life—not mere sentiment. No one could live long in Berlin without being completely disabused of illusions. Something instead, that has seen the difficulties of life in Berlin but chose to accept them, that continues to build this good and proud city in contrast to a surrounding totalitarian presence that refuses to release human energies or aspirations. Something that speaks with a powerful voice of affirmation, that says yes to this city, yes to the future, yes to freedom. In a word, I would submit that what keeps you in Berlin is love—love both profound and abiding.

Perhaps this gets to the root of the matter, to the most fundamental distinction of all between East and West. The totalitarian world produces backwardness because it does such violence to the spirit, thwarting the human impulse to create, to enjoy, to worship. The totalitarian world finds even symbols of love and of worship an affront. Years ago, before the East Germans began rebuilding their churches, they erected a secular structure: the television tower at Alexander Platz. Virtually ever since, the authorities have been working to correct what they view as the tower's one major flaw, treating the glass sphere at the top with paints and chemicals of every kind. Yet even today when the sun strikes that sphere—that sphere that towers over all Berlin—the light makes the sign of the cross. There in Berlin, like the city itself, symbols of love, symbols of worship, cannot be suppressed.

As I looked out a moment ago from the Reichstag, that embodiment of German unity, I noticed words crudely spray-painted upon the wall, perhaps by a young Berliner: "This wall will fall. Beliefs become reality." Yes, across Europe, this wall will fall. For it cannot withstand faith; it cannot withstand truth. The wall cannot withstand freedom.

And I would like, before I close, to say one word. I have read, and I have been questioned since I've been here about certain demonstrations against my coming. And I would like to say just one thing, and to those who demonstrate so. I wonder if they have ever asked themselves that if they should have the kind of government they apparently seek, no one would ever be able to do what they're doing again.

Remembering the Wall

Wolfgang Thierse

The 1998 election of Wolfgang Thierse as president of
the Bundestag, Germany's lower house of parliament,
was one of the first actions by the western German political establishment to truly integrate eastern Germany after
German reunification on October 3, 1990. Thierse was
the first German Democratic Republic (GDR) politician
to reach one of the highest political positions in reinte-
grated Germany's democratic system. Before German reunification, Thierse taught literature and was a prominent civil rights activist in the GDR. While president of
the Bundestag, Thierse called for a "unification of memories," asking Germans of east and west to overcome their
divided past and become aware of their common history.

In August 1961 the Berlin Wall was erected to prevent East Germans who rejected communism from escaping to West Germany through West Berlin. Thierse, a
Berliner, tells how the wall shaped his life and the lives of
his family and friends in the following address given on
April 4, 2002. The whole world was transformed when
the wall fell on November 9, 1989, and Germany was
unified on October 3, 1990, he says. Thierse hopes the
fragments of the wall, which were presented to UN secretary general Kofi Annan, will keep the memory of the
peaceful revolution of 1989 alive. He hopes the fragments will not only preserve the memory of those within
the GDR who died protesting confinement behind the
wall, but further efforts to overcome divisions throughout
the world that threaten peace and human rights.

Wolfgang Thierse, address to Kofi Annan, Secretary General of the United Nations,
New York, April 4, 2002.

What once divided Germany also divided the United Nations. International tensions, the arms race and the ideological rivalry of the Cold War were played out here in the Security Council too. The Wall was present in many hearts and minds long before it became a physical reality. And when the Berlin Wall was finally consigned to history, it was not only the Germans who benefited. The United Nations, too, gained greater freedom, responsibility and creative scope. It can now resume its original purpose—which, after all, also had to do with Germany.

A Symbol of Suffering

For almost three decades, the Berlin Wall was by far the most visible monument to the division of Germany and the world. From the outset, it was a concrete metaphor for an inhuman policy. And from the outset, it was a symbol, for everyone to see, of a political cynicism, which was inherently prepared to inflict human suffering.

The Wall was built in August 1961. The GDR's German Democratic Republic's Communist leaders sought to present the intra-German border as the "anti-Fascist protection wall", claiming it was designed to fend off a preventive strike by the Western powers and preserve peace in Europe. Yet in reality, the brutal border installations had a very different purpose: to stop the mass exodus of East German citizens to the West. Between October 1949 and August 1961, around 2.7 million people had voted with their feet and fled the GDR. It was a damning indictment of the Communist regime.

When the Wall was built, I was 17 years old. When it finally came down, I was 46. The Wall has written itself into my personal history and has shaped my life and the lives of my family and friends in profound and painful ways. This is why it is so important to me personally to ensure that the memory of this time is kept alive. We owe it, above all, to the people whose protests against the Wall and opposition to being confined within the borders of the GDR cost them their lives.

Almost 1000 people died along the border between the two Germanies. More than 230 of them lost their lives at the

Berlin Wall. Some were shot dead by the GDR border guards, some drowned or died at road blocks, others plunged to their deaths from rooftops or even from homemade hot-air balloons. We still do not know exactly how many lives the border claimed.

The fall of the Berlin Wall in the peaceful revolution of autumn 1989 was one of the most joyous moments in European and German history. The restoration of our country's unity on 3 October 1990 was an event, which transformed not only Germany but also Europe and the world. Thanks to the policy of détente, thanks to sensible international compromises, and thanks to the peaceful revolution, it was possible to put an end to the division of the world into two hostile camps. And it was not only Germany but the entire international community, which benefited from this unprecedented historic act, to which so many contributed.

Overcoming Divisions

Yet not all the optimistic expectations have been fulfilled. Our shared hope that the end of the East-West conflict would usher in a Golden Age of Peace has proved elusive. The much-vaunted peace dividend has turned out to be extremely fragile. Here at the United Nations, you are familiar with the problems: I need only mention the Balkan conflicts and the Middle East. The challenge posed by terrorism—which, after the events of 11 September 2001, cannot be ignored—has still not been resolved, even though the changes taking place in Afghanistan give us cause for hope.

Secretary-General, Kofi Annan, on behalf of the German Bundestag, it is a great pleasure and honor for me to present you with three original segments of the Berlin Wall today, as a gift from the German people. Together with other symbols and sculptures, let them be a reminder to us all that lasting peace can only be achieved if we overcome divisions. That is one of the most important lessons we have learned from the cruel and horrific 20th century. And it is precisely this lesson which is symbolized by the image on the concrete, which shows two people embracing across the Wall.

The three sections come from the area around Potsdamer

Platz in the center of Berlin. They bear witness in stone to the Communist regime's contempt for human rights and dignity. But they also bear witness to the power of the popular will, civil courage, and the power of human reason.

These segments of the Wall are a tangible legacy of one of the most significant political turning points in post-war history. Germany did not acquire full equality under international law until 3 October 1990. It was not possible to draw a line under the Second World War in international law until German unity had been restored. Today, for the very first time in Germany's history, there is mutual recognition of all Germany's existing borders. At last, we have learned—and I hope we have learned this lesson well—how to deal with the fact that we are the European country with the highest number of immediate neighbors. Germany is now encircled by friends—a gratifying and novel experience for us.

The example of Berlin shows that building walls, locking a people in or shutting it out can never be a concept for lasting success. Walls can be made permeable. Walls can be torn down. Walls can be overcome. All that is needed is patience, persistence, determination, and friends and allies. That is the message which will be sent out by this political monument in the future. And perhaps it is also an encouraging symbol for your own work, Secretary-General, and for the work of the United Nations as a whole.

Appendix of Biographies

Edward J. Bloustein

Edward J. Bloustein, an educator and university administrator, was born in New York, New York, on January 20, 1925, the son of Polish Jewish immigrants. In 1943, Bloustein entered the U.S. Army as a private and was discharged in 1946 as a sergeant. After World War II, he entered New York University, later studying at Oxford on a Fulbright scholarship. He was awarded a Ph.D. from Cornell University in 1954 and continued his studies in law at Cornell, receiving his law degree in 1959.

While pursuing his degrees, Bloustein was an instructor of legal philosophy at Cornell and a political analyst for the U.S. Department of State. He served as a law clerk to Judge Stanley H. Fuld of the New York State Court of Appeals from 1959 to 1961 and joined the faculty of New York University School of Law in 1961. Bloustein was chosen to assume the presidency of Bennington College in Vermont in 1965. His success at Bennington led to his appointment as president of Rutgers in 1971, a position Bloustein held until his death in 1989. Bloustein achieved his goal of making Rutgers one of the nation's premier universities when Rutgers was invited to join the prestigious Association of American Universities in February 1989. Ten months later, on December 9, 1989, Bloustein suffered a fatal heart attack while on a business trip to the Bahamas.

Bloustein served as editor in chief of the *Cornell Law Review,* wrote articles for law, education, and psychology journals, and published several books, including *Nuclear Energy: Public Policy and the Law* and *The University and the Counterculture.*

Winston Churchill

Winston Churchill, considered one of the greatest political figures of the twentieth century, served as Great Britain's prime minister from 1940 to 1945 and 1951 to 1955, and led Britain to victory over Nazi Germany during World War II. Churchill was also a renowned orator and a Nobel Prize–winning author.

Churchill was born in Blenheim Palace, Oxfordshire, England, on November 30, 1874. He served in the British army in India and the Sudan but left the army in 1899 to become a war correspondent. He was taken prisoner during the Boer War and made headlines when he escaped. Churchill began his political career as a member of the Conservative Party but shifted to the Liberal Party when he saw a need for social reform. Churchill became First Lord of the Admiralty in 1911, in which capacity he helped modernize the British navy. He was one of the first to understand the potential of airplanes in war. Unable to influence the government's war policy during World War I, he rejoined the army. However, Prime Minister David Lloyd George brought Churchill back into government as Minister of Munitions, responsible for the production of tanks, airplanes, guns, and shells.

At the outbreak of World War II, Churchill, a staunch opponent of appeasement with Nazi Germany, was again appointed First Lord of the Admiralty. When Neville Chamberlain resigned as prime minister in May 1940, Churchill replaced him. Churchill formed an all-party government to unite public opinion behind the war effort and developed a strong relationship with U.S. president Franklin D. Roosevelt. Churchill eventually persuaded the United States to take part in the war against Germany and Italy.

After the war, Churchill was replaced by Clement Attlee. It was during this period when Churchill came to America to make his famous "Sinews of Peace" speech, in which he expressed his concern over the "iron curtain" that was descending across Europe, dividing democratic and Communist nations. Some analysts claim that the speech defined the East-West divisions that marked the beginning of the Cold War. Churchill was forced to concede a Soviet-dominated Eastern Europe, but his fear of Communist expansion never ceased.

Churchill returned to power in 1951 and was awarded the Nobel Prize for Literature for his six-volume treatise *The Second World War*. He retired from politics in 1955 and died on January 24, 1965.

Thomas J. Dodd

Thomas J. Dodd was born in Norwich, Connecticut, and received his degree in law from Yale University in 1934. During the Great Depression, Dodd served in the FBI and was appointed state director of the National Youth Administration. In 1938, Dodd became special assistant to the attorney general, prosecuting espionage and sabotage cases during World War II. After the war, when the Allies convened an international military tribunal to prosecute Nazi war criminals in Nuremberg, Germany, Dodd was appointed vice-chairman of the review board and later executive trial counsel. Dodd not only helped shape policy and prove the charges against

Nazi war criminals but revealed to the world the horrors of the concentration camps and the activities of the Gestapo and the SS.

On his return to the United States, Dodd became active in Democratic politics, serving as a U.S. congressman in 1952 and 1954 and as a senator from 1959 to 1970. As a member of the House, Dodd became an outspoken foe of communism and opposed any conciliation with Soviet leaders. He led the opposition to Nikita Khrushchev's visit to America. As a member of the Senate Foreign Relations Committee, Dodd was a champion of nations he believed were held captive by communism, particularly Eastern European nations such as Lithuania, Poland, and Hungary. Dodd was also President Lyndon B. Johnson's leading foreign policy spokesman in the Senate, vigorously defending the U.S. presence in Vietnam.

In 1962, Dodd published a collection of the speeches he made during the early years of the Cold War, *Freedom and Foreign Policy*. Dodd died at his Old Lyme, Connecticut, home on May 24, 1971.

Albert Einstein

Albert Einstein is often identified as the father of the theory of relativity. He was also a major contributor to quantum theory and in 1921 won the Nobel Prize in physics for his study of photoelectric effect. Einstein was born in Ulm, Germany, on March 14, 1879. Einstein's family moved to Milan, Italy, but Einstein remained in Munich to study mathematics and calculus. Despite barely-passing marks, he entered the Eidgenössische Technische Hochschule in Zurich, Switzerland, graduating in 1900 as a teacher of mathematics and physics. While his peers taught at universities, Einstein had not performed well enough to get a university position. He taught mathematics at private schools and found a position in the patent office in Bern from 1902 to 1909. Einstein earned his doctorate from the University of Zurich in 1905.

After publishing several papers on theoretical physics, Einstein became a lecturer at the University of Bern in 1908 and a professor of physics at the University of Zurich in 1909. He was appointed a full professor at the Karl-Ferdinand University in Prague, Czechoslovakia, in 1911. By 1913 Einstein had won international fame as a theoretical physicist. After winning the Nobel Prize, Einstein began to make international visits. While visiting the United States for the third time in 1932, Einstein was offered a post at Princeton. He was to spend seven months in Berlin each year and five months at Princeton. However, shortly after Einstein left Germany, the Nazis came to power, and he never returned. He had become a

Swiss citizen in 1902, and while retaining his Swiss citizenship, he became a U.S. citizen in 1940.

Einstein was a pacifist and supported conscientious objection. He became an active leader in the international antiwar movement in the 1920s. As a witness to the rise of Nazi power, however, Einstein came to advocate military preparedness against the threat of Nazism and wrote a famous letter to President Franklin D. Roosevelt, urging him to initiate a nuclear research program. However, Einstein soon recognized that nuclear weapons posed a threat to humanity, and so during the last decade of his life, he was an advocate of nuclear disarmament and international cooperation to prevent war. One week before his death, Einstein wrote a letter to fellow pacifist Bertrand Russell agreeing to put his name on a manifesto that urged all nations to give up nuclear weapons.

During World War II, Einstein contributed to the war effort by hand writing his 1905 paper on special relativity, which raised six million dollars at auction and is now in the Library of Congress. He left his scientific papers to the Hebrew University in Jerusalem before he died on April 18, 1955, in Princeton.

Dwight D. Eisenhower

Dwight D. Eisenhower was born on October 14, 1890, in Denison, Texas. In 1891 his parents moved to Abilene, Kansas, where he and his six brothers were raised on a salary that never exceeded $100 a month. In order to survive on a limited income, the Eisenhowers raised their own food and sold surplus for cash. The boys began work early to earn their own spending money. Despite these humble beginnings, all six Eisenhower boys achieved success.

Eisenhower graduated from West Point in 1915 and served with General Douglas MacArthur in the Philippines from 1935 to 1939. In 1942, while working under General George C. Marshall in the War Department, Eisenhower was placed in command of the invasion of North Africa, and in 1944, Marshall named Eisenhower the Supreme Allied Commander for the invasion of Europe. As the invasion's principal architect, Eisenhower is often best remembered for its success.

After the success of Operation Overlord and the drive through France and Germany, Eisenhower headed the European occupation forces for six months, later succeeding George C. Marshall as chief of staff. In 1949 Eisenhower accepted the presidency of Columbia University, in New York. However, in 1950 President Harry S. Truman recalled Eisenhower to active duty and put him in command of the North Atlantic Treaty Organization forces in Europe, a post he held until May 1952, when he won the Republican Presidential nomination. Eisenhower defeated Adlai Stevenson in both the 1952 and 1956 elections.

Eisenhower had aspirations to end the Cold War during his presidency, and he quickly halted the fighting in Korea, negotiating an uneasy truce on July 27, 1953. Efforts to ease tensions with the Soviet Union, however, were difficult to negotiate while still taking a firm stand against communism. Promises to free oppressed people behind the "iron curtain" involved more talk than action in Eisenhower's administration. Not only did the United States fail to support a 1956 anti-Communist revolt in Hungary, it also failed to support its allies—France, Great Britain, and Israel—in an attack on Egypt in that same year.

During Eisenhower's second term, Communist Fidel Castro successfully seized power in Cuba, and Soviet premier Nikita Khrushchev boycotted a summit conference at Paris in May 1960 after the Soviets shot down an America U-2 reconnaissance plane over the Soviet Union. Democrats believed Eisenhower was jeopardizing peace with these spy missions and also argued that the United States was falling behind the Soviet Union in the development of missiles and other weapons of the space age. Public support for Eisenhower's brand of foreign policy was waning, and although Eisenhower had groomed Richard Nixon as his successor, John F. Kennedy defeated Nixon in 1960.

During his retirement, Eisenhower was treated as an elder statesman, and Presidents Kennedy and Lyndon B. Johnson sought his advice on international problems. A serious heart attack in August 1965 ended his participation in public affairs. Eisenhower died at Walter Reed Army Hospital in Washington, D.C., on March 28, 1969.

Mikhail Gorbachev

Mikhail Gorbachev was born on March 2, 1931, in Privolnoye, a city in the Stavropol province of the Soviet Union. After studying law at Moscow University, where he met his wife Raisa, he joined the Communist Party, gradually increasing his influence. In 1970, Gorbachev was elected to the Supreme Soviet and in 1978 became the party's secretary of agriculture. Gorbachev joined the Politburo as Yuri Andropov's protégé in 1980. When Andropov became leader of the Soviet Union in 1983, Gorbachev assumed responsibility for the economy.

In 1985, following the death of Konstantin Chernenko, who had succeeded Andropov, Gorbachev became the leader of the Soviet Union and began a political, economic, and social program that radically altered the Soviet government. The slogans of Gorbachev's new program were *glasnost*, openness, and *perestroika*, restructuring. Under *glasnost*, the Soviet government began to allow greater freedom, which led to the release of political prisoners, an increase in emigration, an examination of corruption, and a reexamination of Soviet history. Gorbachev also began to improve relations with the United States in a series of summits with President Ronald Reagan, and in 1987 Gorbachev and Reagan signed an intermediate nuclear forces limitation treaty. In 1989 Gorbachev ended the Soviet occupation of Afghanistan and began withdrawing Soviet political control of Eastern Europe. For his contribution to reducing tension between the East and West, Gorbachev was awarded the Nobel Peace Prize in 1990.

The newly created Congress of People's Deputies voted Gorbachev executive president, but in 1990 and 1991 reform efforts seemed to stall, and remaining hardline Communists tried unsuccessfully to unseat Gorbachev. Shortly after the failed coup, Gorbachev dissolved the Communist Party and granted independence to the Baltic states. The federal Soviet government lost its influence. After the Commonwealth of Independent States was established in 1991, Gorbachev resigned as president.

Since his resignation, Gorbachev has headed international organizations, including Green Cross International, and has written several books, including his memoirs and *Perestroika: New Thinking for Our Country and the World*.

Ernesto "Che" Guevara

Ernesto "Che" Guevara was born in Rosario, Argentina, on June 14, 1928. Suffering from asthma, Guevara spent a lot of time at home reading the works of Karl Marx, Friedrich Engels, and Sigmund Freud. Guevara's family was opposed to the dictatorship of Juan Perón, and his mother was an activist. During a long series of political crises in Argentina, Guevara learned to despise military politicians, the influence of the U.S. dollar, and imperialism.

During his studies to be a doctor at the University of Buenos Aires, Guevara took several motorcycle journeys thorough Argentina, Peru, Colombia, and Venezuela, during which he encountered Latin American poverty. As a result of what he saw on these journeys, Guevara decided he did not want to become a middle-class general practitioner after passing his qualifying exams in 1953.

Guevara went to Guatemala but did not join the Communist Party, which meant he had little chance of gaining a medical appointment, so Guevara found himself penniless. It was during this time that he witnessed CIA involvement in the overthrow of Guatemala's social reform president, Jacob Arbenz, and came to believe that only armed insurrection would lead to successful revolutions against imperialism. From Guatemala, Guevara went to Mexico where he met Fidel Castro, whom he followed to Cuba. Guevara first served as a doctor and later as a successful guerrilla officer.

When Castro's revolutionaries succeeded in overthrowing Cuban dictator Fulgencio Batista in 1959, Guevara became Castro's second in command and was appointed governor of the national bank. In 1961 Guevara was made minister of industry and became increasingly hostile toward U.S. interests in the Cuban economy and began strengthening his relationship with the Soviet Union. During this time he signed a trade pact with the Soviets that freed Cuban industry from U.S. dependence. From 1961 to 1965 Guevara traveled the world as Cuba's ambassador with his wife Aledia March and was turning away from Soviet communism toward the teachings of Communist Chinese leader Mao Tse-tung. He encouraged revolution in Africa and began to attack the Soviet government for its revisionist philosophy and its policy of coexistence with capitalism. Guevara's increasing rebellion forced Castro to distance himself from Guevara. Guevara's last revolutionary venture was an attempt to oust Bolivian dictator General René Barrientos, but Guevara was captured and executed on October 9, 1967.

Guevara's refusal to bend to any kind of establishment, even if Communist, and his dedication to action made him an idol for the discontented American youth of the late 1960s and early 1970s who hoped to end what they believed to be a world of bourgeois industrial capitalism. Guevara wrote several books, including *Guerrilla Warfare, Man and Socialism in Cuba*, and *Reminiscences of the Cuban Revolutionary War.*

John F. Kennedy

John F. Kennedy was the nation's youngest and its first Roman Catholic president, elected in November 1960. During his brief time in office, Kennedy faced some of the most difficult challenges of the Cold War yet also achieved one of the first steps in relaxing Cold War tensions when he negotiated a nuclear test ban treaty in 1963. The U.S. space program advanced significantly during Kennedy's administration, which earned the United States worldwide prestige. Tragically, however, his term was brief; while riding in a motorcade in Dallas, Texas, he was assassinated on November 22, 1963.

Kennedy was born on May 29, 1917, in Brookline, Massachusetts, the second of nine children. Kennedy's forebears immigrated to Boston from Ireland, and his grandfather became a Boston political leader. Kennedy's father, Joseph, graduated from Harvard and became a bank president at twenty-five, slowly increasing the family fortune and encouraging the advancement of his children until the Kennedys became one of the most prominent families not only in Massachusetts, but in U.S. political history.

Kennedy's experiences at school and in Europe developed his understanding of foreign policy. He studied at the London School of Economics in 1935 and entered Harvard University in 1936. Several trips to Europe during the late 1930s gave Kennedy an opportunity to witness international politics first hand. In 1939, on a trip with his father, who was ambassador to Britain, Kennedy stayed at American embassies where he talked to newspapermen, political leaders, and diplomats. When Kennedy graduated *cum laude* from Harvard in June 1940, he published a well-received thesis, *Why England Slept*, which examined the British policies that led to the Munich Pact of 1938.

Kennedy served in the navy as a lieutenant in command of a PT boat during World War II. When his boat was rammed by a Japanese destroyer, he rallied the survivors to escape to an island where he risked his life to engineer their rescue. For these heroic acts Kennedy received the Purple Heart and the Navy and Marine Corps Medal. Unfortunately, during the rescue, Kennedy aggravated a back injury he had received while playing football at Harvard and was discharged in 1945.

After the war, Kennedy decided to pursue a career in politics. He was elected to the House of Representatives in 1946, 1948, and 1950. He became a senator in 1952 and on September 12, 1953, he married Jacqueline Bouvier. In 1958 he was reelected to the Senate and in 1960 formally announced his presidential candidacy. Kennedy defeated Nixon by a narrow margin.

Kennedy's inaugural address was devoted almost entirely to international affairs, and in the few short years of his presidency, he faced some of the nation's most memorable Cold War crises. In April 1961, a force of anti-Castro Cubans trained by the CIA failed to establish a beachhead in Cuba at the Bay of Pigs. This American interference in Cuba's affairs was criticized abroad but received support in the United States. Also during this time, Nikita Khrushchev, leader of the Soviet Union, threatened to sign a treaty with East Germany that would limit access to West Berlin. Kennedy advised Khrushchev that access to Berlin was extremely important to the West. When East Germany blocked access to West Berlin and began construction of a wall to prevent East Berliners from escaping to the West, Kennedy obtained money for armaments and ordered National Guard and reserve units into active service. Although Khrushchev did not sign a treaty, many within the United States and abroad felt that Kennedy's administration was not aggressive enough against Communist expansion.

In the eyes of much of the world, the 1962 Cuban Missile Crisis was the event that brought the East and West to the brink of nuclear war. U.S. aerial reconnaissance had revealed Soviet offensive missile bases under construction in Cuba. Despite assurances that these bases were defensive, not offensive, continued reconnaissance revealed the contrary. Kennedy demanded their removal, announced a quarantine on Soviet shipments to Cuba, and maintained U.S. armed forces at combat readiness. After an exchange of a series of letters between Kennedy and Khrushchev, the Soviet Union dismantled and withdrew its offensive weapons. Many credit Kennedy and his advisors with this major victory for the West in the Cold War.

Kennedy also fought Communist expansion in other parts of the world in a variety of ways. Kennedy provided aid to Latin American nations whose economic troubles he believed made them vulnerable to Communist revolution. Known as the Alliance for Progress, his ten-year plan for developing the Americas was signed by all Latin American countries except Cuba. Kennedy also strengthened defenses in Southeast Asia to combat Communist guerrilla warfare and increased the number of U.S. military advisers in Vietnam. He established the Peace Corps in March 1961. Headed by his brother-in-law, Sargent Shriver, the Peace Corps worked to improve the way of life and lay a foundation for freedom in underdeveloped nations of the world.

Kennedy was assassinated on November 22, 1963, by Lee Harvey Oswald. Oswald himself was fatally shot by Jack Ruby, a nightclub owner, as Oswald was being escorted through the basement of a Dallas police station. The Warren Commission concluded that neither Oswald nor Ruby "was part of any conspiracy, domestic or foreign, to assassinate President Kennedy." In 1979, however, the House Assassinations Committee concluded that Lee Harvey Oswald was probably part of a conspiracy that may have included members of organized crime.

Nikita Khrushchev

Nikita Khrushchev was one of the most colorful Soviet leaders, remembered for his dramatic gestures and enthusiastic belief that communism would ultimately triumph over capitalism. Khrushchev was born in Kalinovka, Russia, in 1894, the son of an illiterate peasant and coal miner. Unable to survive by farming, the family moved to an industrial center in Ukraine where Khrushchev began working at an early age. He became an activist at eighteen after helping a group of workers organize a strike protesting working conditions. Khrushchev continued his activism and after the Russian Revolution, in 1918 joined the Red Army and the Communist Party.

After the war, Khrushchev received formal training in Marxism and was appointed to a political post in Ukraine. As a result of his support for Stalin's struggle against Leon Trotsky and Nikolai Bukharin, Khrushchev advanced rapidly in the party, serving as a member of the Central Committee in 1934 and advancing to the Politburo in 1939. This was, however, a dark period in Soviet history known as the Great Terror. Soviet leader Joseph Stalin conducted a series of bloody purges to ensure his power, in which Khrushchev played a part.

After Joseph Stalin's death on March 5, 1953, a new "collective leadership" was instituted in the Soviet Union, and Khrushchev emerged as the secretary of the Communist Party. In a "secret" speech to the Party Congress in 1956, Khrushchev denounced Stalin and his policies, instituting a program that restored legal procedures, reduced the threat of the secret police, closed labor camps, and to some degree restored public debate. During Khrushchev's leadership, Alexandr Solzhenitsyn published his tale of life in the gulag camps, *One Day in the Life of Ivan Denisovich*, resulting in an entire movement of dissident writers and intellectuals. Although they remained underground, they would not have survived under Stalin. Destalinization created unrest in other Communist nations of Europe, resulting in defiance in Poland and Hungary, but Khrushchev quelled these revolutions. When Khrushchev replaced Nikolai Bulganin as premier, he became leader of both the state and the party.

Soviet relations with the rest of the world changed under the leadership of Khrushchev. Unlike Stalin, Khrushchev advocated peaceful coexistence with the West, although he continued to maintain the Soviet Union's strong control over Eastern Europe. Khrushchev met with President Dwight D. Eisenhower at Camp David and toured the United States in 1959. At the same time, however, the appeal of communism spread throughout Asia, Africa, and Latin America as the result of aid in forms such as dams and stadiums donated by the Soviet Union at the urging of

Khrushchev. When the Soviet Union was the first to launch a space satellite, *Sputnik*, the West began to fear that the Soviet Union was surpassing the technological superiority of the West. Khrushchev's philosophy of peaceful coexistence also brought him into conflict with Communist China and its belief in international revolution.

When the Soviet Union agreed to remove nuclear missiles placed in Cuba during the Cuban Missile Crisis, Khrushchev lost face at home and abroad and never regained his prestige. As a result of international crises and problems with agricultural production within the Soviet Union, Khrushchev was removed from power in October 1964 and retired to rural Russia where he died in 1971.

Henry Kissinger

Henry Kissinger was U.S. secretary of state from 1973 to 1977 and played a major role in formulating American foreign policy during this period. He established a policy of détente with the Soviet Union and pursued the normalization of relations with China. Kissinger also helped initiate the Strategic Arms Limitation Talks. A skilled negotiator, Kissinger arranged cease-fires between Israel and Egypt and between North Vietnam and the United States in 1973, for which he received the Nobel Peace Prize.

Kissinger was born in Fuerth, Germany, on May 27, 1923, but came to the United States in 1938, becoming a naturalized citizen in 1943. He studied at Harvard University, receiving a Ph.D. in 1954, and was a member of the Harvard University faculty in the Department of Government and at the Center for International Affairs between 1954 and 1971.

During World War II, Kissinger served in the U.S. Army Counter-Intelligence Corps and after the war, until 1949, was a captain in the Military Intelligence Reserve. During the 1960s Kissinger served as a consultant to the Department of State, the National Security Council, and the United States Arms Control and Disarmament Agency.

In addition to the Nobel Prize for Peace, Kissinger won the Presidential Medal of Freedom, the Medal of Liberty, the Veterans of Foreign Wars Dwight D. Eisenhower Distinguished Service Medal, the Hope Award for International Understanding, and awards for his writings, which include *Nuclear Weapons and Foreign Policy, The Necessity for Choice, The White House Years, Years of Upheaval,* and *Diplomacy*. Kissinger continues to lecture and serve as a consultant on international affairs.

Douglas MacArthur

One of the most controversial military figures in American history, Douglas MacArthur was born on January 26, 1880, the son of Arthur MacArthur Jr., who had led troops in the Civil War and the Spanish-American War. Douglas MacArthur lived his entire life in the United States Army. "My first memory was the sound of bugles," he recalls. After he graduated from West Point at the head of his class in 1903, MacArthur's first assignment as a young lieutenant was working with the corps of engineers in the Philippines. When MacArthur toured Asia with his father and mother shortly thereafter, he was convinced America's future lay in Asia.

After his father died, MacArthur was transferred to the War Department in Washington to be near and to care for his mother. While there, he was promoted to major and became the army's first public relations officer. MacArthur managed to sell the American people on the Selective Service Act of 1917 as the nation moved closer to involvement in World War I. During the war, MacArthur was promoted to brigadier general, helping lead the Rainbow Division in France. His feats of courage made him the most decorated American soldier of the war. MacArthur kept his rank after the war when he became superintendent of West Point where he initiated a program to produce officers at the Academy who could lead in modern warfare.

In 1930 MacArthur was appointed chief of staff of the U.S. Army, serving under both Presidents Herbert Hoover and Franklin D. Roosevelt. This was a troubling time for MacArthur as it was difficult to convince Americans about the dangers of fascism in Europe and Asia when people were struggling during the Great Depression. His reputation was damaged by the Bonus March of 1932, during which he led army troops to disperse impoverished World War I vets who had marched on the capital to demand the bonus they were promised for their military service during the war.

In 1935 MacArthur was again called to the Philippines to help establish the islands' independence. Unfortunately, MacArthur did not have enough time to build a force to defend the Philippines against the growing strength of Japan. After the attack on Pearl Harbor on December 7, 1941, by Japanese planes, MacArthur's air force was destroyed, and by January 1942, his forces had retreated to the Bataan Peninsula. Roosevelt ordered MacArthur to withdraw to Australia, which ran counter to MacArthur's sense of duty, and his promise "I shall return" became synonymous with the war in the Pacific.

Roosevelt then made MacArthur commander in chief of U.S.

forces in the Far East. MacArthur led his forces to victory in the battles of Midway, the Coral Sea, and Guadalcanal, and he liberated New Guinea and, eventually, the Philippines. On September 2, 1945, MacArthur presided over the Japanese surrender on board the *U.S.S. Missouri*, which brought an end to World War II. For the next five years, MacArthur was the Supreme Commander of the Allied Powers in Japan, during which he helped Japan rebuild.

When North Korea invaded South Korea in 1949, President Harry S. Truman named MacArthur commander of the United Nations forces. MacArthur drove North Korean forces beyond the 38th parallel to the Yalu River that divided North Korea from Communist China despite warnings that it would provoke Chinese intervention. When China did, in fact, intervene, MacArthur asked permission to bomb Chinese bases in Manchuria. Fearing war with China and the Soviet Union, Truman opposed MacArthur's strategy. When MacArthur made his disagreement with Truman public, Truman removed him from command on April 11, 1951.

MacArthur received a hero's welcome on his return to the United States, however. He lived a quiet life in New York until his death in 1964.

Mao Tse-tung

Mao Tse-tung was the chairman of the Chinese Communisty Party and founder of the People's Republic of China. An idealist who remained committed to the theory of Marxist-Leninism, Mao was thoroughly devoted to the Communist revolution in his country. Authorities estimate that over three million people were killed for voicing their opinion against Mao's policies during the first years of his regime.

The son of a prosperous peasant, Mao was born in the Hunan province of China on December 26, 1893. He received enough schooling to spark an interest in education, but in 1911 Sun Yat-sen led a revolution to overthrow the imperial government. After serving in the revolutionary army, Mao completed his studies, but rather than become a teacher, Mao went to Peking to work as an assistant in a university library.

While working in the library, Mao became active in radical student groups and in 1921 became a founding member of the Chinese Communist Party. Soon after, Mao developed his theory of the revolutionary potential of the peasantry, which deviated from the Soviet emphasis on the industrial proletariat. Mao put his theory to the test when he organized the peasantry for a guerrilla war against the Nationalist armies of Chiang Kai-shek between 1927 and 1945.

Chiang Kai-shek led a drive against Mao's Red Army of workers and peasants that forced them to escape to the northwest, but later Mao's army used its rural foundation to overwhelm the Nationalists. Mao proclaimed the People's Republic of China on October 1, 1949, establishing himself as Chairman of the party.

Mao immediately began to implement his economic and ideological plans. His regime is known for two movements: The Great Leap Forward, Mao's attempt to organize peasants into communes that some authorities claim resulted in starvation, and the Cultural Revolution, a campaign for ideological purity that authorities claim resulted in repression and death. The ideology of the Cultural Revolution was articulated in *The Little Red Book*, published in 1964 and compiled by army marshal Lin Piao. The book contains hundreds of excerpts from Mao's Communist philosophy. Quoting the book from memory, marauding bands of young people known as the Red Guard attacked anyone opposed to Marxist-Leninism, which led to anarchy in many Chinese cities. In 1969 the army was brought in to end the crisis.

Both China and the Soviet Union supported Communist forces in North Korea. China did not officially intervene, however, until UN forces drove North Korean forces to the Chinese border. Chinese forces retaliated and drove the UN forces back to the 38th parallel, and the war became a bloody stalemate. After two years both sides agreed to an armistice and a truce was signed on July 27, 1953.

Although China and the Soviet Union signed a defense pact in 1950, Sino-Soviet relations deteriorated as each nation vied for pre-eminence in the Communist movement. Nikita Khrushchev accused Mao of straying from true Marxist doctrine, and in 1960 Russian technicians and economic aid were withdrawn. In 1969 the Soviet Union and China fought a brief border war. In the 1970s the Sino-Soviet split helped Mao's regime accept normalization of relations with the United States. In 1972 President Richard Nixon visited Peking, and in 1976 President Gerald Ford also visited China. Mao died on September 9, 1976.

Eugene McCarthy

Eugene McCarthy is often remembered as a soft-spoken liberal senator who ran as an independent candidate for president in 1976, but he was also one of the first in government to articulate his opposition to President Lyndon B. Johnson's Vietnam War policy.

McCarthy was born in Watkins, Minnesota, in 1916. He received his B.A. from St. John's University in 1935 and his M.A. in sociology from the University of Minnesota in 1938. During World

War II, McCarthy served as a technical assistant for military intelligence. After the war, he returned to Minnesota to teach at the College of St. Thomas in St. Paul. McCarthy began his political career serving as a Democratic member of the U.S. House of Representatives from 1949 to 1959. He became a senator in 1959 and gained a reputation as an intellectual.

It was his opposition to President Lyndon B. Johnson's policies in Vietnam that won him the support of many liberals who supported his candidacy for the Democratic nomination in 1968. McCarthy began to observe confusion and inconsistencies in U.S. policy toward Vietnam. For example, Secretary of State Dean Rusk would announce that everything was under control in Vietnam, but the media would indicate turmoil within the South Vietnamese government. McCarthy also noted that Secretary of Defense Robert McNamara made confusing and contradictory estimations about the bombing and infiltration of North Vietnam. Despite these contradictions, McCarthy recalls, Johnson kept sending in more and more troops. Those who criticized Johnson's administration were accused of giving aid and comfort to the Communists.

By 1967 more than fifteen thousand U.S. servicemen had been killed in Vietnam, and large numbers of people in America and around the world were protesting the war. McCarthy's race for the presidential candidacy was backed by many college students, increasing numbers of whom were becoming opposed to what they believed was an immoral war. McCarthy was successful in early primaries, but he lost the nomination to Hubert Humphrey at the Democratic National Convention in Chicago, during which antiwar protests led to a violent riot with police.

McCarthy retired from the Senate in 1973 and resumed teaching. He has written several books, including *The Limits of Power* and *The Year of the People*.

Joseph R. McCarthy

Joseph R. McCarthy was born on November 14, 1908, in Grand Chute, Wisconsin. He graduated from Marquette University in Milwaukee, Wisconsin, in 1935. McCarthy practiced law in Wisconsin, becoming a circuit judge in 1940. During World War II, McCarthy fought in the Pacific as a captain in the U.S. Marines. After the war, he returned to Wisconsin and defeated twenty-two-year incumbent Robert La Follette Jr. for a seat in the U.S. Senate in 1946. McCarthy was reelected in 1952.

McCarthy's early years as a junior senator were rather unremarkable. However, his speech on February 9, 1950, at the

Women's Republican Club in Wheeling, West Virginia, won the senator national attention and established him as a crusader against Communist infiltration. In his speech McCarthy claimed to possess a list of 205 card-carrying Communists employed in the U.S. Department of State. Although the State Department personnel were eventually exonerated of his charges, McCarthy continued to make his allegations on radio and television appearances. When asked to produce evidence, he refused, making new accusations. Although his tactics were criticized, when the Republicans assumed control of the Congress in 1953, they appointed McCarthy chairman of the Senate Permanent Investigation Subcommittee. As chairman, he conducted widely publicized hearings on Communist subversion.

According to many authorities, McCarthy ruthlessly pursued people and often ruined careers based on flimsy evidence and unidentified informers. On December 2, 1954, the Senate voted to censure him, describing his actions as "contrary to senatorial tradition." McCarthy died in Bethesda, Maryland, on May 2, 1957. His notoriety, however, survived. The political practice of publicizing accusations of disloyalty or subversion with insufficient regard to evidence is now known as McCarthyism.

Walter F. Mondale

Walter F. Mondale was born in Ceylon, Minnesota, on January 5, 1928, the son of a Methodist minister. After serving in the U.S. Army during the Korean War, Mondale returned to the United States to earn his law degree from the University of Minnesota Law School in 1956. After serving as Minnesota's attorney general for two years beginning in 1960, he was elected governor in 1962. In 1964, he was asked to fill Hubert H. Humphrey's U.S. Senate seat when Humphrey was elected vice president. Mondale was reelected to the Senate in 1966 and 1972. While in the Senate, he initially supported U.S. involvement in Vietnam, but he later opposed the war.

Mondale served as Jimmy Carter's vice president from 1976 to 1980. During his service as vice president, Mondale was an influential foreign-affairs adviser to the president and acted as his emissary abroad.

Mondale ran as the Democratic presidential candidate in 1984, and was the first major-party candidate to select a woman, Geraldine Ferraro of New York, as his running mate. However, he faced an uphill battle against the popular incumbent, Ronald Reagan. After losing the 1984 presidential election, Mondale returned to his private law practice but remained involved in international affairs. In the spring of 1993, he was elected director of the Council on Foreign Relations and on August 13, 1993, was appointed U.S. ambassador to Japan. After his service ended in December 1997, Mondale again returned to private practice.

Richard M. Nixon

Richard M. Nixon was born in Yorba Linda, California, on January 9, 1913, to Quaker parents. Nixon served as undergraduate president while attending Whittier College in California. After he graduated from Whittier in 1934, Nixon received a scholarship to attend Duke University Law School in North Carolina, where he graduated third in his class. Nixon joined the navy in August 1942, serving as an air transport officer in the South Pacific. He was discharged in 1946 as a lieutenant commander.

During that same year, Nixon was elected to Congress. He became a member of the House Un-American Activities Committee and made a name for himself during the investigation into the Communist activities of Alger Hiss, a well-respected former official of the State Department and president of the Carnegie Endowment for International Peace. Hiss denied the charges but Nixon persisted, and Hiss was eventually convicted of perjury for his testimony. Nixon won a Senate seat in 1950, and his anti-Communist stance influenced his selection to be Dwight D. Eisenhower's running mate in 1952. The Eisenhower and Nixon ticket won in both 1952 and 1956.

While vice president, Nixon visited fifty-six countries. In 1958, Nixon and his wife, Pat, were the target of hostile demonstrations in Peru and Venezuela. Eisenhower dispatched troops to the Caribbean to protect Nixon, but instead Nixon canceled further appearances and was heralded for his courage in the face of such hostility. Nixon also gained the public's attention in 1959 during a visit to Moscow when he unexpectedly encountered Soviet leader Nikita Khrushchev in front of the kitchen exhibit of a model American house at the American National Exhibition. There Nixon successfully defended American interests in a verbal clash known as the "kitchen debate" with Khrushchev.

Although Nixon lost the 1960 election to John F. Kennedy and failed in a bid to become California's governor, he maintained his Republican Party ties and won the 1968 Republican presidential nomination and the election. It was during his first term as the nation's thirty-seventh president that Nixon achieved the successes in foreign policy for which he is remembered. As vice president he had became familiar with the international scene, and because of his broad understanding of foreign affairs and his skills as a negotiator, Nixon improved relations with Moscow and opened doors to China that had been closed for many years.

In his "Vietnamization" program, Nixon reduced the American role in the war in Vietnam, leaving the South Vietnamese to do their own fighting. He cut back American ground forces, which fell from 540,000 in 1972 to zero in 1973, when the draft was ended. A series of unannounced negotiations between North Vietnamese diplomats and Nixon's secretary of state, Henry Kissinger, revealed Nixon's willingness to make concessions, eventually resulting in a cease-fire on January 28, 1973. Nixon also obtained the release of nearly six hundred U.S. prisoners of war.

In January 1973, after his reelection, news of a government cover-up emerged during the trial of burglars who broke into the Democratic National Committee headquarters at the Watergate office building in Washington, D.C. The burglars and two coplotters—G. Gordon Liddy and E. Howard Hunt—were indicted on charges of burglary, conspiracy, and wiretapping. H.R. Haldeman and John D. Ehrlichman, two of Nixon's top aides, resigned. White House counsel John Dean, who had been dismissed, became the star witness during televised Senate hearings that exposed the White House cover-up and illegalities in Republican fund raising. On July 24, 1974, the U.S. Supreme Court ordered Nixon to surrender tapes he had made of office meetings and telephone conversations, and on August 5, Nixon released the tapes. The tapes indicated that he had halted an FBI probe of the Watergate burglary, which was essentially an admission of obstruction of justice. Impeachment appeared inevitable. For the first time in American history, on August 9, 1974, a president resigned. A month later, after assuming the presidency, Gerald R. Ford pardoned Nixon for any offenses he might have committed, which ended any possible prosecution.

After years of seclusion in San Clemente, California, in 1977 Nixon appeared in televised interviews conducted by journalist David Frost. Although the public remained divided in their opinions of Nixon, he resumed public appearances and traveled abroad on personal diplomatic missions. Nixon published several books, including *RN: The Memoirs of Richard Nixon*, *No More Vietnams*, and *The Real War*. He died in New York City on April 22, 1994.

Ronald Reagan

Ronald Reagan was born in Tampico, Illinois, on February 6, 1911. After he graduated from Eureka College near his home in

Dixon, Illinois, he began his entertainment career as a radio sports announcer in Davenport, Iowa. In 1937, while covering baseball's spring training in California, Reagan was "discovered" by an agent from Warner Brothers, who signed him to play a radio announcer in *Love is on the Air*. Reagan went on to appear in over fifty movies in a film career that lasted nearly thirty years.

Reagan took a break from his acting career during World War II while he served in the U.S. Army making training films. In 1947 he became president of the Screen Actors Guild, and it was during this time that he came to believe that Communist infiltration was a serious threat to the nation. In consequence, his liberal political philosophy became transformed into a more conservative one. He joined the Republican Party in 1962. Reagan impressed a group of businessmen who had heard his inspiring speech in support of Senator Barry Goldwater's campaign for the presidency, and they suggested he run for governor of California. During his campaign against the popular incumbent Edmund G. Brown Sr., Reagan took a stand against campus radicals and welfare cheaters and won by a substantial margin. During his eight years as California's governor, Reagan learned the realities of political leadership. Despite a hostile Democratic legislature, he managed to achieve some of his goals, including welfare reform and reducing funding of California universities, which he believed were too lenient with student demonstrators.

After serving as California's governor, Reagan decided to run for president. During the 1980 campaign, while Reagan attacked what he claimed were President Jimmy Carter's failed economic policies, Carter argued that Reagan was likely to lead the United States into war with the Soviet Union. During most of the campaign, polls showed neither candidate had captured the public's interest, but in the final days of the campaign, Reagan managed to pull ahead of Carter and win the election. In the 1984 campaign, Reagan won every state but Minnesota and gathered the greatest number of electoral votes ever tallied by a presidential candidate.

Although the Nixon and Ford administrations supported a foreign policy of détente with the Soviet Union, Reagan took a harder line against communism. During his first term, relations between the Soviet Union became strained. In 1983, the United States began to deploy intermediate-range missiles in Western Europe, and in October of that same year, Reagan ordered the invasion of Grenada, fearing the country had become a potentially dangerous Cuban-Soviet military base.

During Reagan's second term his growing friendship with Soviet leader Mikhail Gorbachev improved U.S.-Soviet relations. In 1985, however, Reagan proposed the Strategic Defense Initiative (SDI), the technological pursuit of defensive weapons in space, which led to stalled negotiations between the United States and the Soviet Union on an intermediate-range nuclear forces (INF) treaty. However, the treaty was ultimately signed by both leaders in 1987.

Reagan's policy of assisting anti-Communist guerrillas in Nicaragua resulted in the most damaging event of his presidential career. In 1986, members of his administration admitted that they had been secretly selling arms to Iran in exchange for hostages, using some of the profits to finance the Contras in Nicaragua. These policies led to an investigation, and a presidential commission concluded that Reagan's relaxed policy with his advisors kept him uninformed of the diversion of funds. Although his role in the affair could not be determined, he failed to ensure that the law was upheld.

Reagan's involvement in the questionable affair did not seem to influence his popularity with the American people, however, and he came to be known as the Teflon-coated president—nothing stuck to him, not Iran-Contra nor allegations that he was influenced by astrology. Although Reagan was wounded in an assassination attempt in 1981 and underwent surgery for colon cancer in 1985, he always remained positive.

Reagan retired with his wife, Nancy, to Bel-Air, California. He had been in retirement for five years when he learned he had Alzheimer's disease. Reagan withdrew from public view on November 5, 1994, after writing a poignant open letter about his diagnosis to the American people.

Dean Rusk

Dean Rusk was born in Cherokee County, Georgia, on February 9, 1909. He graduated from Davidson College in North Carolina in 1931 and received a Rhodes scholarship that allowed him to study at Oxford, where he focused on international affairs. Rusk returned to the United States to teach government at Mills College, in Oakland, California, where he also served as dean of faculty. He studied law at the University of California, Berkeley, graduating in 1940. In the same year, he was called to active duty. During World War II, Rusk served in the U.S. Army in the China-Burma-India theater and was discharged as a colonel.

After World War II, Rusk served in several positions within the Department of State. He was assistant secretary of state for Far Eastern affairs, playing a role in the decision to take military action in Korea. From 1952 to 1961, Rusk was president of the Rockefeller Foundation and was later appointed secretary of state by John F. Kennedy after the 1960 election. Rusk remained in this position until 1969.

While secretary of state, Rusk advocated military force to prevent Communist expansion and was a staunch defender of the war in Vietnam. He also encouraged economic aid to underdeveloped nations to prevent the spread of communism. Rusk advocated negotiations that culminated in the 1963 nuclear test ban treaty with the Soviet Union and supported low tariffs that would encourage world trade.

When Rusk retired from public service in 1970, he returned to Georgia where he taught international law at the University of Georgia until 1984. He established the Dean Rusk Center for International and Comparative Law at the university and remained active in university affairs until his death on December 20, 1994.

In 1963, Rusk published selections of his speeches in his book *The Winds of Freedom* and in 1990, the book *As I Saw It*, coauthored with his son Richard.

Margaret Chase Smith

Margaret Chase Smith was born in Skowhegan, Maine, on December 14, 1897. As a young woman, Smith showed an independence uncommon for women at the time. During the 1920s, she founded the Skowhegan Business and Professional Women's Club. Smith taught school, served as a textile mill executive, and managed circulation for the Skowhegan newspaper, the *Independent Reporter*. She was elected to the U.S. House of Representatives in 1940, succeeding her husband upon his death. After four terms in the House, Smith became a U.S. Senator in 1948.

Early in her career as a legislator, Smith served on the House Naval Affairs Committee and won status for women in the military. During Cold War tensions in 1954, she personally financed a trip to twenty-three countries to inform herself about conditions in the postwar world. Smith conferred with leaders such as Winston Churchill, Charles DeGaulle, V.B. Molotov, and Chiang Kai-shek. Her interviews and reports brought Smith respect as a world leader when they were aired on *See It Now*, a program hosted by famed journalist Edward R. Murrow. Later in her career she sponsored legislation that committed the federal government to medical research and also supported the space program, serving as a charter member of the Senate Aeronautical and Space Committee.

Smith first gained national attention when in a Senate speech she denounced Senator Joseph McCarthy's crusade to purge the government of Communists. She was the only woman in the Senate when she signed a declaration made by seven Republican senators that denounced McCarthy's tactics. Smith also found herself in the national spotlight as a result of her criticism of the Kennedy administration's foreign policy when she exposed inconsistencies in the policies of Secretary of Defense Robert S. McNamara. As a result of her opposition, Smith was the first woman nominated for the U.S. presidency. At the Republican National Convention, Smith placed second to Barry Goldwater, who was defeated by Lyndon Johnson in November 1964.

During the remainder of her political career, Smith continued to exercise her influence. She played a significant role in Senate deliberations over the Anti-Ballistic Missile Treaty and other arms control efforts. Smith finally lost reelection in 1972 and retired to Skowhegan where she continued to meet with constituents, politicians, policy makers, and school children in the Margaret Chase Smith Library. She died at her home on Memorial Day, May 29, 1995.

Adlai Stevenson

Adlai Stevenson was born in Los Angeles, California, on February 5, 1900, and six years later his family moved to Bloomington, Illinois. Stevenson grew up in a political family. His grandfather had served as vice president to Grover Cleveland, and the presence of politicians and talk of politics were part of family life.

In 1922 Stevenson graduated from Princeton, and in 1926 received his law degree from Northwestern University. He practiced law in Chicago and began his career in government service in the 1930s during the Great Depression. Stevenson served as special counsel to the Agricultural Adjustment Administration and then was assistant general counsel to the Federal Alcohol Bureau. During World War II, Stevenson was assistant to the U.S. secretary of the navy and became special assistant to Secretary of State Edward Stetinius in 1945. Also in 1945, Stevenson attended the San Francisco Conference that founded the United Nations, to which he would later serve as U.S. ambassador until his death on July 14, 1965 in London.

Stevenson was elected governor of Illinois in 1949. During his term as governor, his reforms gained him notoriety, and he became the Democratic presidential candidate in 1952 and 1956. According to many authorities, Stevenson was not running against Republican Dwight D. Eisenhower in 1952 but against the problems of the previous Democratic administration of Harry S. Truman—allegations of Communist infiltration, corruption in government, and the war in Korea. Stevenson was soundly defeated by Eisenhower in both elections.

Despite these defeats, Stevenson continued to have significant influence within the United States and abroad. Although he aspired to be John F. Kennedy's secretary of state, when Kennedy was elected in 1960, Kennedy appointed Stevenson ambassador to the UN. However, Kennedy did make Stevenson's appointment a cabinet position to ensure Stevenson would have a voice in making policy and to emphasize the importance of the UN as a forum for foreign policy. While ambassador, Stevenson worked to strengthen the UN and to resist Soviet efforts to weaken the office of secretary general. While ambassador, Stevenson emphasized the importance of halting the arms race and putting an end to nuclear testing. Partly as a result of Stevenson's efforts, in 1963 the Kennedy administration banned nuclear testing in the atmosphere, under water, and in space.

Stevenson was admired and respected by many. He was considered an excellent orator with a sharp wit who raised the level of political debate among voters in the United States. Stevenson was also a prolific writer. His works include *Call to Greatness*, *Friends and Enemies*, and *Putting First Things First*.

Wolfgang Thierse

The son of an attorney, Wolfgang Thierse was born on October 22, 1943, in Breslau, Germany. He studied culture at Humboldt University in East Berlin, and after he graduated he worked as an assistant in the cultural theory and aesthetics department at the university. Thierse was also a prominent civil rights activist in the German Democratic Republic (GDR). After taking part in a civil rights protest in 1976, Thierse was dismissed from government service and went to work at the Central Institute for Literary History at the Academy of Sciences.

In 1989, as the GDR was crumbling, Thierse joined the Party of Democratic Socialism (SPD), and when Germany was reunited on October 3, 1990, Thierse was elected to the Bundestag and selected to be the deputy chairman of the SPD. During his time in the Bundestag, Thierse spoke out against his party for its lack of sensitivity to the problems of eastern Germans. The election of Thierse as president of the Bundestag, however, was one of the first actions by the west German political establishment to truly integrate east Germany after German unification. While president of the Bundestag, Thierse called for a "unification of memories," asking Germans of east and west to overcome their divided past and become aware of their common history.

On November 9, 1999, at the tenth anniversary of the fall of the Berlin Wall, Thierse spoke of the significance of the wall in the modern history of the world while standing beside former Soviet president Mikhail Gorbachev, former U.S. president George Bush, German chancellor Gerhard Schroeder, and Schroeder's predecessor Helmut Kohl. Thierse presented fragments of the wall to UN secretary general Kofi Annan on April 4, 2002, suggesting that the fragments would keep the memory of the peaceful revolution of 1989 alive.

Harry S. Truman

Harry S. Truman was born in Lamar, Missouri, on May 8, 1884. Truman served as a field artillery captain in France during World War I. After the war, he began his political career in Kansas City. He became a senator in 1934 and during World War II headed the Senate committee that investigated waste and corruption during the war, thereby helping the United States save as much as $15 billion.

After only a few weeks as vice president, Truman assumed the presidency upon the death of Franklin D. Roosevelt on April 12, 1945. Roosevelt, beloved by many, had been the nation's president since 1932, throughout the Great Depression and most of World War II. Truman told reporters at that time, "I felt like the moon, the stars, and all the planets had fallen on me." With little briefing, Truman indeed faced some difficult wartime problems. Although the war in Europe ended less than one month later, Japan would not surrender. Truman made the difficult decision to order atomic bombs dropped on Hiroshima and Nagasaki, and, shortly after, Japan surrendered. Although Truman witnessed the signing of the United Nations Charter in June 1945, he was forced to deal with the threat of Communist expansion throughout his presidency.

Truman is perhaps best remembered for his Cold War foreign policy. The Truman Doctrine provided aid to Greece and Turkey, nations that appeared to be under pressure from the Soviet Union. The Truman Doctrine was followed by a more expansive plan named for Truman's secretary of state, George C. Marshall. The Marshall Plan stimulated economic recovery in Western Europe, which had been ravaged by war. After his election in 1948, Truman created a massive airlift to supply Berliners with food and supplies when the Soviets blockaded West Berlin and in 1949 negotiated a military alliance among Western nations, the North Atlantic Treaty Organization. In June 1950, North Korea invaded South Korea, and Truman and his advisors agreed that the United States and the UN could not back away from this Communist aggression. However, Truman limited the war to Korea, refusing to risk a major conflict with either China or the Soviet Union.

Truman did not run for another term but retired to Independence, Missouri. He died on December 26, 1972.

Chronology

1943
November 28: The Big Three—Churchill, Stalin, and Roosevelt—meet for the first time to begin discussing the shape of the post–World War II world.

1945
February 4–11: The Big Three meet again at Yalta. Stalin pledges to enter the war against Japan. The Declaration on Liberated Europe, promising free elections in postwar Europe, is signed.

July: The Soviet Union insists on occupying territories in Eastern Europe at the Potsdam Conference.

August 6 and 9: The United States detonates atomic bombs over Hiroshima and Nagasaki, Japan, bringing an end to the war in the Pacific.

October: U.S. Secretary of State James Byrnes and Soviet foreign minister V.B. Molotov meet to begin discussions on the fate of postwar Europe.

1946
March 15: During a speech delivered in Fulton, Missouri, Winston Churchill warns that an "iron curtain" divides the nations of Europe.

June: Congress establishes the Atomic Energy Commission under the Atomic Energy Act of 1946.

October: Soviet-American negotiations over a World War II peace settlement stall.

1947
March: Congress provides aid to Greece and Turkey, implementing the Truman Doctrine, which calls for the United States to offer financial assistance to countries resisting Soviet takeover.

June: In accordance with the Marshall Plan, developed by

Secretary of State George Marshall, the United States offers assistance for the economic recovery of sixteen European nations ravaged by World War II.

1948

February: Supported by the Soviet army and Soviet influence, both of which were already strong in Czechoslovakia, Czech Communists carried out a coup in Prague.

June: Soviet troops block Western access to Berlin. The United States, Britain, and France airlift more than 2 million tons of food and supplies to the city for fifteen months.

August: Congressman Richard Nixon and the House Un-American Activities Committee charge Alger Hiss, a respected official formerly with the State Department, with treason.

1949

April 4: Several Western nations form the North Atlantic Treaty Organization (NATO), a common defense alliance to counterbalance Soviet forces in Eastern Europe and to check further Soviet expansion.

August 29: The Soviet Union explodes an atomic bomb at Semipalatinsk in Kazakhstan.

September: In alliance with the Soviet Union, Communists under Mao Tse-tung seize control of China from U.S. ally, Chiang Kai-shek.

October 7: The German Democratic Republic, also called East Germany, is formed.

1950

February: Senator Joseph McCarthy pursues an anti-Communist crusade, also known as the Red Scare.

June 25: Communist North Korea invades South Korea. The United Nations authorizes deployment of soldiers, including U.S. troops, to support South Korea. The Korean War begins.

December: An infusion of Chinese forces checks the success of American-led UN forces commanded by General Douglas MacArthur.

1951
April: President Harry S. Truman relieves MacArthur of command for insubordination in pressing for an invasion of China.

1952
November 1: The United States tests its first hydrogen bomb.

November 4: Dwight D. Eisenhower is elected president of the United States.

1953
March 5: Joseph Stalin dies.

June: Soviet troops quell anti-Communist revolts in East Germany.

June: The CIA engineers the overthrow of an Iranian regime unfriendly to the United States, installing the shah of Iran.

July 27: A truce in the Korean War is reached.

August 14: The Soviet Union explodes its first hydrogen bomb.

September 12: Nikita Khrushchev becomes chairman of the Communist Party of the Soviet Union.

1954
June: The CIA engineers the overthrow of a regime unfriendly to the United States in Guatemala.

July: The Geneva Accord partitions Vietnam at the 17th parallel, dividing the nation into Communist North Vietnam and democratic South Vietnam.

September 8: The Southeast Asian Treaty Organization is established, unifying Australia, Great Britain, France, New Zealand, Thailand, the Philippines, Pakistan, and the United States in an agreement to support each other against aggression.

1955
May 14: The Soviet Union and seven Eastern European countries sign the Warsaw Pact to ensure a unified command against NATO.

June 15: Nationwide civil defense exercises begin in the United States to prepare against nuclear attack.

July 18–23: Eisenhower and Khrushchev meet for the first time in Geneva, Switzerland.

1956

February 14: In his "secret speech" at the Twentieth Party Congress, Khrushchev details Stalin's crimes against the Soviet Union, including the murder of political opponents and criminal misleadership in World War II.

October 29: British, French, and Israeli troops attack Egypt to take back control of the Suez Canal; the United States refuses to help.

November: Soviet tanks crush a national rebellion against communism in Hungary and thousands flee to the West.

1957

October 4: The Soviet Union launches the first space satellite, *Sputnik*, challenging the United States's scientific supremacy.

1958

July: U.S. Marines land in Lebanon in support of local pro-Western government.

November: Khrushchev demands that the United States withdraw troops from West Berlin and declare it a "free city."

1959

February: Fidel Castro seizes control of Cuba, overthrowing right-wing dictator Fulgencio Batista, despite U.S. support for Batista.

September 15: Khrushchev begins his visit to the United States; he is denied access to Disneyland because, he is told, adequate security preparations could not be made.

1960

May 1: An American U-2 spy plane is shot down over the Soviet Union. Khrushchev demands an apology, but Eisenhower denies it was a spy plane. An East-West summit in Paris is ruined. The pilot, Gary Powers, was convicted of espionage and sentenced to three years imprisonment and seven years of hard labor in the Soviet Union.

November 8: After a campaign calling for an intensified American commitment to fighting the Cold War, John F. Kennedy is elected president of the United States.

1961

January: President Eisenhower's farewell address warns against the dangers of the "military-industrial complex" in the United States.

March: President Kennedy proposes the Alliance for Progress to extend economic aid to Latin America.

April: A U.S.-sponsored attempt by fifteen hundred Cuban exiles to oust Fidel Castro fails at the Bay of Pigs.

April: Soviet cosmonaut Yuri Gagarin gains worldwide fame as the first man to travel in space aboard the *Volstok1* spacecraft.

June: Kennedy and Khrushchev meet in Vienna, Austria. Khrushchev calls for support for "wars of national liberation" and demands Western withdrawal from Berlin.

August: East Germany erects the Berlin Wall to stem the flight of its citizens to the West.

1962

The Kennedy administration intensifies its military commitment to South Vietnam, which is trying to stop Communist North Vietnam's drive to conquer the whole country with the assistance of China, Russia, and South Vietnam's Communist Vietcong.

October: President John F. Kennedy orders a blockade of Cuba to prevent Soviet shipments of nuclear missiles. Threat of nuclear war recedes when Khrushchev halts work on launch sites and removes missiles already in Cuba.

1963

June 26: Kennedy visits Berlin and makes the proclamation that he says represents the world of freedom: "*Ich bin ein Berliner*—I am a citizen of Berlin."

July 25: The United States and the Soviet Union ratify a nuclear test ban treaty that prohibits tests in the atmosphere, underwater, and in space.

November 1: President Ngo Dinh Diem of South Vietnam is assassinated.

November 22: President John F. Kennedy is assassinated in Dallas, Texas; Lyndon B. Johnson takes over the presidency.

1964

August 7: Congress authorizes expansion of involvement in Vietnam by passing the Gulf of Tonkin Resolution after a questionable attack of two American destroyers by North Vietnamese torpedo boats in the Gulf of Tonkin.

October 15: Leonid Brezhnev replaces Khrushchev as chairman of the Communist Party of the Soviet Union.

October 16: China tests an atomic bomb.

November 3: Lyndon B. Johnson is elected President of the United States.

1965

April: U.S. Marines are sent to the Dominican Republic in the name of anticommunism.

July: President Johnson announces that 150,000 U.S. troops will be dispatched to Vietnam.

1967

Anti-war rallies are staged in several U.S. cities and in Europe.

June: President Johnson and Soviet leader Alexei Kosygin meet at Glassboro, New Jersey. The meeting accomplishes very little. An attempt is made to move toward an anti-ballistic missile (ABM) treaty, but Kosygin does not want to discuss the issue.

July: American troops in South Vietnam number four hundred thousand.

1968

January 23: North Korean patrol boats seize the U.S.S. *Pueblo*, a U.S. Navy intelligence-gathering vessel, in international waters in the East Sea off Wonsan. Strong public demand arises in the United States for retaliatory action against North Korea.

February: The Tet Offensive, a massive Vietcong and North Vietnamese offensive strike against the cities of South Vietnam, reveals the continuing strength of the North Vietnamese army. The attacks are broadcast into the living rooms of Americans who begin to see sights such as South Vietnam's General Luan raising his revolver to the head of a captured Vietcong and killing him.

August 22: In Prague, Czechoslovakia, Soviet troops crush a revolt against the nation's Communist government.

August 26–29: Police and National Guard troops use tear gas and clubs to keep "hippies" and militants away from the Chicago Democratic Convention.

November 5: Richard M. Nixon is elected president of the United States.

1969

March: The United States begins heavy bombardment in Cambodia in an effort to eliminate Communist supply routes.

June 5: U.S. Secretary of State Henry Kissinger and Xuan Thuy of North Vietnam begin secret meetings to discuss peace.

July 20: *Apollo II* lands on the moon.

November 3: Nixon declares his Vietnamization plan, reducing the American role in Vietnam and leaving the South Vietnamese to do their own fighting.

1970

January: Nixon announces a doctrine requiring American allies to assume some of the military and financial burdens for the containment of communism.

May 4: Four Kent State University students are killed in a demonstration against intervention in Cambodia.

June 11: The Soviet Union agrees to continue support of North Vietnam.

December 7: The chancellor of West Germany, Willie Brandt, signs a cooperation treaty between Poland and West Germany.

1971
April 10: The U.S. ping-pong team arrives in China, the first group of Americans allowed into China since the Communist takeover in 1949.

1972
February: President Nixon reopens severed ties with China during a ten-day official visit.

April 10: The United States and the Soviet Union sign a biological weapons ban treaty.

May 26: Nixon and Brezhnev sign the SALT I treaty, which freezes the number of nuclear missiles possessed by each superpower.

December 21: West and East Germany sign a mutual relations treaty.

1973
January: The United States and North Vietnam agree on a cease-fire.

March: U.S. army troops withdraw from Vietnam.

September: The United States helps engineer the overthrow of the leftist regime of Chilean president Salvador Allende.

October: Egypt and Syria attack Israel; Egypt's president Anwar Sadat requests Soviet aid.

November 7: Congress passes the War Powers Act, mandating that "in every possible instance" the president must consult with Congress before sending American troops into a war.

December: Oil producers in the Persian Gulf double the price of oil.

1974
July: Congress passes the Jackson-Vanik amendment, tying Soviet-American trade to Soviet willingness to permit Jewish dissidents to leave the Soviet Union.

August 9: Nixon resigns in the wake of the Watergate scandal; Gerald R. Ford becomes president.

1975
April 30: Vietnam War ends as Communist North Vietnamese forces occupy Saigon without resistance.

July 15–24: Joint efforts by Soviet and U.S. scientists, astronauts, and cosmonauts result in the *Apollo-Soyuz* rendezvous in space.

August 1: The Helsinki Accord is signed. Thirty-five countries, including the United States and the Soviet Union, accept the Eastern European boundaries as permanent. Soviets agree to adopt a more liberal human rights policy.

November 11: Angola achieves independence from Portugal. Soviets fly Cuban troops to Angola in a move Kissinger describes as a dangerous escalation of the Cold War.

1976
November: Jimmy Carter is elected president of the United States.

1978
September: Carter successfully mediates the Egyptian-Israeli Camp David Accords, which assure Israel's withdrawal from the strategically important Sinai Peninsula.

1979
January: The United States and China begin to establish diplomatic bonds.

July: Carter and Brezhnev agree to SALT II, which limits each country to twenty-four hundred nuclear arms launchers.

November: The shah of Iran is overthrown; American hostages are seized in Iran.

December 25: The Soviet Army invades Afghanistan on Christmas Day. Soviets will suffer sixty thousand casualties in its nine-year war against Afghan guerrillas.

1980

January 4: The United States stops wheat sales to the Soviet Union.

February 20: Carter announces a boycott of the Moscow Olympic Games.

April 24: An attempt to rescue U.S. hostages in Iran fails.

September: The independent trade union Solidarity is founded in Poland under Lech Walesa.

November 4: Ronald Reagan is elected president of the United States.

1981

November: Reagan signs the secret National Security Decision Directive 17 authorizing the CIA to train and equip the Contras in their war with the Sandinistas in Nicaragua.

November 18: President Reagan announces his "zero-option" offer to the Soviets: The United States will not deploy cruise missiles in Europe if the Soviets remove their intercontinental ballistic missiles (IBMs). The Soviets reject the offer.

1982

November 10: Brezhnev dies and is replaced by Yuri Andropov.

1983

March: Reagan proposes the Strategic Defense Initiative (SDI). SDI technology would shoot down enemy nuclear missiles before they reach their targets.

March 8: Reagan refers to the Soviet Union as an "evil empire."

August: Soviets shoot down a Korean civilian airliner they claim violated Soviet air space.

October: A terrorist explosion kills 239 U.S. soldiers in their barracks in Lebanon.

October: U.S. troops are sent to Grenada to eliminate a regime friendly to Moscow and Cuba.

1984

January 17: Arms limitation talks between NATO and Warsaw Pact begin.

February 9: Andropov dies and is replaced by Konstantin Chernenko.

March: Reagan visits China, agreeing to sell sophisticated weapons to the Chinese.

August: Many Eastern European countries boycott the Los Angeles Olympic Games.

1985

January: Reagan calls upon the United States to defend "freedom and democracy . . . on every continent."

February 4: Reagan requests three times the military budget to support SDI.

March 10: Chernenko dies and is replaced by Mikhail Gorbachev, who launches an economic and political restructuring program called *perestroika.*

April 7: Gorbachev declares a definitive stop to missile deployment in Europe.

1986

Gorbachev begins to withdraw economic support from Soviet satellite states, including Cuba.

October 11: Gorbachev and Reagan meet in Reykjavik, Iceland, and shock the world by agreeing to remove all intermediate-range nuclear missiles from Europe.

November: The Iran-Contra affair is revealed to the American people. Members of Reagan's administration sold arms to Iran and extended clandestine support to the Contras in Nicaragua through the profits from the arms sales.

1987

December: Reagan and Gorbachev meet in Washington to sign a treaty to remove all medium- and short-range nuclear missiles.

1988

July 16: The Warsaw Pact demands a three-step decrease of conventional weapon units in Europe.

November: George Herbert Walker Bush is elected president of the United States.

December: Gorbachev renounces the Brezhnev Doctrine, thereby permitting greater freedom to the states of Eastern Europe.

1989

January: Soviet troops withdraw from Afghanistan.

June: The Communist regime in China responds with force to protests for democracy in Tiananmen Square.

June: Poland becomes independent of Soviet influence, and Lech Walesa and Solidarity come to power.

September: Hungary becomes independent of Soviet influence and the new regime permits East Germans to escape through Hungary to West Germany.

November: The Berlin Wall falls and the East German government opens the country's borders.

December: Communist regimes fall in Czechoslovakia, Bulgaria, and Rumania; the Soviet empire ends.

Bush and Gorbachev meet in Malta; Bush proposes treaties on nuclear and conventional arms reductions.

1990

March: Lithuania becomes independent of the Soviet Union.

May: The foreign ministers of East and West Germany and the World War II Allies pave the way for the reunification of Germany.

May 29: Boris Yeltsin is elected president of the Russian republic.

May 30–June 2: Gorbachev and Bush meet in Washington for a four-day summit. The two leaders sign more than a dozen bilateral agreements, including the framework for reducing nuclear weapons, a ban on chemical weapons, and agreements normalizing trade.

August 31: East and West Germany sign the Unification Treaty.

October 3: Germany is reunited.

November: Gorbachev meets with German chancellor Helmut Kohl: The two countries sign a nonaggression pact and an accord governing Soviet troop withdrawal from eastern Germany. Germany and Poland later agree to guarantee the permanence of their current borders.

1991

January: The Persian Gulf War, in which the United States and the Soviet Union are allied against Iraq, is the first post–Cold War war.

March: The United States withdraws the last of its intermediate-range nuclear missiles from Europe, completing the terms of the 1987 treaty.

April: The Warsaw Pact ends.

July: Hard-line Communists try, but fail, to overthrow Gorbachev and the new Soviet government.

August: The Soviet Union collapses, ending seventy-four years of Soviet communism.

September 27: Bush announces that the United States will destroy twenty-four thousand nuclear warheads and ends the twenty-four-hour alert status of U.S. strategic bombers.

December: The republics of the Soviet Union ally together as the Commonwealth of Independent States. Gorbachev resigns. The government of Russia, led by Yeltsin, takes over most of the former Soviet government's functions.

For Further Research

Oratorical Collections

ALBERT CRAIG BAIRD, ED., *American Public Addresses, 1740–1952*. New York: McGraw-Hill, 1956.

BERNARD K. DUFFY AND HALFORD R. RYAN, EDS., *American Orators of the Twentieth Century: Critical Studies and Sources*. New York: Greenwood, 1987.

STEVEN R. GOLDZWIG, *In a Perilous Hour: The Public Addresses of John F. Kennedy*. Westport, CT: Greenwood, 1995.

JOHN GRAHAM, ED., *Great American Speeches, 1898–1963*. New York: Appleton-Century-Crofts, 1970.

DONALD GRUNEWALD, ED., *"I Am Honored to Be Here Today."* New York: Oceana, 1985.

BRIAN MACARTHUR, ED., *The Penguin Book of Twentieth-Century Speeches*. New York: Penguin Books, 1999.

RONALD REAGAN, *Speaking My Mind*. New York: Simon and Schuster, 1989.

WILLIAM SAFIRE, *Lend Me Your Ears: Great Speeches in History*. New York: W.W. Norton, 1992.

GREGORY R. SURIANO, ED., *Great American Speeches*. New York: Gramercy Books, 1993.

General Studies

JIAN CHEN, *Mao's China and the Cold War*. Chapel Hill: University of North Carolina Press, 2001.

LEE EDWARDS, *The Collapse of Communism*. Stanford, CA: Hoover Institution Press, 2000.

NORMAN FRIEDMAN, *The Fifty-Year War: Conflict and Strategy in the Cold War*. Annapolis, MD: Naval Institute Press, 2000.

JOHN LEWIS GADDIS, *We Now Know: Rethinking Cold War History.* New York: Oxford University Press, 1997.

RAYMOND L. GARTHOFF, *A Journey Through the Cold War: A Memoir of Containment and Coexistence.* Washington, DC: Brookings Institution Press, 2001.

ROBERT C. GROGIN, *Natural Enemies: The United States and the Soviet Union in the Cold War, 1917–1991.* Lanham, MD: Lexington Books, 2001.

ALLEN HUNTER, ED., *Rethinking the Cold War.* Philadelphia: Temple University Press, 1998.

IAN JACKSON, *The Economic Cold War: America, Britain, and East-West Trade, 1945–63.* New York: Palgrave, 2001.

EDWARD H. JUDGE AND JOHN W. LANGDON, EDS., *The Cold War: A History Through Documents.* Upper Saddle River, NJ: Prentice-Hall, 1999.

WALTER LAFEBER, *America, Russia, and the Cold War, 1945–2000.* Boston: McGraw-Hill, 2002.

SCOTT LUCAS, *Freedom's War: The American Crusade Against the Soviet Union.* New York: New York University Press, 1999.

RONALD E. POWASKI, *The Cold War: The United States and the Soviet Union, 1917–1991.* New York: Oxford University Press, 1998.

Cultural Studies

MICHAEL BARSON AND STEVEN HELLER, *Red Scared! The Commie Menace in Propaganda and Popular Culture.* San Francisco: Chronicle Books, 2001.

NANCY E. BERNHARD, *U.S. Television News and Cold War Propaganda, 1947–1960.* New York: Cambridge University Press, 1999.

WALTER L. HIXSON, *Parting the Curtain: Propaganda, Culture, and the Cold War, 1945–1961.* New York: St. Martin's Press, 1997.

PETER J. KUZNICK AND JAMES GILBERT, EDS., *Rethinking Cold War Culture*. Washington, DC: Smithsonian Institution Press, 2001.

SHAWN J. PARRY-GILES, *The Rhetorical Presidency, Propaganda, and the Cold War, 1945–1955*. Westport, CT: Praeger, 2002.

RICHARD ALAN SCHWARTZ, *Cold War Culture: Media and the Arts, 1945–1990*. New York: Facts On File, 1998.

DAVID SEED, *American Science Fiction and the Cold War: Literature and Film*. Chicago: Fitzroy Dearborn, 1999.

ROBERT R. TOMES, *Apocalypse Then: American Intellectuals and the Vietnam War, 1954–1975*. New York: New York University Press, 1998.

Cold War Diplomacy

ROBERT D. ENGLISH, *Russia and the Idea of the West: Gorbachev, Intellectuals, and the End of the Cold War*. New York: Columbia University Press, 2000.

HENRY KISSINGER, *Years of Renewal*. New York: Simon and Schuster, 1999.

NORRIE MACQUEEN, *The United Nations Since 1945: Peacekeeping and the Cold War*. New York: Addison Wesley Longman, 1999.

ADLAI STEVENSON, *Friends and Enemies: What I Learned in Russia*. New York: Harper, 1959.

JOHN VAN OUDENAREN, *Détente in Europe: The Soviet Union and the West Since 1953*. Durham, NC: Duke University Press, 1991.

ODD ARNE WESTAD, *Brothers in Arms: The Rise and Fall of the Sino-Soviet Alliance, 1945–1963*. Stanford, CA: Stanford University Press, 1998.

Major Conflicts

GERARD J. DE GROOT, *A Noble Cause? America and the Vietnam War*. New York: Longman, 2000.

GILBERT N. DORLAND, *Legacy of Discord: Voices of the Vietnam War.* Washington, DC: Brassey's, 2001.

LAWRENCE FREEDMAN, *Kennedy's Wars: Berlin, Cuba, Laos, and Vietnam.* New York: Oxford University Press, 2000.

MICHAEL HICKEY, *The Korean War: The West Confronts Communism.* Woodstock, NY: Overlook Press, 2000.

ROGER HILSMAN, *The Cuban Missile Crisis: The Struggle over Policy.* Westport, CT: Praeger, 1996.

CHRISTOPHER HILTON, *The Wall: The People's Story.* Stroud, UK: Sutton, 2001.

DAVID E. KAISER, *American Tragedy: Kennedy, Johnson, and the Origins of the Vietnam War.* Cambridge, MA: Harvard University Press, 2000.

ROBERT F. KENNEDY, *Thirteen Days: A Memoir of the Cuban Missile Crisis.* New York: W.W. Norton, 1999.

STEPHEN G. RABE, *The Most Dangerous Area in the World: John F. Kennedy Confronts Communist Revolution in Latin America.* Chapel Hill: University of North Carolina Press, 1999.

STANLEY SANDLER, *The Korean War: No Victors, No Vanquished.* Lexington: University Press of Kentucky, 1999.

ORRIN SCHWAB, *Defending the Free World: John F. Kennedy, Lyndon Johnson, and the Vietnam War, 1961–1965.* Westport, CT: Praeger, 1998.

EZRA T. SIFF, *Why the Senate Slept: The Gulf of Tonkin Resolution and the Beginning of America's Vietnam War.* Westport, CT: Praeger, 1999.

W.R. SMYSER, *From Yalta to Berlin: The Cold War Struggle over Germany.* New York: St. Martin's Press, 1999.

RICHARD C. THORNTON, *Odd Man Out: Truman, Stalin, Mao, and the Origins of the Korean War.* Washington, DC: Brassey's, 2000.

ANN TUSA, *The Last Division: A History of Berlin, 1945–1989.* Reading, MA: Addison-Wesley, 1997.

MARK J. WHITE, *The Cuban Missile Crisis.* Basingstoke, Hampshire, England: Macmillan, 1996.

The Arms Race

LISA A. BAGLIONE, *To Agree or Not to Agree: Leadership, Bargaining, and Arms Control.* Ann Arbor: University of Michigan Press, 1999.

STEPHEN J. CIMBALA, *Deterrence and Nuclear Proliferation in the Twenty-first Century.* Westport, CT: Praeger, 2001.

KEN COATES, *The Last Frontier: Preparing War in Space.* Nottingham, England: Bertrand Russell Peace Foundation, 2001.

JOHN LEWIS GADDIS, ED., *Cold War Statesmen Confront the Bomb: Nuclear Diplomacy Since 1945.* New York: Oxford University Press, 1999.

HENRY KISSINGER, *Nuclear Weapons and Foreign Policy.* New York: Harper, 1957.

ANDREW ROJECKI, *Silencing the Opposition: Antinuclear Movements and the Media in the Cold War.* Urbana: University of Illinois Press, 1999.

Biographical Studies

JEFF BROADWATER, *Adlai Stevenson and American Politics: The Odyssey of a Cold War Liberal.* New York: Twayne, 1994.

DAVID BURNER, *John F. Kennedy and a New Generation.* New York: HarperCollins, 1988.

IRA CHERNUS, *Eisenhower's Atoms for Peace.* College Station: Texas A&M University Press, 2002.

ERIC CHOU, *Mao Tse-tung: The Man and the Myth.* New York: Stein and Day, 1982.

HAROLD FOOTE GOSNELL, *Truman's Crises: A Political Biography of Harry S. Truman*. Westport, CT: Greenwood, 1980.

SERGEI N. KHRUSHCHEV, *Nikita Khrushchev: And the Creation of a Superpower*. Shirley Benson, trans. University Park: Pennsylvania State University Press, 2000.

JOHN B. MARTIN, *Adlai Stevenson and the World*. New York: Doubleday, 1977.

RICHARD M. NIXON, *RN: The Memoirs of Richard Nixon*. New York: Simon and Schuster, 1990.

DAVID M. OSHINSKY, *A Conspiracy So Immense: The World of Joseph McCarthy*. New York: Macmillan, 1983.

WILLIAM E. PEMBERTON, *Harry S. Truman: Fair Dealer and Cold Warrior*. Boston: Twayne, 1989.

GEOFFREY PERRETT, *Old Soldiers Never Die: The Life of Douglas MacArthur*. New York: Random House, 1996.

ROBERT D. SCHULZINGER, *Henry Kissinger: Doctor of Diplomacy*. New York: Columbia University Press, 1989.

MARY E. STUCKEY, *Playing the Game: The Presidential Rhetoric of Ronald Reagan*. Westport, CT: Praeger, 1990.

KENNETH W. THOMPSON, ED., *The Ford Presidency*. Lanham, MD: University Press of America, 1988.

Websites

A&E TELEVISION NETWORKS, *The History Channel—Speeches*, www.historychannel.com/speeches.

CNN, *Cold War: CNN Perspective Series*, www.cnn.com/SPECIALS/cold.war.

COLD WAR MUSEUM, *The Cold War Museum*, www.coldwar. org.

PUBLIC BROADCASTING SYSTEM, *Great American Speeches*, www.pbs.org/greatspeeches.

Index